A TIME TO ATTACK

A TIME

TO

ATTACK

THE LOOMING IRANIAN NUCLEAR THREAT

MATTHEW KROENIG

palgrave
macmillan

A TIME TO ATTACK
Copyright © Matthew Kroenig, 2014.
All rights reserved.

First published in 2014 by PALGRAVE MACMILLAN® in the United States—a division of St. Martin's Press LLC, 175 Fifth Avenue, New York, NY 10010.

Where this book is distributed in the UK, Europe and the rest of the world, this is by Palgrave Macmillan, a division of Macmillan Publishers Limited, registered in England, company number 785998, of Houndmills, Basingstoke, Hampshire RG21 6XS.

Palgrave Macmillan is the global academic imprint of the above companies and has companies and representatives throughout the world.

Palgrave® and Macmillan® are registered trademarks in the United States, the United Kingdom, Europe and other countries.

ISBN 978-1-137-27953-8

Library of Congress Cataloging-in-Publication Data is available from the Library of Congress.

A catalogue record of the book is available from the British Library.

Design by Letra Libre, Inc.

First edition: May 2014

10   9   8   7   6   5   4   3   2   1

Printed in the United States of America.

CONTENTS

LIST OF ABBREVIATIONS AND ACRONYMS

AEOI	Atomic Energy Organization of Iran	DoD	Department of Defense (United States)
AIPAC	American Israel Public Affairs Committee	EU	European Union
		FA	*Foreign Affairs* magazine (United States)
AUMF	authorization for the use of military force		
BOG	Board of Governors (International Atomic Energy Agency)	GCC	Gulf Cooperation Council
		HEU	highly enriched uranium
CFR	Council on Foreign Relations	IAEA	International Atomic Energy Agency
CIA	Central Intelligence Agency (United States)	IAEA AP	International Atomic Energy Agency Additional Protocol
DIA	Defense Intelligence Agency (United States)		
DNI	Director of National Intelligence (United States)	IC	intelligence community (United States)

ICBM	intercontinental ballistic missile	PNE	peaceful nuclear explosion
IDF	Israel Defense Forces	PSI	Proliferation Security Initiative
IRGC	Iranian Revolutionary Guard Corps	SAM	surface-to-air missile
LEU	low-enriched uranium	SLBM	submarine-launched ballistic missile
MAD	Mutually Assured Destruction	SPR	Strategic Petroleum Reserve (United States)
MOP	Massive Ordnance Penetrator	SRBM	short-range ballistic missile
MRBM	medium-range ballistic missile	TRR	Tehran Research Reactor
MW	megawatt		
NATO	North Atlantic Treaty Organization	UAE	United Arab Emirates
		UN	United Nations
NIE	National Intelligence Estimate (United States)	UNSC	United Nations Security Council
NNWS	non-nuclear-weapon state	UNSCR	United Nations Security Council Resolution
NPT	Treaty on the Nonproliferation of Nuclear Weapons	USSR	Union of Soviet Socialist Republics
NSG	Nuclear Suppliers Group	WGU	weapons-grade uranium
NWS	nuclear weapon state	WMD	weapons of mass destruction
OPEC	Organization of the Petroleum Exporting Countries		

ACKNOWLEDGMENTS

FOR MUCH OF THE PAST DECADE, I HAVE WORKED AS a researcher and teacher in various universities in the United States. While I was more engaged in US national security policy than many in the so-called ivory tower, I still spent much of the past ten years conducting scholarly research and publishing in peer-reviewed academic journals. As a nuclear nonproliferation specialist, I was, of course, very interested in the Iran nuclear issue and read the analysis of people who followed the issue closely on a day-to-day basis, but I did not myself devote much time to studying or writing on Iran. By 2010, a strong consensus had developed among experts focusing on Iran that went something like this: the United States lacked the ability to destroy Iran's deeply buried and hardened nuclear facilities; any attempt to attack Iran would result in devastating military retaliation and a region-wide war; a strike would be futile if not counterproductive because Iran would simply redouble its efforts to build nuclear weapons after a strike; even if Iran acquired nuclear weapons, it wouldn't be that bad because we could simply deter and contain Iran much as we deterred and contained the Soviet Union during the Cold War; and, finally, when all was said and done, deterring and containing a nuclear-armed Iran, while difficult, would be vastly preferable to a military strike. Not following the issue closely myself, I was largely convinced by these claims.

Then, in May 2010, I accepted a Council on Foreign Relations (CFR) International Affairs Fellowship that took me to the Pentagon as an adviser on Iran policy in the Office of the Secretary of Defense. Due to my academic expertise in the area of nuclear weapons proliferation and nuclear deterrence, this placement made a lot of sense. Shortly after arriving in the office and getting up to speed on the myriad defense issues related to Iran and its nuclear program, however, I was surprised to realize that many of the claims undergirding the conventional wisdom about Iran policy were way out of line. Of course, some of the most important disagreements about Iran boil down to judgment calls, but many of the judgment calls were strongly biased against military action. I was amazed at how many smart people took an incredibly nuanced issue and reduced it to an open-and-shut case: a nuclear-armed Iran would not be that bad, but attacking Iran would be an unmitigated disaster. As you will see in this book, the reality is much more complicated.

Moreover, many of the most important issues are not about judgment calls at all, but about basic facts, and I was shocked at the degree to which the public debate on this issue was being dominated by people who simply had their facts wrong. I was determined to set the record straight.

Shortly after leaving the Pentagon, I published an article in the January/February 2012 issue of the venerable magazine *Foreign Affairs*, entitled "Time to Attack Iran: Why a Strike Is the Least Bad Option."[1] In the piece I argued that, if forced to choose, a limited US military strike on Iran's nuclear facilities would be less bad than attempting to deter and contain a nuclear-armed Iran. It is not easy to be among the first people to make a controversial argument on matters of war and peace—even if one's position is correct—and the article generated much controversy, leading many of my colleagues to disagree strongly with me in response pieces published in policy journals, newspaper columns, and online blogs, and in debates at various public events and on radio and television programs in the weeks that followed.

Then, only two months later, in an interview with Jeffrey Goldberg of *The Atlantic*, President Barack Obama staked out a position that was similar to mine. He said that a nuclear-armed Iran was unacceptable and that the United States would do everything in its power, including using military force if necessary, to keep Iran from the bomb. Over the course of the subsequent two years, I have spent countless hours presenting my analysis of the Iran nuclear problem to officials in the executive branch and Congress, at think tanks and universities around the world, and on radio and television. During that time, the politically relevant discourse in Washington has done a near 180-degree turn. There is now a widespread bipartisan consensus that a policy of preventing Iran from acquiring nuclear weapons using all necessary means is preferable to containing a nuclear-armed Iran; I hope I played at least some small part in contributing to a more informed debate about our options for dealing with Iran's nuclear program.

The Iran nuclear issue, however, is an intricate subject, and I had only a few thousand words to address it in the FA piece. This book allows me the opportunity to present my complete understanding of the issue in its full complexity. More importantly, I believe this book is the most comprehensive and authoritative source available anywhere on the Iranian nuclear challenge.

Writing a book is always an enormous undertaking, and it is not something that I could have done alone. I would like to thank my wonderful colleagues in the Department of Government at Georgetown University in Washington, DC.

I would also like to recognize the Brent Scowcroft Center on International Security at the Atlantic Council, where I recently took up a position as a nonresident senior fellow. I'm particularly grateful to Frederick Kempe, Damon Wilson, Barry Pavel, and Jeffrey Lightfoot for bringing me on board the strong and increasingly vibrant think tank they are building. This book would not have been possible were it not for the Council on Foreign Relations, which provided me with not one, but two unique fellowship experiences that helped to bring this project together. First, I was a recipient of the CFR International Affairs Fellowship, which allowed me to spend a year working on Iran policy at the Department of Defense. I would like to thank Michèle Flournoy, James Miller, Alexander Vershbow, Colin Kahl, Mike Holmes, and Pat Antonelli, the senior leadership in the Office of the Secretary of Defense (Policy) at the time, who graciously allowed me to spend my fellowship year in the Middle East office. In addition, I would also like to recognize my talented colleagues on the Iran desk at DoD: Ylber Bajraktari, Ilan Goldenberg, Jana Kay, and Bill Van Atten. The debates we had in our cubicles about how best to resolve the Iranian nuclear challenge were as exhaustive, entertaining, and heated as anything I have encountered before or since.

After leaving DoD, I spent a year as a Stanton Nuclear Security Fellow at the Council on Foreign Relations. There I spent my time thinking, writing, briefing, and doing media appearances on Iran. I am grateful to CFR's leadership, including Richard Haass and James Lindsay, for the opportunity to have been part of CFR's studies program. CFR's fellowship programs would not be such a success were it not for the tireless work of Janine Hill and Victoria Alekhine. Kate Collins provided deft research and administrative support. I would also like to thank the other fellows who helped to challenge and advance my thinking on Iran, including Elliott Abrams, Robert Blackwill, Steve Biddle, Robert Danin, Richard Falkenrath, Michael Levi, Meghan O'Sullivan, and Ray Takeyh.

I have previously written on Iran in articles in *Foreign Affairs, Foreign Policy* online, the *Washington Post, The American Interest,* and *USA Today* and in a book chapter published by CFR.[2] I thank the editors of these outlets for permission to reprise some of the themes from these articles in this book and my co-authors of the pieces in the *Post* and *The American Interest,* Jamie Fly and Robert McNally, respectively.

I've also received incisive comments and criticisms that have sharpened my thinking on this issue in lectures at think tanks and universities around the world. I would like to thank the Alexander Hamilton Society; Carnegie-Tsinghua Center; Cato Institute; Center for National Policy; Center for Strategic and International Studies; Council on Foreign Relations; Georgetown University; Foreign Policy Initiative; Henry Jackson Society; Körber Foundation; World Affairs Council of Washington, DC; University of California at Berkeley; and Yale University.

While writing up the draft manuscript, I benefited from the research assistance of Christian Chung. He is one of my most capable colleagues and he is only twenty years old. Needless to say, he has a very bright future ahead of him.

When I began searching for a literary agent to work with me on this project, two words were frequently used to describe Will Lippincott: the best. I feel fortunate to be included in his stable of authors. I would also like to thank Lippincott Massie McQuilkin's skilled agency assistants, Derek Parsons and Amanda Panitch.

Karen Wolny, editorial director of Trade at Palgrave Macmillan, immediately recognized the value of this book and shared my vision for it. It has been a delight to work with Karen and her team, including Donna Cherry, Lauren Janiec, and Lauren LoPinto, to bring this book to press.

I am fortunate to have supportive friends who were always willing to provide a distraction when I wanted something to do other than talk about Iran—although we often did that too. Thanks to Nitin Chadda, Kevin Chaffee, Guido Licciardi, Mike Mosettig, and David Stein.

Finally, I owe everything to my warm and loving family: Dale and Martha Burns, Mark and Barb Kroenig, Brad Kroenig, and Julie Kroenig Forbes. Each and every one of you is incredibly accomplished in your own way, and you inspire to me do better each and every day. Thank you.

INTRODUCTION

IT WAS A MUGGY JULY AFTERNOON WHEN PRESIDENT
Barack Obama strode to the microphone in the Rose Garden to face the
sea of reporters that had gathered to hear this momentous announcement.
Even the famously cool president appeared to be shaken. Maybe it was the
Washington, DC heat, or perhaps it was the gravity of what was about to
be said. This was a speech he had hoped to avoid.

He began slowly, recounting the history of the long-running crisis
over Iran's nuclear program. He explained how a nuclear-armed Iran
would pose a grave threat to international peace and security. Channeling
the language of previous US presidents, he stated that a nuclear-armed
Iran would be "unacceptable" and that he had pursued many avenues in
an attempt to stop Iran's nuclear progress. He explained how he had built
an unprecedented international coalition to put pressure on Iran's leaders. In eight separate United Nations Security Council Resolutions, the
United States, Russia, China, Britain, France (countries that don't often
see eye-to-eye), and other representatives of the international community came together to demand that Tehran stop its uranium enrichment
activities. He described how his administration had attempted to address

this problem diplomatically, but that Tehran continued to defy its international legal obligations under the Nuclear Nonproliferation Treaty. He reminded his audience that his policy has always been to prevent Iran from acquiring nuclear weapons, with diplomacy if at all possible, but by force if necessary.

He had pursued negotiations until the last possible moment, but the window for diplomacy was now effectively shut. Iran was on the verge of a nuclear weapons capability.

Only days earlier, the president had issued an ultimatum to Iran's leaders. Either they could suspend their uranium enrichment activities and give international inspectors unrestricted access to their country, or they would face the full wrath of the US military. They were given forty-eight hours to respond. Now that window had also closed.

"The decision to use force is not one that I come to lightly," said the president. He was coming to the heart of his speech. "But Iran's leaders have left me with no choice. Therefore, on my orders, US and coalition forces will begin airstrikes on Iran's nuclear facilities tonight." He cautioned that this was not a dispute between the United States and the Iranian people, but rather a conflict between an international community that values peace and security and an Iranian leadership that prizes its reckless pursuit of a nuclear weapons capability over its international obligations and the welfare of its own people. "It is my sincerest hope that this conflict will end swiftly and decisively with the destruction of Iran's nuclear facilities. But, if Iran's leaders choose to retaliate against the United States and our allies, we will be forced to defend ourselves. In either case, we will accept no outcome short of victory. May God bless our brave men and women in uniform and may God bless the United States of America."

After a decade-long standoff, the United States and Iran were going to war.

This is a scenario that has not yet come to pass, but it very well could in the near future. In his 2014 worldwide threat assessment, Director of National Intelligence James Clapper declared that Iran's advanced nuclear program constitutes one of the greatest emerging national security challenges to the United States of America.[1] Deciding on how to address the threat, therefore, is among the most important choices currently facing the US government. As I see it, there are only three possible outcomes of the crisis. First, the United States and Iran could come to a mutually satisfactory diplomatic settlement. Second, Washington could simply acquiesce to a nuclear-armed Iran. Or, third, the United States and/or Israel could take military action designed to prevent Iran from acquiring nuclear weapons.

Clearly a diplomatic solution to this crisis would be best. That is why the United States has pursued negotiations with Iran over its disputed nuclear program for the past decade. In November 2013 the United States and a group of other world powers struck an "interim" nuclear deal with Iran that was widely lauded as a historic breakthrough. Yet, as President Obama clearly explained, the interim deal is only a "first step." To truly solve the problem, the two sides must strike a more comprehensive diplomatic accord that fully resolves the Iranian nuclear crisis. But the successful negotiation of such a far-reaching agreement will be difficult. President Obama himself estimated that the odds of a successful diplomatic accord are "no better than 50/50." Moreover, it is possible that even a comprehensive diplomatic accord will not succeed in neutralizing the Iranian nuclear threat.

This means that at some point in the foreseeable future, a US president might be forced to choose between the less attractive options of acquiescing to a nuclear-armed Iran and conducting a military strike on Iran's key nuclear facilities.

. President Obama has declared that he has already made his choice. He has repeatedly said that his policy is to prevent, not contain, a nuclear-armed Iran and that all options, including the use of force, are on the table to achieve that outcome. Those who know him well, including those who have worked with him in the White House on this issue, swear that they have no doubt that the president is sincere when he says he is willing to bomb Iran if necessary to stop the spread of nuclear weapons in the Middle East. This position also has overwhelming support in the US Congress.

But is this the right call? How did we even get to this point? How close is Iran to having nuclear weapons, really? Is the United States truly prepared to fight another war over suspected WMD programs in the Middle East so soon after we went to war over trumped-up charges of WMD proliferation in Iraq only a decade ago? Can't we just solve this problem diplomatically? Will Iran's new president, Hassan Rouhani, a relative moderate within Iran's theocratic system, improve the prospects for a comprehensive negotiated settlement? Would a nuclear-armed Iran ever use its nuclear weapons? If not, does a nuclear Iran really represent such a grave threat? Can the United States simply deter and contain a nuclear-armed Iran in the same way that we deterred and contained a much more powerful Soviet Union during the Cold War? How stable is the Iranian government? Is it possible that the regime could collapse from within, thus solving the Iranian nuclear challenge for us? Can we use covert tools like cyberattacks, assassinations, and sabotage, to stop Iran's nuclear program without going to war? Would a military strike against Iran's nuclear facilities be effective? If we must strike, why not let Israel attack Iran's nuclear facilities and do the dirty work for us? Wouldn't any attack on Iran be a disaster?

These are the questions this book will address. I argue that a diplomatic settlement to this crisis would be the best possible outcome and that we should all hope for the successful negotiation of a lasting diplomatic accord. I also argue, however, that it is possible, if not likely, that diplomacy will fail to head off the Iranian nuclear challenge. Therefore, I reason, if the United States is forced to choose between an Iran with the bomb and bombing Iran, then Washington should conduct a limited strike on Iran's key nuclear facilities, pull back and absorb an inevitable round of Iranian retaliation, and quickly seek to de-escalate the crisis. It is not a good option, but, when compared to the dangers of living with a nuclear-armed Iran for decades to come, it is the least bad option.

More important than the central conclusion of the book, however, is the process by which I arrive at it. This book will carefully and systematically analyze the history of US-Iranian relations and the historical development of Iran's nuclear capabilities from the 1950s to the present. Then it will reorient the reader's point of view and consider Iran's security environment, strategic goals, intentions, and capabilities to better understand what Tehran might hope to achieve from this crisis.

Next, it will describe in great detail all of the possible options for resolving the Iranian nuclear challenge and the likely consequences of these various approaches, including waiting for domestic political regime change in Iran; allowing Iran to maintain an advanced nuclear capability without nuclear weapons, aka "the Japan Model"; the contours of possible diplomatic settlements; a strategy for deterring and containing a nuclear

Iran if our policy of prevention fails; and the various military options for destroying Iran's nuclear facilities. Most, if not all, of these will be live options for the foreseeable future. In this way, the book will serve as a guide and instruction manual to scholars, policymakers, and the general public regardless of how the Iranian nuclear issue continues to evolve.

Finally, the book will conclude by systematically comparing the options against one another, making policy recommendations, and then expanding our frame of reference to speculate on what the Iranian nuclear challenge means for the future of nuclear proliferation, the Middle East, and America's role in the world.

There are few, if any, subjects more important than the issue covered in this book. Iran is arguably the most influential country in what might be the most critical geographic region on the planet. Its history, culture, geography, and resources make it a natural contender for the title of the leading state in the Middle East. Furthermore, the crisis spurred by its advanced nuclear program is literally a matter of war and peace. Nuclear weapons in Iran could have horrendous consequences, including possible nuclear war against Israel or even the US homeland. A military strike designed to stop Iran's nuclear progress might be a superior alternative, but it still means an armed attack on another country and, especially if managed poorly, could result in a broader Middle Eastern conflict.

The choices we might face, therefore, are not between the status quo and conflict, but between more dangerous future worlds. The president will ultimately make the final call, but we all have a right to a say in that decision.

This book is intended to make sure that we choose wisely.

CHAPTER ONE

FROM ATOMS FOR PEACE TO ATOMS FOR WAR

ON MARCH 5, 1957, THE UNITED STATES AND IRAN signed a nuclear cooperation agreement under which Washington promised to provide Tehran with various nuclear technologies, including a nuclear research reactor. Roughly a half-century later, the US Department of Defense was drawing up plans to bomb Iran's nuclear facilities.[1] Why the change of heart?

Some have suggested that this apparent 180-degree turn is proof that the United States is fickle, if not downright hypocritical, in the way it views the development of nuclear programs in other countries. As I will explain in this chapter, however, the United States has actually been remarkably consistent in its approach to the spread of nuclear technology around the world since 1945. It has always promoted the diffusion of nuclear technology for peaceful purposes while simultaneously opposing its military application.

Its policy toward Iran has been consistent with this broader pattern. The United States encouraged the development of nuclear research and energy in Iran beginning in the 1950s but actively sought to discourage Iran from acquiring the most sensitive nuclear capabilities since that time. The fall of the shah and the rise to power of an anti-American Islamic government under Ayatollah Khomeini in 1979 transformed the two countries from close friends to sworn enemies almost overnight. But the current Iranian nuclear crisis did not really begin until 2002, when it was revealed that Iran had secret plans to enrich uranium, a sensitive activity that can be used to generate fuel for nuclear reactors or, as Washington and the rest of the international community fears in Iran's case, nuclear weapons. This chapter tells the story about we got from there to here.

ATOMS FOR PEACE, 1945–1979

Nuclear weapons made their first appearance on the world stage in 1945 when the United States dropped atomic bombs on the Japanese cities of Hiroshima and Nagasaki to bring World War II to a close. The horrifyingly destructive power of nuclear weapons quickly became apparent to all, and the United States and later the Soviet Union (the other Cold War superpower, which would test its own nuclear weapon in 1949) soon attempted to prevent other countries from acquiring the world's most dangerous weapons.

There was a problem, however. Nuclear technology is dual use in nature, meaning that the exact same technology can be used for both military and peaceful purposes. At the beginning of the nuclear age, many people were quite optimistic about the potential transformational benefits of the peaceful uses of nuclear technology. A controlled nuclear chain reaction can produce electricity. While today we are well aware of the costs as well as the benefits of nuclear power, experts in the early nuclear age were overly optimistic about nuclear energy's potential upsides, gushing about the possibility of providing endless sources of electricity that would be "too cheap to meter."[2] In addition, controlled nuclear reactions can produce radioactive isotopes that have important medical applications. Moreover, in the early nuclear era, experts even predicted that peaceful nuclear explosions (PNEs) could be used instead of dynamite to move vast quantities of earth in order to construct roads, bridges, dams, and other major infrastructure projects. It seemed impossible, if not unethical, therefore, to deny the vast benefits of this promising new technology to developing countries around the world.

The United States attempted to square the circle. On December 8, 1953, President Dwight D. Eisenhower gave his now-famous "Atoms for Peace" speech before the UN General Assembly. In the speech, Eisenhower announced that Washington would help other countries develop nuclear technology for peaceful purposes while simultaneously resisting any attempts to build nuclear weapons. (While somewhat more sophisticated in form, this is essentially the same tightrope that the United States attempts to walk in its nuclear nonproliferation policy to the present day).

Iran, like many other countries around the world, was eager to access the benefits of peaceful nuclear technology, and just over three years after Eisenhower's speech, on March 5, 1957, Washington and Tehran signed a nuclear cooperation agreement under the auspices of the Atoms for Peace program.

At the time, Iran was under the leadership of Shah Mohammad Rezā Pahlavī. The shah was a pro-Western secular monarch and an American ally. In the shah's Iran, Washington saw a Middle Eastern partner capable of balancing against the growing influence of the Soviet Union among Arab countries in the region. The provision of civilian nuclear technology was one of many tools that the United States used in an attempt to bind friendly countries to its side in its Cold War competition with Moscow.

As part of the nuclear deal, the United States helped the shah lay the foundations for a peaceful nuclear program. Washington built the Tehran Nuclear Research Center at Tehran University and supplied Iran with the 5-megawatt Tehran Research Reactor, which began operation in 1967.

Under Atoms for Peace, the United States helped Iran with basic nuclear science and research, but this assistance in no way suggests that Washington was somehow supportive of the shah's building nuclear weapons as some commentators misleadingly imply. After all, the United States provided the same basic nuclear technology to dozens of other countries around the world, including Congo, Mexico, and Vietnam. Washington clearly did not intend to proliferate nuclear weapons to all of these countries. Moreover, the technology transferred under Atoms for Peace was far too rudimentary to get the recipients anywhere close to a nuclear weapons capability. Indeed, if building nuclear weapons is like running a marathon, receiving a nuclear research reactor is like taking one's first baby step. As I show in my previous book *Exporting the Bomb: Technology Transfer and the Spread of Nuclear Weapons,* countries that get help with basic civilian nuclear technology of the kind that the United States provided to Iran are no more likely to build nuclear weapons than countries that do not receive any such help.[3]

Neither was Iran particularly interested in building nuclear weapons at the time. Indeed, Iran's leaders publicly pledged not to build nuclear weapons on July 1, 1968, when they signed the Treaty on the Non-Proliferation of Nuclear Weapons (NPT). The NPT, as the name suggests, is an international treaty designed to prevent the spread of nuclear weapons to additional countries. It is arguably the most successful international treaty ever created; nearly every country on Earth is a member, and the treaty has been quite effective at keeping countries out of the nuclear club. Later, in 1974, Tehran concluded its safeguards agreement with the International Atomic Energy Agency (IAEA). The IAEA serves as the UN's nuclear watchdog, and the safeguards agreement grants international inspectors the authority to periodically visit Iran's declared nuclear facilities and verify that Iran is using its nuclear facilities strictly for peaceful purposes.

The NPT creates two classes of states. The five states that tested nuclear weapons before 1968 (the United States, the Soviet Union—now Russia—Great Britain, France, and China) are grandfathered in as "nuclear-weapon states." They have the legal right under international law to possess nuclear weapons. All other states that sign the treaty, including Iran, join as "non-nuclear-weapon states." They agree not to develop nuclear weapons in exchange for various benefits, including a pledge from all states to pursue negotiations toward eventual nuclear disarmament; and, most importantly in Iran's case, the inalienable right to develop nuclear technology for "peaceful purposes."

By the 1970s, Iran was interested in expanding the "peaceful purposes" of its nuclear program beyond mere research to include the production of nuclear energy. In 1974, the Iranian parliament, the Majlis, passed the Atomic Energy Act of Iran and established the Atomic Energy Organization of Iran (AEOI). Iran subsequently entered into negotiations with

Western countries to have nuclear power reactors built on Iranian territory. In 1976, West Germany began the construction of two light-water nuclear power reactors in the Iranian town of Bushehr and, in 1977, Tehran concluded a contract with France to have two additional power reactors erected near the city of Ahvaz in southwest Iran.

The United States and Iran also discussed the possibility of further nuclear cooperation. Throughout the Nixon, Ford, and Carter administrations, the two countries attempted to come to terms on a major nuclear cooperation deal that would have included the provision of eight nuclear power reactors to Iran. Negotiations stalled, however, over Iran's interest in reprocessing plutonium. Reprocessing has legitimate civilian applications, but, like uranium enrichment, it also gives countries the ability to produce fuel for nuclear weapons. The eight light-water power reactors the United States was willing to export did not provide a significant weapons proliferation risk, but the ability to reprocess would have put Iran only a hair's breadth away from the atomic bomb. By the late 1970s the United States had a strict policy of preventing the spread of uranium enrichment and plutonium-reprocessing technologies to new countries, including Iran, due to this proliferation risk.

In the end, the Iranians agreed to give up their hopes of reprocessing, but the nuclear cooperation agreement was never consummated for a different reason: US-Iranian relations were about to undergo a seismic shift.

THE IRANIAN REVOLUTION, 1979

On November 4, 1979, a gang of Iranian students and protestors stormed the US embassy in Tehran and took hostage fifty-two American diplomatic personnel working inside. This was a major breach of international law and a violent and direct challenge to the United States. For over a year, Americans tuned in to their nightly television newscasts hoping to get word of the hostages' release, only to be disappointed night after night. The hostage crisis was becoming a major political liability for President Jimmy Carter, and in April 1980 he ordered a secret military mission, Operation Eagle Claw, to rescue the American prisoners. The mission was a complete debacle, resulting in a failure to rescue the hostages in addition to the loss of two US aircraft and eight military service personnel. Finally, on January 20, 1981, just after the inauguration of President Ronald Reagan and 444 days after they were first taken captive, the hostages were released by Iran.

The hostage crisis, however, was only one small event in a larger political transformation taking place in Iran. The shah had never been terribly popular, and his secular and Western orientation did not sit well with many in a country that is a spiritual home of the Shia branch of Islam. This dissatisfaction, combined with economic problems and widespread government corruption, had led to a campaign of civil resistance and anti-government protests in Tehran in late 1977 and 1978. Finally, convinced that he could no longer hang on to power, the shah left Iran in January 1979.

The next month, in February 1979, Ayatollah Ruhollah Khomeini triumphantly returned to Iran from exile in Paris. Khomeini was a politically active Shia cleric and a longtime political opponent of the shah. In November of that year, a new constitution was adopted proclaiming Ayatollah Khomeini the supreme leader of the new Islamic Republic of Iran. Within a year, Iran had been transformed from a secular, pro-American monarchy to a Muslim theocracy that viewed the United States as its foremost foe.

US-Iranian relations would never be the same.

The Iranian Revolution not only had implications for Iran's geopolitical orientation, however, but also for its nuclear program, which stalled in the immediate wake of the revolution. Western contracts were torn up. Germany pulled out of Iran and never completed the nuclear reactors at Bushehr. France and the United States did not follow through on the nuclear agreements they had negotiated with the shah.

Iran's new supreme leader was not terribly interested in nuclear power or, at least initially, in nuclear weapons. But a devastating decade-long war with a neighboring country would help change his mind.

IRAN-IRAQ WAR, 1980–1988

Seeking to take advantage of the turmoil inside an Iran wracked by revolution, Iraqi leader Saddam Hussein ordered his armed forces to invade Iran in September 1980. The resulting eight-year conflict was one of the longest and most gruesome wars of the twentieth century.

The war resembled World War I in that the two sides engaged in years of bloody trench warfare that had the effect of barely moving the front lines. In an attempt to break through the stalemate, both sides resorted to desperate measures. To clear Iraqi minefields, Iran used human minesweepers. These units of teenage and pre-teenage boys were recruited to charge unarmed through minefields in advance of Iranian soldiers. They wore the white headbands of martyrs and cried out in joy as they marched to their impending death.

The war also saw attacks against nuclear facilities. A US attack on Iran's nuclear facilities, therefore, would not be the first time that the country has suffered such a fate. Iraq bombed Iran's partially completed Bushehr reactors, and Iran returned the favor, striking Iraq's French-built nuclear reactor at Osiraq. The Iranian strike was only partially successful, however, and Israel followed up with a more decisive attack of its own in the following year.

Perhaps the most notable feature of the conflict, however, was Iraq's widespread use of chemical weapons. Over the course of the war, it is estimated that Saddam inflicted up to 50,000 casualties on Iran through the use of mustard gas and other lethal chemical agents.[4] Ayatollah Khomeini had initially declared weapons of mass destruction to be contrary to the tenets of Islam, but he eventually concluded that they might be necessary to defend his newly created Islamic Republic. In a letter to supporters in 1988 announcing his decision to drink from the "poisoned chalice" and sign a ceasefire with Iraq, he explained that Iran's military position at the time was hopeless, but that he looked forward to the day when Iran could renew the fight with the help of "atomic weapons which will be the necessity of the war at that time."[5]

A. Q. KHAN AND IRAN'S NUCLEAR SHOPPING SPREE, 1987–2003

A. Q. Khan might very well be one of the most nefarious villains of the second half of the twentieth century. From 1987 to 2003, he was instrumental in spreading dangerous nuclear weapons technology to four rogue states: Pakistan, Iran, Libya, and North Korea.

As a Pakistani scientist working in the Netherlands in the 1970s, he smuggled uranium enrichment technology back to Pakistan. As mentioned above, uranium enrichment technology can be used to make fuel for nuclear power plants or for nuclear weapons. Pakistan used it for both, assembling its first nuclear bomb in the late 1980s.

Dr. Khan then turned his nuclear smuggling ring outward, transferring build-your-own-atomic-bomb kits to Iran, Libya, and North Korea. Khan and his cronies became rich selling sensitive nuclear technology; the rest of the world became imperiled. But Khan wasn't acting alone. The Pakistani government encouraged the exports because they believed the United States had become too powerful following the collapse of the Soviet Union; it was intent on constraining American power by creating an alliance of "strategic defiance" against the United States, linking China and a band of nuclear-armed rogue states.

Representatives of the Iranian government first met with Khan in 1987. Over the next several years, Pakistan gave Iran uranium enrichment designs and component parts and possibly a Chinese design for a nuclear warhead. The advanced nuclear program that Iran possesses today would not have been possible were it not for Dr. Khan.

Iran was a spendthrift nuclear customer, however, and didn't limit its purchases to one supplier. In 1992, it attempted to buy plutonium-reprocessing capabilities from Argentina (the same capabilities it had tried to get from the United States in 1978), but Buenos Aires denied the request. In 1995, it signed a nuclear cooperation agreement with Russia. Moscow contracted to finish the construction of the Bushehr reactors that Germany had left unfinished in the 1970s. More shockingly, Russia offered to help Iran build a uranium enrichment plant. Washington went ballistic over Moscow's plan to export such a sensitive nuclear technology to its old foe, and Russia canceled the uranium enrichment portion of the deal under American pressure. There is reason to believe, however, that Russia may have continued to provide Iran with covert nuclear assistance, including nuclear weapons designs.[6] China also helped to fuel Iran's nuclear ambitions. In the late 1980s and early 1990s, Beijing helped Iran with uranium-conversion capabilities and provided Tehran with calutrons, a key technology for laser isotope separation.[7]

At this point, one might ask why other countries would help Iran acquire the world's most dangerous weapons. This is an excellent question and one to which I devote an entire book.[8] The answer is that states export sensitive nuclear technology when it doesn't threaten themselves but does threaten their adversaries. Since Russia, China, and Pakistan lack the ability to project military power in Iran, they are not directly threatened by a nuclear-armed Iran. But since Washington does have the power to project force in Iran, these countries understand that they can constrain American military might by providing Iran with the ultimate security guarantee. As the title of my PhD dissertation had it, "The Enemy of My Enemy Is My Customer."[9]

Due in part to Iran's nuclear spending spree, US officials were suspicious of Iran's nuclear intentions throughout the 1990s, but a dissident group within Iran removed all (or at least most) doubt about Iran's nuclear transgressions in a fateful 2002 announcement.

REVELATION, 2002

On August 14, 2002, a spokesman for the National Council of Resistance of Iran, an Iranian opposition group, publicly revealed that Iran was building two secret nuclear facilities: a uranium enrichment facility near the city of Natanz and a heavy-water reactor near the city of Arak.

This behavior was doubly suspicious. First, as a member of the NPT, Iran is obligated to declare the construction of any new nuclear facilities to the IAEA, but Iran was attempting to construct these facilities in secret. Second, these were not the innocent facilities devoted to basic research like those Washington had shared decades earlier, nor were they well suited to energy production. These were two facilities tailor-made to make fuel for nuclear weapons. The international community, including the United States, was understandably disturbed by this development.

The Iranian nuclear crisis had begun.

CHAPTER TWO

WHAT DOES IRAN WANT?

IN MY "POLITICS OF NUCLEAR WEAPONS" COURSE AT Georgetown University, I teach my students that nuclear weapons proliferation is all about supply and demand. In order to build nuclear weapons, a country's leaders must want nuclear weapons (demand) and they must also have the technical capability to produce them (supply). Some countries in the world today, like Japan, have the ability to produce nuclear weapons but don't have an interest in doing so. Other countries, like Colonel Gaddafi's Libya in the 1990s, badly want nuclear weapons but lack the ability to build them. In order for nuclear weapons to spread, supply and demand must come together.

Understanding the supply of and demand for nuclear weapons is also helpful in formulating nuclear nonproliferation policy. If we want to prevent Iran from building nuclear weapons, we must adopt policies that address Tehran's demand for nuclear weapons, its ability to produce them, or both.

Before we can consider our various policy options for stopping Iran from building nuclear weapons, therefore, we must begin by analyzing whether Iran wants nuclear weapons and if so, why. We must also examine Iran's ability to produce nuclear weapons should it decide to do so. These are the issues that this chapter will address.

IRAN'S NUCLEAR PROGRAM TODAY

How good are Iran's nuclear capabilities today? The answer is that Iran has come a long way since it penned its first nuclear cooperation agreement with the United States in 1957. It has not quite reached the ability to produce nuclear weapons, but it is close. Under the terms of the interim nuclear deal signed by Iran and the group of international powers known as the P5+1 in November 2013, Iran agreed to freeze key aspects of its nuclear program in place. If the diplomatic track breaks down, however, and Iran decides to ramp up its nuclear activities, it could dash to a nuclear weapons breakout capability in just a few short months.

To understand this point, let's begin by considering Iran's current nuclear infrastructure. These are the facilities that would potentially need to be shut down or limited and closely monitored in a comprehensive diplomatic settlement, or, alternatively, attacked in a military strike.

Some of Iran's nuclear facilities have legitimate peaceful purposes and do not pose a weapons proliferation risk. Iran continues to operate the Tehran Research Reactor, built with US help in 1967. Iran uses the reactor to create radioactive isotopes for the treatment of cancer patients. Iran also operates a light-water nuclear power reactor at Bushehr. As discussed in the previous chapter, this plant has had a slow and painful birth and, in May 2011, nearly forty years after it was first envisioned, it finally went critical. Research reactors and light-water power reactors are not very useful for building nuclear weapons, however, and these facilities are not a major cause of concern for US officials.

Iran is, however, engaging in other, much more troubling behavior. There are two methods of producing fuel for nuclear weapons: generating plutonium in a heavy-water reactor or enriching uranium. Iran is hedging its bets and pursuing both paths.

As was mentioned in the previous chapter, Iran is building a heavy-water reactor at Arak. Iran claims that, like the reactor at Bushehr, the one at Arak will be used to produce electricity. Unlike the light-water reactor at Bushehr, however, heavy-water reactors are bomb-making machines because they produce large quantities of plutonium. France, Israel, India, and North Korea are among the countries that have used plutonium from heavy-water reactors to build their first atomic bombs. The United States has repeatedly said that Iran can have as many light-water reactors as it wishes but that heavy-water reactors are out of the question. The United Nations Security Council (UNSC) has demanded that Iran suspend all work on this reactor. As part of the 2013 interim nuclear deal, Iran has agreed not to finish installing major component parts, such as the control panel, or to start up the reactor, but other work at the site continues. If and when the Arak reactor is completed, it is estimated that it could produce enough plutonium for two nuclear weapons per year.

Iran also operates two uranium enrichment facilities. Iran claims that these facilities are intended to produce fuel rods for their reactors in Tehran, Bushehr, and Arak, but the United States and much of the international community fear that these facilities will be used to make fuel for nuclear weapons. The first enrichment facility is near the Iranian city of Natanz and was revealed by a dissident group in 2002. The plant has two parts, an above-ground pilot plant that became operational in 2003 and a larger underground plant that began enriching uranium in 2007. In 2009, Iran was discovered to be trying to build a second, secret enrichment facility. The Fordow facility, near the Iranian holy city of Qom, is built into the side of a mountain and began operation in early 2012. Iran is enriching uranium at both locations. As part of the 2013 interim deal, Iran has agreed to put limits on its enrichment activities at both sites, but if Tehran reverses that decision for any reason, it would only take it two to three months to produce enough fuel for its first nuclear weapon.

The international community has repeatedly explained to Iran that it doesn't need enrichment facilities for a peaceful program because it can, like the vast majority of countries in the world with nuclear energy programs, simply buy fuel rods from countries that already operate enrichment facilities, like the United States, France, or Russia. Iran insists, however, on enriching uranium itself. The UNSC has demanded that Iran suspend all of its enrichment work.

Before natural uranium can be enriched, it must first be converted into gaseous form. Iran operates a uranium-conversion facility at Isfahan that produces uranium hexaflouride gas that is then fed into the uranium-enrichment plants at Natanz and Qom.

These four facilities, the nuclear reactor at Arak, the enrichment facilities at Natanz and Qom, and the uranium-conversion facility at Isfahan, are the most important nuclear sites in Iran. These facilities greatly increase Iran's ability to build the bomb. Indeed, they are genuine choke points; without these facilities it would be impossible for Iran to make nuclear weapons. It might be hard to believe, but the entire Iranian nuclear crisis is essentially a dispute about these four plants.

Iran operates a number of other nuclear-related facilities of some concern, but they are far less important than the Big Four. Iran operates uranium-mining and -milling facilities to extract natural uranium from the Earth's crust to process it for eventual conversion at Isfahan and enrichment at Natanz or Qom. In addition, Iran has various plants in Tehran and Natanz that manufacture the centrifuges and other component parts that go into the uranium enrichment facilities. Finally, there is an Iranian military base at Parchin where the IAEA suspects Iran may have conducted explosive tests related to the design of nuclear warheads in the past. These facilities are less problematic because Iran can mine all the natural uranium and conduct all the explosive tests it wants, but without plutonium or highly enriched uranium provided by the Big Four, it can't build the bomb.

This brief summary represents the full extent of Iran's known nuclear facilities.

SECRET FACILITIES

What if Iran has secret facilities? If Iran is operating nuclear facilities that we don't know about, then the program I describe above might only be the tip of the iceberg. This would have profound implications for our understanding of Iran's nuclear program and for our ability to stop it. The idea that we might not know everything about Iran's nuclear program is not so far-fetched. After all, we have been surprised about nuclear developments in rogue states in the past. The United States went to war against

Saddam Hussein's Iraq in 2003 on suspicions (which later turned out to be false) that Iraq was developing weapons of mass destruction (WMD). The US intelligence community has also missed the mark in its estimates of other nuclear programs since 1945.[1] In the cases of the Soviet Union, India, Pakistan, and Iraq during the First Gulf War in 1991, we were surprised at how far those programs had come so quickly. In other cases, like Iraq in 2003, we estimated that countries were much closer to the bomb than they actually were. Given this record, one might wonder how we can have any confidence in our assessments of Iran's program.

By definition, we don't know what we don't know and it is certainly within the realm of possibility that Iran has secret nuclear activities that we don't know about. It is also, however, highly unlikely. As required by Iran's NPT commitments, Iran's nuclear facilities are subject to IAEA inspections and, given Iran's spotty record on these matters, the IAEA devotes special attention to Iran. International inspectors are permanently on the ground in Iran, visiting Iran's declared nuclear facilities frequently and writing up detailed reports that are published on the IAEA website every three months.[2] These reports contain information on exactly where these facilities are located; exactly how many and what kind of centrifuges are operating; and exactly how much enriched uranium Iran has stockpiled. In stark contrast, in the cases of intelligence failures on nuclear issues in the past, we did not have an IAEA presence on the ground. Saddam Hussein had kicked out inspectors, and the other countries were not NPT members. In short, the IAEA gives us a very good window into Iran's nuclear operations.

Of course, if there were truly secret facilities in operation, then not even the IAEA would know about them. This too is possible, but also unlikely. Let me explain why. It is important to point out that concerns about secret facilities primarily concern the enriched-uranium, not the pluto-nium, path to the bomb. Heavy-water reactors are large, above-ground facilities that generate huge amounts of energy. It would be simply impossible to hide those signatures. Uranium enrichment facilities on the other hand, give off less heat, can be smaller, and can be placed underground. In other words, they could be hidden.

But it is unlikely that Iran has any secret facilities that are producing enriched uranium. To understand why, let's reflect on Iran's efforts to hide its enrichment activities in the past. The enrichment facility at Natanz was intended to be a secret facility, but it was discovered in 2003 and it didn't begin operating on an industrial scale until 2007. Then Iran tried to build another secret facility at Qom. Again, this operation was uncovered in the planning stages in 2009, and the facility didn't became operational until 2012. To believe that Iran has a secret uranium enrichment facility in operation, therefore, we would have to assume that Iran began building multiple secret underground facilities in parallel many years ago and that we only uncovered some of them. This interpretation borders on implausibility for several reasons. First, Iran has not been very successful at hiding its nuclear facilities in the past. Second, Iran does not have unlimited resources and over the past ten years it has already constructed two large underground uranium enrichment facilities. It is hard to imagine that it was building multiple secret facilities in parallel. Third, if Iran were building a secret facility, it would likely need to transfer equipment and materials from its operating facilities to the new secret facility (it does frequently make transfers between its declared facilities at Natanz and Qom), and the IAEA and Western intelligence agencies would likely spot any attempts at diversion from the declared facilities. Fourth, as our experience with

Natanz and Qom demonstrates, there is a long time lag between when a country starts laying the foundation for an enrichment facility and when that facility actually starts producing enriched uranium. It is possible, therefore, that Iran is digging a hole in the side of a mountain somewhere in the hopes that this would one day become a uranium enrichment facility, but it is hard to imagine that Iran already has a secret uranium enrichment facility up and running. In sum, there is good reason to believe that we know the full extent of Iran's nuclear program.

HOW LONG UNTIL IRAN HAS THE BOMB?

We now know the state of Iran's nuclear program, but, given these capabilities, how long would it take Iran to build the bomb? For years, analysts and politicians have put forward various timelines for how long it will take Iran to build nuclear weapons. Some of my friends remark that it seems like Iran has been a year or two away from the bomb for as long as they can remember. They conclude from this that current predictions that an Iranian bomb is just around the corner are similarly inaccurate. While it is true that many contradictory or alarmist predictions have been floated about Iran's timeline to a bomb, the vast majority of these estimates were made by people who (to be quite frank) really didn't know what they were talking about. Below you will find a clear and accurate accounting.

In order to build nuclear weapons, Iran must do three things: first, it must produce sufficient quantities of weapons-grade fissile material, either plutonium or highly enriched uranium. Second, it must use this material to construct a functioning nuclear warhead. Third, it must have some means of delivering the warhead to its intended target. Let's consider each step in turn.

The IAEA states that 8 kilograms of plutonium or 25 kgs of weapons-grade uranium is sufficient for producing nuclear weapons.[3] At present, Iran does not have any plutonium, but if and when the Arak reactor goes critical, Iran will be able to produce 10–12 kgs of plutonium a year. This is roughly enough for a bomb every six months and something we should continue to keep our eye on. Iran halted major work on the reactor in accordance with the terms of the interim deal, but if Iran decides to resume work at the site it would likely take less than one year for the reactor to become operational.

For now, Iran's efforts are focused on enriching uranium.[4] To build a nuclear weapon, a country would need 25 kgs of uranium enriched to 90 percent purity. (Your eyes may be glazing over at this point, but pay attention! This is important.) The nuclear reactors at Bushehr require fuel made from uranium enriched to 3.5 percent and the Tehran Research Reactor requires 20 percent. By convention, low-enriched uranium (LEU) is the term given to enriched uranium below the 20 percent level. Highly enriched uranium (HEU) means uranium enriched above 20 percent. And weapons-grade uranium (WGU) denotes 90 percent HEU. (To distinguish between various levels of LEU, some journalists covering Iran have begun calling 20 percent LEU medium-enriched uranium, but this is an unusual term and I will not use it in this book.)

Previously, Iran had been enriching to 20 percent because this is the maximum purity required for its stated peaceful purposes. Under the terms of the interim deal, Iran agreed not to enrich above 5 percent. Enriching much above these thresholds, especially toward the 90 percent level, would be a telltale sign that Iran was dashing for a bomb. It should be noted, however, that Iran has the capability to enrich to 90 percent if its leaders decided to do so. Enriching uranium is kind of like riding a bike. The hard part is getting up, but once you have your balance and are moving forward, it is not that difficult to increase your speed. The best outside experts estimate that if Iran decided to enrich to 90 percent today, it would take roughly two to three months to produce one bomb's worth of WGU.[5] Moreover, experts estimate that the type of "comprehensive" nuclear deals under discussion between Iran and the international community would only add a few months to this timeline, bringing Iran's dash time to enough WGU for one bomb to about six months if such a deal is successfully concluded.[6]

With sufficient quantities of weapons-grade uranium, Iran would next have to build the bomb. This brings us to step two. There are two basic nuclear weapons designs: gun-type and implosion. The gun-type design is simple. Indeed, it is so simple that the United States did not even test it before using it on Japan in World War II because we were so confident that it would work. A gun-type weapon is well within Iran's capability and, after producing sufficient quantities of WGU, it might take Tehran an additional month or two to fashion a workable warhead.

An implosion weapon, on the other hand, is much more complicated, but Iran has been making progress. Iran's scientists likely have access to a Chinese design for an implosion nuclear weapon given to them by A. Q. Khan.[7] Iran has also conducted research and a number of experiments related to building an implosion-type nuclear weapon.[8] Experts estimate that it would take Iran roughly a year or so to build an implosion weapon.[9]

Third, and finally, Iran would need some means of getting a nuclear weapon to its intended target. The advanced nuclear powers rely on three primary means of delivery: bomber aircraft, ballistic missiles, and submarine-launched ballistic missiles (SLBMs). Iran does not have SLBMs, so this method of delivery is out of the question. Iran does have an air force, but it is not very good.[10] Aircraft, therefore, would not be a reliable means of delivering nuclear weapons for Iran. Iran does, however, have a large stockpile of ballistic missiles.[11] At present, these missiles have ranges capable of reaching all of the Middle East and parts of southern Europe. Meanwhile, Iran is currently working to develop longer-range missiles.[12] The US Department of Defense estimates that by 2015, Iran could have a ballistic missile capable of reaching Western Europe and the East Coast of the United States.[13] Constructing a nuclear warhead small enough to fit on the nose cone of a ballistic missile is quite difficult, and experts estimate that it could take Iran several years to accomplish this feat. [14]

In addition to the three primary means of delivery, it is possible that a country could choose an unconventional delivery method, such as putting a nuclear weapon in a truck or a cargo container and driving or shipping the weapon to its intended target. This is an option that Iran could exercise immediately upon building its first nuclear weapon.

In sum, therefore, it would take Iran two to three months from the decision to do so to produce weapons-grade uranium, one year to construct an implosion weapon, and several years to develop a reliable means of delivery. Some analysts look at these timelines and thus claim that we have several years to solve the Iranian nuclear challenge.[15]

This conclusion, however, is profoundly incorrect because the first step is all that really matters. From a nonproliferation perspective, the longer timelines that include perfection of nuclear weapon design and delivery vehicles are completely irrelevant. Once Iran has sufficient quantities of WGU, the game is over.

To better understand the issue, let's begin with some simple military analysis. At present, the United States has the ability to conduct airstrikes on Iran's nuclear facilities to prevent it from producing enriched uranium. We know where its declared facilities are and we can destroy them. There are downsides to a strike to be sure, but we have a viable military option. If Iran produces significant quantities of weapons-grade uranium, however, all is lost. Iran could move that material anywhere, including secret and deeply buried bunkers. We would not know where the material is located, and even if we did, we would not be able to destroy it. At that point, Iran could construct nuclear weapons without fear of US intervention. Our only remaining options would be launching a full-scale ground invasion to search the entire country for hidden nuclear material or praying that Iran never decides to weaponize. Neither option is attractive. This is essentially the situation we have been facing for several years in North Korea. While North Korea might or might not have the ability to construct and deliver a functioning nuclear warhead, it already possesses sufficient quantities of weapons-grade fissile material and we therefore have no viable means of rolling back the nuclear program.

In short, therefore, we must act before Iran develops significant quantities of weapons-grade uranium. If we wait until Iran is turning the screws on a nuclear device, we will be too late.

If we are serious about stopping Iran from building nuclear weap-ons, we must not let them acquire sufficient quantities of WGU. The operative question then is: How long would it take Iran to produce one bomb's worth of HEU? As I stated above, the answer today is two to three months from the time Iran decides to enrich to 90 percent and, with a comprehensive deal in place, that timeline would only be extended to about six months. As long as Iran's supreme leader, Ayatollah Ali Khamenei, does not make the decision to enrich to higher levels, however, we will have more time.

There is another possibility to take into account as well. Iran might decide to ramp up its nuclear activities, but not immediately dash to one bomb's worth of WGU. Rather, if the interim agreement collapses or Iran decides to cheat on its terms, it could slowly build up its stockpiles of LEU, install more centrifuges at Natanz and Qom, and install more advanced centrifuges. All of these advancements would reduce the time it would take Iran to dash to one bomb's worth of WGU. At some point, Iran's dash time could compress to be shorter than the time it would take the United States to respond. Some have referred to this point as an "undetectable breakout" capability.[16] Whatever you want to call it, this development would force an important decision point on the United States. If we let Iran go beyond this point, we will essentially be acquiescing to a nuclear-armed Iran because if it ever decided to build the bomb, there would no longer be anything we could do to stop it.

Fortunately, as long as the nuclear freeze negotiated in the interim deal remains in place, the march to undetectable breakout is not much of a concern. But if the agreement falls apart and Iran resumes its nuclear activities, then it would likely take Iran less than a year to arrive at an "undetectable breakout" capability.

In short, this systematic review of Iran's nuclear capabilities suggests that if the diplomatic track breaks down and Iran ramps up its nuclear program, then we would only have an estimated two to twelve months to solve the Iranian nuclear challenge. In other words, if diplomacy fails, then we will not have much time before we need to consider other options.

DOES IRAN WANT THE BOMB?

The United States and much of the rest of the international community fear that Iran is developing a robust nuclear program in order to build nuclear weapons, but Iran insists that it is merely interested in developing a peaceful nuclear energy program. Which side is telling the truth? The answer is simple: Iran would like to build nuclear weapons. The only people Tehran is fooling at this point are people who want to be fooled.

To proceed, we can approach this issue like social scientists. We can treat each claim as a hypothesis and evaluate which is better supported by the available evidence. This exercise will reveal that the evidence is simply not consistent with the notion that Iran is interested in a peaceful energy program.

We can begin by considering Iran's strategic objectives and how they might be served by nuclear weapons. Iran's two primary strategic goals are (1) to be able to deter a foreign attack from its adversaries like Israel and the United States, and (2) to become the most dominant state in the Middle East. [17] Nuclear weapons help them achieve both of those goals. A peaceful nuclear energy program gives them neither.

Nuclear weapons would provide Iran with the ultimate security guarantee. If another country attacked, or threatened to attack, Tehran's leaders could threaten to retaliate with a devastating nuclear war. The prospect of inviting a terrible nuclear catastrophe would be enough to deter Israel, the United States, or any other state from directly attacking Iran. This is a significant strategic benefit.

Nuclear weapons would also contribute to Iran's desire to be the Middle East's regional hegemon. Freed from concerns about existential threats to its national security, it could expand its conception of its national interest, throw its weight around more in the region, and even explicitly brandish nuclear weapons in crises in an attempt to coerce adversaries. Even if nuclear weapons didn't contribute to these broader goals, the mere possession of nuclear weapons would place Iran in an elite group. It would be one of only ten states on Earth and one of two in the Middle East to gain access to the nuclear club.

In addition, Iran's leaders also badly want to protect their theocratic government and, as we will discuss in more detail in future chapters, the acquisition of nuclear weapons could give the regime a longer lease on life.

In his seminal study, Stanford University political scientist Scott Sagan lists security, prestige, and domestic politics as the three most important reasons why countries decide to build nuclear weapons.[18] All three motivations are pushing Iran toward the bomb.

A peaceful nuclear energy program is much less relevant to Iran's strategic goals. One cannot threaten to respond to foreign invasion by generating electricity. One does not become the most dominant state in the Middle East by developing a seventy-year-old technology that is so commonplace that it is used to produce power in dozens of countries around the world. And one does not generate regime stability by inviting unprecedented international pressure and scrutiny over something as trivial as the means one uses to generate electricity.

In short, if one takes Iran's leaders at their word about what their goals are, one would have to assume that they would badly want to build nuclear weapons.

But if we don't want to take Iran's leaders at their word, then let's look at the country's needs and its behavior. First, it is not clear that Iran has a need for nuclear energy. Nuclear power is a vital source of power for countries like Japan that have very few natural resources. But Iran sits on huge oil and gas reserves. Why would Iran need nuclear energy? Leaders in Tehran claim that they want to develop nuclear power to provide energy domestically to free up oil and gas for export. This is a plausible story. Still, it remains a fact that Iran does not badly need nuclear power to meet its energy needs.

Second, Iran does not need to enrich uranium domestically. The vast majority of countries on Earth that operate nuclear reactors do not enrich their own uranium. Instead, they have a more advanced nuclear power, like the United States, France, or Russia provide them with nuclear fuel-cycle services. In these arrangements, the more advanced nuclear power sends the recipient enriched-uranium fuel rods to run in their nuclear reactors. Then, when the fuel rods are spent, they are shipped back to the supplier for storage or reprocessing. The international community has offered to provide Iran with fuel-cycle services time and time again in international negotiations, but these offers have always been rejected by Iran's leaders. They claim that these arrangements are insufficient because they cannot trust other countries to follow through on their commitment to provide them with nuclear fuel. Therefore, they claim, for reasons of energy security, they need to enrich uranium domestically. But given the small size of Iran's nuclear program and its lack of large domestic uranium reserves, an indigenous uranium enrichment program does not make economic sense. In short, if Iran really wanted nothing more than to generate nuclear power, then it could simply have another country provide it with fuel services. It would be better off economically and the crisis over Iran's uranium enrichment program would be over. Yet Iran insists on enriching its own uranium.

Third, Iran doesn't need to enrich to such high levels. When Iran began enriching uranium in 2003, it only enriched to 3.5 percent. It claimed that it needed 3.5 percent fuel for the nuclear reactor at Bushehr. At the time, the international community was very concerned about Iran's enrichment capability and would have been shocked if Iran claimed that it needed to enrich to higher levels. Then, in 2010, Iran did just that. It claimed that it needed 20 percent enriched uranium to fuel the TRR. Iran already has a ten-year supply of fuel for the TRR, but it insisted that it needed more. Under the terms of the interim deal, Iran agreed to limit enrichment to 5 percent, but then it immediately threatened to enrich to higher levels if negotiations eventually fail. In December 2013, Iran's parliament introduced legislation that would require Iran to enrich to 50 to 60 percent to make fuel for nuclear-powered submarines. This despite the fact that Iran does not even have nuclear-powered submarines or immediate plans to acquire them. Rather than justifiable reasons, it appears that Iran is merely searching for excuses to enrich to ever-higher levels.

Fourth, Iran doesn't need to build a heavy-water reactor. Light-water reactors and heavy-water reactors can both produce energy, but heavy-water reactors are also bomb-making machines. The international community has said that Iran is welcome to have as many light-water reactors as it would like, but that heavy-water reactors are off the table. Under the terms of the interim deal, Iran agreed to temporarily halt some construction on the heavy-water reactor, but other work at the site continues. Iran could negotiate to dismantle the heavy-water reactor altogether and, in return, have an advanced nuclear supplier come in and build multiple light-water reactors in its place. Yet Iran insists on building a heavy-water reactor.

Fifth, if Iran were really interested in producing nuclear energy, it wouldn't need to be so sneaky. Iran tried to hide its first uranium enrichment facility at Natanz. It didn't admit to its existence until it was exposed by a dissident group. Then it attempted to secretly build the Qom enrichment facility. Again, it didn't admit to the existence of the facility until it was called out. Iran has an obligation under its IAEA safeguards agreement to report the construction of new facilities. If these were really facilities intended for the production of nuclear energy for peaceful purposes, why try to hide them?

Sixth, it doesn't make sense that Iran would go through such hardship in order to have a nuclear energy program. Due to its insistence on pursuing such dangerous nuclear technologies over the past decade, an international coalition has formed against Iran, making it an international pariah and badly damaging its economy. In order to endure such hardship, Iran's current supreme leader, Ayatollah Ali Khamenei, must believe that there is a very bright light at the end of this tunnel. It is implausible to think that a leader would willingly destroy his country's reputation and economy over the means used to produce energy. But having the ultimate security guarantee might very well be worth it.

Seventh, Iran is building ICBMs. No country on Earth, not even the United States, mounts conventional warheads on ICBMs. Traditionally, ICBMs have had one purpose: to deliver nuclear warheads thousands of miles away. If Iran is not developing nuclear weapons, then why does it have such a robust ICBM development program?

Finally, if Iran weren't interested in building nuclear weapons, it wouldn't need to design nuclear weapons. Yet, the IAEA has evidence that Iran possesses the design for an implosion-type nuclear weapon and that

Iran has conducted experiments on engineering its own nuclear warhead on the Parchin military base.[19]

Some experts question the intensity with which Iran is pursuing the design and construction of nuclear weapons, but serious examination of these doubts only serve to reinforce the notion that Iran would like to build nuclear warheads. In a widely reported 2007 National Intelligence Estimate (NIE), the US intelligence community famously assessed that Iran had stopped its research on nuclear warhead design in 2003.[20] Many people incorrectly concluded from this assessment that Iran gave up its nuclear weapons program a decade ago, but that is the wrong lesson to draw. This is because the NIE also stated very clearly that Iran was pushing full steam ahead on the other two elements of building nuclear weapons: enriching uranium and improving its ballistic missile delivery systems. Since enriching uranium is the most difficult and important part of building nuclear weapons, the NIE was essentially saying that the heart of Iran's nuclear program was very much alive and well. Moreover, since it is simply not possible to assemble a nuclear warhead without sufficient quantities of WGU, stopping the warhead design work at that point was essentially irrelevant to Iran's overall progress toward a nuclear weapons capability. Most importantly, however, we now have reason to believe that the 2007 NIE's controversial assessment about weaponization was incorrect. The intelligence agencies of our European allies disagreed with the 2007 assessment from the start; they have always believed that Iran's warhead design work continued after 2003.[21] In addition, the IAEA has made a number of subsequent statements suggesting that Iran's warhead design work was not halted in 2003.[22] It appears, therefore, that Iran has been steadily advancing all three elements of its nuclear weapons program, including nuclear warhead design.

In sum, the evidence is overwhelming. Iran would like to build nuclear weapons.

The US intelligence community (IC) has frequently said, however, that we have no firm evidence that Iran's leaders have yet made a final decision to build nuclear weapons.[23] Many people who badly want to avoid a confrontation with Iran and therefore desperately want to believe Iran's cover story point to this assessment as proof that Iran is not doing anything wrong. But the IC's assessment is more about the limits of intelligence than it is about Iran's intentions. After all, we can't get inside the supreme leader's head. Just because we have no firm evidence does not mean that Khamenei has not already made his decision. It is likely that he has—after all, he has been building up his country's nuclear infrastructure for over twenty years. It would be naïve for us to think that he hasn't thought long and hard about what he intends to do with it. Moreover, this strange focus on a final decision to build nuclear weapons is largely beside the point. As I made clear in the above discussion on building the bomb, a country can only assemble a nuclear weapon after producing significant quantities of weapons-grade fissile material. Since Iran has not yet produced enough WGU for a bomb, it couldn't possibly make a final decision to build nuclear weapons even if it wanted to. Indeed, by rapidly increasing its ability to enrich uranium over the past decade, Iran's behavior was completely consistent with that of a country that has made the final decision to build nuclear weapons.

Many DC-based experts, in an abundance of caution, argue that the evidence I have laid out so far only suggests that Iran's supreme leader wants a nuclear weapons *option.* They argue that it is clear that he is interested in something more than nuclear energy and that he is putting in place all the pieces that would allow him to build nuclear weapons quickly if he decided to go in that direction, but that we cannot yet conclude definitely that he will ultimately decide to go for the bomb. But, why would the supreme leader go through so much trouble and endure so much international pressure to put the pieces in place if he didn't intend to do anything with them? It is simply implausible that Iran would go to such great lengths to get one screwdriver's turn away from the most powerful weapons on Earth—a weapon that would help Iran meet its foremost geopolitical goals—and then suddenly once the international community was no longer in a position to intervene, voluntarily stop short.

Others claim that the supreme leader has issued a fatwa, a religious edict, declaring nuclear weapons to be inconsistent with the tenants of Islam, but this is incorrect. Rather, Khamenei has publicly discussed the political difficulties involved in building nuclear weapons, but there is no evidence of a formal religious edict.[24] Moreover, even if he had issued a fatwa, it wouldn't matter that much. Shia clerics often change or even reverse fatwas. The supreme leader could easily issue a new fatwa declaring that Iran must acquire nuclear weapons and that this action is justified to serve a greater religious good, namely, the supreme interests of the Iranian Revolution.

But, you may be asking, what about the interim deal agreed to in November 2013? Isn't this proof that Iran is not interested in building nuclear weapons and is prepared to demonstrate this to the international community? It is of course possible that after pursuing a nuclear weapons capability for over twenty years, Iran has made a sudden strategic decision to abandon its nuclear weapons ambitions altogether and this is what motivated it to sign the nuclear deal with the P5+1. Unfortunately, as we will discuss in more detail in chapter 4, I suspect that the reality is that the interim agreement is likely a tactical maneuver designed to relieve international pressure while maintaining the nuclear program largely intact for a future nuclear weapons bid. So while we can hope that Iran has decided to give up its dream of becoming a nuclear power once and for all, the more careful analysis above gives us good reason to be pessimistic.

In sum, it is my judgment, based on the preponderance of evidence, that Iran has in fact made a final decision to build nuclear weapons if at all possible. Any other interpretation is not supported by the facts. I will end by relaying an analogy told by one of my colleagues, Emanuele Ottolenghi, a fellow at the Foundation for the Defense of Democracies. In January 2013, we were at conference in London, and Ottolenghi asked his audience to imagine for a moment that we had a neighbor who went to a bicycle shop every weekend for thirty years.[25] And every weekend, we saw the neighbor coming home with various bicycle parts: frames, tires, brakes, handlebars, etc. And, then one day, he invited us to his basement to show us his work. There we saw an impressive bicycle-making shop. There were no complete bicycles, but there were a bunch of partially manufactured bicycles in various stage of completion. So, at this point, we naturally ask him, "Are you planning to build bicycles?" And he responds, "I don't know. I haven't decided yet."

Would we believe him?

CHAPTER THREE

THE NONSTARTERS

Covert Ops, Japanese Models,
and Persian Springs

ON JANUARY 11, 2012, MOSTAFA AHMADI-ROSHAN was driving to work in Tehran's morning rush-hour traffic when a man on a motorcycle pulled up next to him and placed a magnetic device on the driver's-side door of his silver Peugeot 405. It was the last thing Ahmadi-Roshan saw. The motorcycle sped away just before the bomb exploded, killing the Iranian nuclear scientist. In addition to targeted assassinations of Iranian nuclear scientists, Iran's nuclear program has experienced many other mysterious accidents that seem to have been pulled directly from the pages of an Ian Fleming novel, including cyberattacks and sabotage, all temporarily delaying Iran's nuclear progress.

The previous chapter made it clear that Iran has an advanced nuclear program that could be used to build nuclear weapons in short order, which raises the question: What can the United States and the rest of the international community do to keep Tehran from the bomb? Since diplomacy might not solve the problem, and because the realistic alternatives (acquiescing or bombing) are so unattractive, many well-intentioned observers have grasped for other possible solutions to the Iranian nuclear challenge. Perhaps the United States could avoid the fallout of an overt military attack by conducting a covert war on the Iranian nuclear program that would have the same effect? Or, alternatively, short of a diplomatic breakthrough, perhaps we can come to some sort of implicit understanding whereby Iran is allowed to maintain an advanced nuclear program but refrain from building nuclear weapons, aka "the Japan model"? Or perhaps we can simply wait out the current government in Iran? Iran's theocratic leaders are not terribly popular and one day they might fall, bringing to power a more pro-Western and democratic leadership ready to trade away the nuclear program.

While all of these options sound nice in principle, they are nonstarters in practice. This chapter will explain why.

COVERT OPS

Dr. Ahmadi-Roshan's untimely end was far from unique. At least two other Iranian nuclear scientists suffered the exact same fate while a fourth, Dr. Dariush Rezaei-Nejad, was gunned down outside the front door of his home by a machine-gun–toting man on a motorcycle.[1] No one has claimed responsibility for the attacks, but many journalists speculate that the assassinations might have been the work of Israel's intelligence service, the Mossad.[2]

The Mossad rises to the top of the short list in part because it has a history of carrying out this type of attack. In the 1950s and 1960s, both Egypt and Israel were racing to build nuclear weapons and ballistic missiles. Egypt's weapons programs employed many German engineers who had gained experience developing V-2 rockets for Nazi Germany during World War II. Due to the Mossad, however, German rocket scientists working in Egypt had a short life expectancy. Among other problems, the letters they received in the mail had a tendency to explode when opened.[3] Later, in the 1980s, Israel's regional rival, Iraq, was pursuing several types of WMD technologies and at least one European scientist working for Saddam Hussein was shot outside of his apartment in Brussels.[4] Again, many believe the Mossad was responsible.

These assassinations, while seemingly cold-blooded, are motivated by several grisly logics. First, it actually does take a rocket scientist to be a rocket scientist; not everyone is qualified for the job. By systematically eliminating the human capital in Iran's nuclear program, one might hope to deny Tehran the ability to complete its weapons projects. Second, even if one cannot hope to kill every Iranian with a PhD, one can at least send a message to the others: being a scientist in Iran's nuclear program may have fringe benefits, but it also has fringe costs. The fear of an untimely death may encourage scientists already in the program to look for other lines of work. Third, and finally, one can hope to make the work of an Iranian nuclear scientist seem so perilous as to deter Iran's best and brightest from going into this profession in the first place.

While there is reason to believe, therefore, that assassinations may harm Iran's nuclear progress, there is also reason to suspect that they will not be enough. Knocking off individuals one by one is a highly inefficient way to slow a large nuclear program in a country with a deep scientific bench. These targeted killings are nothing more than a drop in the proverbial bucket.

For this reason, targeted killings cannot be the only weapon aimed at throwing sand in the gears of Iran's nuclear program. And they are not.

Enriching uranium is incredibly difficult. It involves rotating metal cylinders at the speed of sound—no small feat. Inexperienced engineers often struggle to keep the centrifuges from spinning out of control and crashing on the ground. Indeed, the process is so sensitive that the natural oils from a human hand can be enough to throw everything off. This posed a problem for Iran until their scientists discovered that they needed to don special gloves before handling centrifuges.[5]

Iran therefore created some of its own difficulties as it learned to enrich uranium, but it also appears to have had some outside help.

The CIA has engaged in a campaign of sabotage against Iran's nuclear program for years. Among other measures, it is reported that the CIA has surreptitiously introduced damaged parts and faulty designs into Iran's nuclear supply chain.[6]

By far the most spectacular covert action aimed at Iran's nuclear program, however, was Stuxnet. Stuxnet is a computer worm that infected Iran's nuclear program from 2008 to 2010. The worm targeted the control systems that Iran used to operate its centrifuge facilities. It ordered the control system to variously increase and decrease the speed at which the centrifuges rotated, throwing the delicate machines off balance and causing them to spin out of control and crash. Perhaps just as ingenious, the worm was programmed so that the control system's monitors reported that everything was operating normally. For two years, Iranian scientists were dumbfounded as to why they were having so much difficulty with the centrifuges.

Then, in 2010, due to a design flaw in the software code, the worm began to infect the Siemens control system that Iran used to operate its nuclear facilities in similar machines outside of Iran. Indonesia, India, Pakistan, Azerbaijan, and even the United States all had problems. The existence of Stuxnet suddenly became public, tipping Iran off to their problem and leading them to wipe their machines.

The origin of the Stuxnet worm was kept a mystery for years, although many suspected US or Israeli involvement. Neither state went out of its way to deny the allegations. In a 2010 interview, for example, Gary Samore, then the White House coordinator for Arms Control and Weapons of Mass Destruction, said, "We're glad they are having trouble with their centrifuge machine and that we—the US and its allies—are doing everything we can to make sure that we complicate matters for them."[7]

Then, finally, in June 2012, David Sanger of the *New York Times*, based on interviews with several anonymous administration officials, reported that Stuxnet had indeed been a joint project of US and Israeli intelligence.[8] It is not quite clear why administration officials decided to reveal US involvement in Stuxnet. The decision certainly carried risks. The trumpeting of America's entrance into the cyberwar game caused some to worry that this could set a dangerous precedent and encourage America's enemies to follow suit.[9] Others speculated that the announcement was part of President Obama's re-election strategy and was intended to demonstrate that he had been tough enough on Iran.[10]

Whatever its precise motivations, the disclosure had the effect of revealing fascinating details about Stuxnet. The project was incredibly complex.

For example, the software code that made up the worm was fifty times larger than the average computer worm. In addition, the United States went so far as to build mini-replicas of Iran's enrichment facilities in the United States to test the efficacy of the worm before inflicting it on Iran.[11]

The worm also made history in other ways. For years, cybersecurity experts had warned of an impending "digital Pearl Harbor" in which a sophisticated cyberattack would wreak great physical destruction.[12] Despite these gloom-and-doom predictions, however, various worms, viruses, direct denial of service attacks, and other types of cyberattacks, while causing much disruption, had never caused physical damage. Stuxnet was the first. And you can be certain that it will not be the last.

What does all of this mean, however, for solving the Iranian nuclear challenge? This discussion leaves no doubt that covert options like assassinations and cyberattacks are fascinating, but are they effective? When news of Stuxnet first became public, some experts estimated that the worm had brought as much as a two-year delay to Iran's nuclear progress, but these early reports were overly optimistic.[13] We now know that Iran quickly and fully recovered from the cyberattacks.

Indeed, Iran had been the target of various covert operations for years, yet it continued to make steady progress on its nuclear program. If one simply examines the objective measures of Iran's nuclear development released in the IAEA reports every three months, it is clear that Iran did not suffer any major setbacks. The number of centrifuges operating and the size of the enriched uranium stockpiles continued to increase every three months. Years of intense black operations failed to make a dent.

One might argue that if past efforts have been unsuccessful, perhaps we need to step up our game. If diplomacy fails to solve the problem, then we should just launch a more intense covert campaign that would definitively stop Iran's nuclear progress. Yet, slowing or stopping Iran's nuclear program had been a top national security priority for over a decade. Indeed, the Stuxnet virus exemplifies the extreme lengths to which we were willing to go in an effort to upend Iran's technical progress. It was not enough.

The simple fact of the matter is that there are things you can do with 30,000-pound bombs that you cannot do with computer worms.

Fine, you might be thinking, if cyberattacks, sabotage, and assassination won't do the trick, then what about a covert military attack? As we will discuss in chapter 6, a US military strike would greatly damage Iran's nuclear facilities, but it would also come with many costs. So one might imagine that we can have our cake and eat it too by conducting a covert bombing run on Iran's nuclear facilities. Under such a plan, we could simply bomb Iran's key nuclear facilities but never admit that the United States had been behind the attack.

This is not a serious option either, however. Everyone knows that the United States is the only country capable of carrying out such an attack, especially if it succeeded in destroying Iran's deeply buried and hardened facilities. If we woke up one morning to find that the nuclear facilities at Natanz and Qom had been destroyed, it would be obvious to all who had been behind the attack. It would not, therefore, be possible, or advisable, for us to lie to our friends, our enemies, and the American public about waging war against another country.

In short, the international community waged an aggressive covert campaign against Iran's nuclear program for years, but, in the face of this resistance, Iran continued to inch closer to a weapons capability. Granted, these covert actions had some effect on Iran's program. Indeed, it is likely that Iran's nuclear progress would have been even more precipitous in the absence of such measures. What this section makes clear, however, is that covert operations will not, on their own, be sufficient to solve the problem.

THE JAPAN MODEL

I must apologize to any readers who had expectations to the contrary, but this is not a section about a physically attractive Asian on a catwalk. Rather, the following paragraphs discuss the notion that Japan's nuclear program could serve as a template for Iran to follow.

Japan has had an advanced and peaceful nuclear program since the 1970s. Before the Fukishma-Daichi nuclear meltdown in 2011, Japan produced 30 percent of its energy from domestic nuclear power plants. This is an understandable option for a country that lacks natural energy resources of its own. It operated dozens of nuclear reactors, has the ability to reprocess plutonium, and possesses a stockpile of thirty-five tons of plutonium.[14] This is enough plutonium to produce a large arsenal of nuclear weapons. Japan also possesses a uranium enrichment facility that could conceivably be used to enrich uranium for use in an atomic bomb. In short, Japan has the ability to build nuclear weapons on short order if it decides to do so. Yet, it has so far refrained from building nuclear weapons. For this reason, Japan is often called a "latent," "virtual," or "de facto" nuclear weapons state.

Some analysts see Japan as a possible model for Iran. Iran, like Japan, is on its way to becoming a latent nuclear power. Advocates of the Japan model for Iran argue that we might be able to come to a tacit understanding whereby Iran, much like Japan, is permitted to maintain an advanced nuclear capability so long as it refrains from actually building nuclear weapons.

In April 2013, I appeared on National Public Radio's hour-long call-in show *Talk of the Nation*. Appearing on air with me was Jessica Matthews, president of the Carnegie Endowment for International Peace. During the show, Matthews suggested the Japan model as a way out of the current conundrum. She argued:

> I think . . . the most important outcome . . . that might be mutually acceptable at this point might well be that Iran has sort of an existential nuclear capability, but not an actual one or declared one. And that, while it is by no means a good outcome for us—it's a horrible outcome—is, in my view, much less horrible than the consequences of going to war. . . . A lot of people call this the Japan option: Everything's there. It's sort of a screwdriver turn away.[15]

Matthews is not alone among serious experts who hold this view. Some argue that this might actually be Iran's best option. They suggest that with such an advanced capability, Iran's enemies would have to wonder whether Iran might actually have a nuclear weapon or two stashed away somewhere, so this option might provide Tehran with the full security benefits of actual nuclear weapons. Moreover, they claim, this option wouldn't have the costs associated with openly declaring a nuclear weapons capability, such as inviting the United States and the international community to increase sanctions or launch a military attack.

From the US point of view, they imply that this compromise could be acceptable because if Iran never actually builds nuclear weapons, then we would not have to worry about the most severe negative consequences of Iranian nuclear proliferation, such as nuclear war. This might, they suggest, be a win-win situation.

Alas, upon serious reflection, it becomes clear that the Japan model is also a nonstarter for a variety of reasons. First, it is important to point out that Iran is not Japan. Japan is a formal treaty ally of the United States. Japan has not attempted to hide its nuclear facilities from the international community. It has not lied to IAEA inspectors. It does not provide weapons and money to international terrorist groups. It does not threaten to wipe its neighbors off the map. It did not fight a major naval battle with the United States in 1988, unlike Iran, which engaged the US Navy in its largest naval battle since World War II in Operation Praying Mantis. It has not been behind the killing of US soldiers in Iraq and Afghanistan for the past decade. Japan and Iran are very different countries, and there are very good reasons why the United States should be much more skeptical of Iran's intentions and fearful of its nuclear capabilities.

Second, in order to believe that the Japan model is a workable solution, one must believe that leaders in Iran or the United States, or both, are stupid. The reason the Iranian nuclear issue is a major international crisis is because Washington and Tehran's interests are diametrically opposed. It is a zero-sum game. Leaders in Tehran believe that they can enhance their relative power by acquiring nuclear weapons, and they have been willing to go through much pain in order to acquire them. Leaders in Washington believe that nuclear weapons in Iran would pose such a grave threat to US national security that they say they are willing to go to war to prevent this from happening. If actual nuclear weapons are what changes the game, then Iran does not benefit by stopping short. If, on the other hand, a virtual capability is the game changer, then the United States should not accept a latent capability in Iran. To suggest, therefore, that by stopping a screwdriver's turn away from the bomb, both countries can somehow get what they want is ridiculous.

Third, and most importantly, the Japan option is not actually a distinct option. Rather it is, in essence, exactly the same as acquiescing to a nuclear-armed Iran. This is because once Iran is a screwdriver's turn away from a nuclear bomb, the United States can no longer physically prevent Iran from building nuclear weapons. Once Iran has a virtual capability, we would be reduced to hoping and praying that Iran never decides to actualize its nuclear potential. Whether Iran eventually builds nuclear weapons in this scenario is entirely up to Tehran. We forfeit all control. Moreover, there is no reason to believe that Iran would stop with a virtual nuclear capability. As we discussed in the previous chapter, Iran's most important strategic goals are to deter foreign attack and to become the most dominant state in the Middle East. Actual nuclear weapons help Iran achieve both of those goals. A bunch of nuclear facilities does not help them accomplish either. After all, Japan's sophisticated nuclear power infrastructure does not make it the most dominant state in East Asia. It is silly, therefore, to think that Iran's ambitious geopolitical goals in the Middle East would be satisfied by the Japan model. There is little reason to believe that Iran would be content with the Japan model. It would build nuclear weapons as soon as it thought it could get away with it.

In sum, the Japan model would quickly slip into the Pakistan or North Korea model. Readers interested in learning more about the "Japan model" as a solution to the Iranian nuclear crisis, therefore, should consult chapter 5, "Iran with the Bomb," for they are one and the same.

REGIME CHANGE

Mohamed Bouazizi set himself on fire. It was December 17, 2010, and the Tunisian street vendor, like many in the working class in Tunisia, was frustrated by the high rates of unemployment and lack of economic opportunity in his country. Self-immolation was his way of visibly demonstrating his displeasure. Within weeks, the flames spread from a single human body to engulf an entire region. The Arab Spring had begun.

Disaffected groups in Tunisia quickly took to the streets to protest the economic mismanagement of their government. On January 14, less than a month later, President Zine El Abidine Ben Ali fled the country, paving the way for a new constitution and government in Tunisia.

But the tumult didn't stop there. People in other Arab countries, inspired by the model in Tunisia, rose up. Over the next few months, there were at least minor protests in almost every country in the Arab world and major uprisings in others. Leaders were able to hang on to power in some countries, like the tiny gulf nation of Bahrain, but elsewhere dictators fell. Egypt's strongman, Hosni Mubarak, was forced from power after ruling for thirty years. A civil war erupted in Libya and, with the help of NATO airpower, rebel groups overthrew and then brutally murdered Colonel Muammar Gaddafi, ending his forty-two-year reign. Domestic violence spread to Syria where President Bashar Assad is using every trick in the book, including chemical weapon attacks on his own people, in an effort to retain control. Finally, in Yemen, President Ali Abdullah Saleh survived an assassination attempt in June 2011 but was still forced to cede power.

What if the Arab Spring spread to Iran? If we can't sabotage Iran's nuclear program out of existence and if we can't convince this regime to voluntarily dismantle its nuclear program, perhaps we could help bring to power a different regime that would be more willing to deal with us on the nuclear program? Perhaps we will be blessed by a Persian Spring?

Many claim that as long as the current theocratic government rules Iran, we will have serious conflicts of interest and the solution is to just wait this regime out, or help push it out, and deal with the successor government. To be clear, this is not George W. Bush–style regime change, which calls for invading the country and overthrowing the government by force. Rather, this is a peaceful regime-change option.

There are certainly cracks in the foundation of the current regime. The government is unpopular in large segments of society and the average Iranian is much more secular and pro-Western than the ayatollah and his inner circle of advisers. This is a country with a history of revolutions, and it is possible that at some point the current government will be overthrown and a different, more moderate, government will come to power.

Indeed, it recently seemed that the Persian Spring might be coming, but the groundhog saw its shadow and crawled back into its hole, giving us a longer winter than we would have liked. In the summer of 2009, Iranian president Mahmoud Ahmadinejad was locked in a heated re-election campaign against several challengers, including Mir-Hossein Mousavi, who had been Iran's prime minister in the 1980s during the Iran-Iraq War but was now running as a Reformist candidate.

According to official results, Ahmadinejad won handily, 63 percent to 34 percent, but Mousavi's supporters didn't believe the official tally, suspected fraud, and took to the streets in protest. Many other students, youth, reformers, people dissatisfied with the theocratic government, and some people who simply had nothing better to do, soon joined them. As many as three million protestors filled Tehran's streets wearing green, the color of Mousavi's election campaign, chanting "where is our vote" and "down with the dictator." For a moment, it seemed possible that this Green Movement would sweep Iran's clerics from power.

But the government struck back quickly and forcefully. Government forces arrested hundreds of protestors, several deaths were reported, and Mousavi himself was imprisoned. The Green Movement was crushed. So were any hopes that the theocratic regime in Iran would be forced from power anytime soon.

Since that time, the clerics' grip on power has only increased. Most participants in the Green Movement are either dead, in prison, or in exile overseas. Other sources of domestic opposition within Iran are demoralized.

In the 2013 presidential election, Iranian voters selected Hassan Rouhani, the most moderate of the candidates who were permitted to run, signaling their displeasure with the direction of the country. Nevertheless, the election still underscored the enduring strength of the regime. At the end of the day, the presidency was transferred, without violence or protest, to a cleric and regime insider. From the regime's perspective, therefore, the 2013 election was a vast improvement over the turmoil in 2009. It is difficult to foresee a complete change of Iran's political system coming anytime soon.

There are, of course, mechanisms for changes in leadership *within* Iran's political system, but it is unlikely that these will result in an end to Iran's nuclear program. President Rouhani was able to deliver an interim nuclear deal in November 2013, but, as we will discuss in the next chapter, it is unlikely that he will be willing or able to make the major concessions required to seal a worthwhile "comprehensive" nuclear accord. After all, he still supports the clerical regime's strategic goals, including the continuation of a robust nuclear program; he just has a more moderate style of pursuing them. More importantly, however, despite all the attention lavished on the Iranian presidency by the international press in recent years, Iran's president is a mere figurehead on foreign policy matters. Real power lies with the supreme leader. Iran's president, therefore, only has as much authority on the nuclear issue as the supreme leader is willing to grant.

The slightly more interesting question, therefore, is: What happens when the Supreme Leader dies? Ayatollah Ali Khamenei is seventy-three years old. When he passes, a group of roughly one hundred Islamic clerics, the Assembly of Experts, will gather and elect a new supreme leader. The ayatollah, however, is in good health, and there is no reason to believe he will be leaving us anytime soon. As one expert on Iranian domestic politics told me, "He eats a lot of yogurt and takes long walks." Moreover, even if mortality catches up with him, the conservative process of appointment virtually forecloses any radical change. Anyone who is elected through this process is going to be dedicated to preserving *velayat-e faqih,* or "rule of the jurists," Iran's system of conservative Islamic government. They are also likely to be distrustful of the United States and the West. This is not the kind of person who would dismantle a nuclear program that has become a source of national pride or who would be eager to sign an agreement with Iran's longstanding enemy, the United States.

There are things the United States can do to encourage an indigenous regime change in Iran. Perhaps, most importantly, Washington can serve as an example to would-be reformers in Iran by consistently speaking out against the Iranian government and its gross violations of human rights. Unfortunately, this was not the US response in 2009. The Obama administration had come to power, also in early 2009, believing that it could engage the Iranian government, mend relations between the two countries, and resolve the nuclear dispute peacefully. In order to do this, they needed a partner in Iran's theocratic government. When protests broke out in Iran in the summer of 2009, therefore, the Obama administration's instinct was to stay silent for fear of embarrassing and alienating the mullahs with whom it had hoped to cooperate. In hindsight, it is clear that this was the wrong position to take; the United States should have stood strongly on the side of the reformist movement and against the leaders who have demonstrated themselves to be among our greatest adversaries for the past several decades. Alas, we did not. It is unlikely that our rhetorical support would have made a huge difference on the ground in Tehran, but it is still important for the United States to stand up for its values, which in this case also happened to align perfectly with our interests.

In addition to lending rhetorical support and serving as an example, the West can disseminate information technology to dissidents in Iran, enabling their communications in the face of their government's repression and censorship. Furthermore, Western democracy-promotion groups can meet with reformist elements and teach them techniques that have proved handy for toppling dictators elsewhere. Unfortunately, these are small steps that, while moving in the right direction, are unlikely to have a significant effect on domestic developments in Iran.

Moreover, even if a Persian Spring were to come to Iran, it still might not help us solve the nuclear conundrum. Even Rouhani, often considered a moderate by the Western press, and Mousavi, the leader of Iran's Green Movement, are strong supporters of Iran's nuclear program. Indeed, any leader in Iran, no matter how he or she comes to power, will inherit an Iran in the exact same geopolitical position and will, therefore, have the exact same strategic incentives to pursue and maintain Iran's nuclear capability.

While it is always possible that we could get a radical political change in Iran that will solve the nuclear program for us, we shouldn't hold our breath. Wishing for a miracle is not strategy. It is likely that we will have to make difficult choices on how to deal with Iran's nuclear program well before any new regime takes over the country. In other words, meteorologists are forecasting a nuclear winter before a Persian Spring.

If only there were some way to negotiate a comprehensive agreement with the current government that would solve this problem once and for all.

CHAPTER FOUR

A DEAL WITH THE DEVIL

Diplomacy and Sanctions

WHY CAN'T WE JUST SOLVE THIS PROBLEM DIPLO-matically? It is a question I often hear when I give public lectures on Iran. It is a popular option. In a Gallup poll, 73 percent of Americans say they would like to solve the Iran issue with diplomacy.[1] The vast majority of experts, myself included, believe that a diplomatic resolution to this crisis would be the best possible outcome, if we could get it. Indeed, if I suddenly got word that Iran had decided to give up its nuclear program and we had reason to believe that the agreement would be verifiable and would stick, I would drop everything and go celebrate. Even the leader of the free world, President Obama, wants a diplomatic resolution to this crisis. As a presidential candidate in 2008, then-Senator Obama made waves by vowing to sit down for presidential-level talks with Iran's leaders "without preconditions."[2]

Diplomacy is attractive because it offers an apparent way out of the possible dilemma of choosing between bombing Iran or letting Iran have the bomb. Rather than go to war, the diplomatic option lets us sit down and strike a bargain with which both sides can live.

With such a widespread consensus that a diplomatic resolution to this crisis would be best, why are we even discussing alternatives? The answer is that we might not be able to solve his problem diplomatically. Even President Obama assesses that a comprehensive nuclear accord with Iran is unlikely and it is possible that even a comprehensive accord will not fully neutralize the Iranian nuclear threat. We, therefore, need to be realistic.

But we shouldn't give up hope just yet. Even though the odds are not great, the possible alternatives discussed in chapters 5 and 6 are so much worse that it is worth giving the diplomatic effort everything we've got. So here goes nothing . . .

FROM THE AXIS OF EVIL TO KAZAKHSTAN

THE GEORGE W. BUSH YEARS, 2001–2009

In his 2002 State of the Union address, President George W. Bush named Iran, along with North Korea and Saddam Hussein's Iraq, as part of an "Axis of Evil, arming to threaten the peace of the world." At the time he made those remarks, he didn't even realize the full extent of Iran's villainy. It was a few months later, in August, when it was revealed that Iran was constructing secret nuclear facilities at Natanz and Arak.

This development in Iran's nuclear program posed a major problem, but the United States already had its hands full. By late 2002 and early 2003, the full attention of the US political system and national security apparatus was focused on the ongoing war in Afghanistan and the impending invasion of Iraq. Moreover, the Bush administration was not philosophically inclined to bargain with Tehran's leaders. As Vice President Dick Cheney once said, "We don't negotiate with evil; we defeat it."[3]

The responsibility for negotiating an end to Iran's dangerous activities, therefore, fell to a group that came to be known as the EU-3, made up of the three major European powers: France, Germany, and the United Kingdom. The group quickly made progress. In November 2003, Iran, with Rouhani acting as the country's lead nuclear negotiator, agreed to halt the construction of the Natanz facility as a precondition for further negotiations. Iran initially continued uranium conversion activities at Isfahan and the construction of additional centrifuges, but by November 2004, Iran had stopped conversion as well, meaning that Iran had suspended all activities related to uranium enrichment.

In December 2003, Iran signed the Additional Protocol to the IAEA safeguards agreement. The IAEA AP greatly increases inspectors' ability to detect any covert efforts to build nuclear weapons because it allows inspectors to conduct snap, short-warning inspections of facilities and to inspect any suspicious facilities in the country, even if they are not declared nuclear facilities. Unfortunately, Iran never fully implemented the AP. Nevertheless, at the time, signing the AP was an important step in the right direction.

Iran's cooperative behavior in this period can be explained by a number of factors. First, uranium enrichment in Iran was still something of a dream, not yet a reality, so Iran was not sacrificing much by giving it up. Second, Iran watched in fascination and terror in the spring of 2003 as the

US military made a thunder run to Baghdad to topple Saddam Hussein. The Iranians were stunned that an army they had fought to a protracted stalemate in a brutal ten-year war had been annihilated by American military power in a few short weeks. Reinforcing the point, when asked what lesson Iran's leaders should draw from the US invasion of Iraq, Cheney said simply, "Take a number."[4] Iran's leaders feared as much and wanted to do whatever they could to stay out of the Pentagon's sights. Third, Iran's WMD programs were initially a means to balance against similar capabilities in neighboring Iraq, but now, thanks to Washington, Saddam Hussein was no longer in power and the threat that launched the program in the first place had been eliminated. Fourth, and finally, what appeared to have been Iranian cooperation may have actually been shrewd diplomacy that traded tactical concessions for strategic gains. Indeed, Rouhani later bragged that the 2003 suspension had been a clever ploy that allowed Iran to take the international pressure off while still advancing other elements of the program. In Rouhani's words, "While we were talking to the Europeans in Tehran, we were installing equipment in Isfahan. . . . By creating a calm environment—a calm environment—we were able to complete the work in Isfahan."[5]

Still, this period was characterized by active diplomacy between the EU-3 and Iran. The EU-3 pushed for an agreement in which Iran would dismantle its fuel-cycle facilities and forswear uranium enrichment and plutonium reprocessing activities. In exchange, the EU-3 was prepared to offer many benefits, including light-water nuclear power reactors to meet Iran's stated demand for peaceful nuclear technology. Iran also floated various proposals that would put limits on, but not completely shut down, its enrichment program, but the West was opposed to any deal that allowed uranium enrichment in Iran.

Meanwhile, the United States played bad cop to the EU-3's good cop. The United States had already implemented one of the world's toughest sanctions regimes against Iran in the years following the 1979 Iranian Revolution. Indeed, by 1997, President Bill Clinton had signed Executive Order 13059, virtually prohibiting any and all US trade and investment in Iran.[6]

In order to increase the pressure on Iran further, however, the United States was interested in expanding the sanctions regime. Sanctions are most effective when more countries take part. If the United States were the only country to have sanctions in place, the target of the sanctions, in this case Iran, could simply substitute away from the United States by trading and investing with other countries. If every country in the world got on board, however, then Iran would be in real trouble. Washington wanted therefore to pass a round of sanctions in a United Nations Security Council Resolution (UNSCR). UNSCRs have the force of international law, meaning that every country in the world would be legally obligated to participate in UNSC-mandated sanctions.

The UNSC is made up of five permanent members, the United States, Russia, China, the United Kingdom, and France, also known as the P5, and ten rotating members. Passing a UNSCR, therefore, requires a majority vote of all members and either a "yes" vote or an abstention from the P5 members, each of whom wields veto power.

At this time, however, Washington was unable to convince the other members of the P5 to go along with UN sanctions. The European members,

France and the United Kingdom, held out hope for a near-term negotiated settlement with Iran. More problematically, the Russians and the Chinese stubbornly refused to admit that there was even a problem.

It was during this time that I took my first job in the US government. In the summer of 2004, I was working as an analyst at the Central Intelligence Agency as part of the agency's graduate fellowship program, a kind of internship program for graduate students. My assignment was to analyze how the P5 members were reacting to the Iranian nuclear issue and to forecast what it might take for them to finally come around and support a UNSCR against Iran. I argued that because the other great powers did not have the ability to project military power into the Middle East, they were less threatened by Iran's nuclear program. A nuclear-armed Iran posed a direct challenge to US forces, bases, and allies in the region, but for Beijing, Moscow, Paris, and London, a nuclear Iran was, and remains to this day, more of a theoretical concern. In addition, these countries had greater economic ties with Iran and therefore had more to lose economically by imposing sanctions on Iran. I argued that this latter condition was a function of the first. If the security threat was seen to be serious enough, economic concerns would melt away. This work would later inform the argument in my dissertation and my first book about how countries view the threat posed by nuclear weapons proliferation.

Eventually it was Iran's own provocative behavior that would suffice to spur the international community to action. In August 2005, a new president, Mahmoud Ahmadinejad, came to power and ushered in a new era of confrontation. Ahmadinejad toed a much harder line than his predecessor, Mohammad Khatami. While the presidency in Iran lacks teeth, the selection of Ahmadinejad, at the time a favorite of Iran's supreme leader, signaled a change of direction for Iran's foreign relations. Ahmadinejad brought a new hard-line foreign policy team with him, and it was at this time that Rouhani was replaced as Iran's lead nuclear negotiator. Iran announced its intention to resume uranium enrichment and to reject any deal that didn't acknowledge its right to enrich uranium. It began converting uranium at Isfahan immediately, and centrifuges began spinning at Natanz in early 2006.

Furthermore, at about this time, new revelations came to light about Iran's nuclear program.[7] Not only was Iran engaging in sensitive nuclear-fuel–cycle activity, but for the first time the IAEA acquired hard evidence that Iran had worked on the design and construction of nuclear warheads in 2002 and 2003 and that this work might be continuing to the present day. Over the years, more evidence has come to light suggesting that Iran conducted this work at its military base located at Parchin.[8]

In addition to the international negotiations over Iran's uranium enrichment program, therefore, there is a separate diplomatic track between the IAEA and Iran over access to the Parchin facility. In what has now become a well-choreographed dance, the IAEA repeatedly demands that Iran clear up questions about its past and present nuclear weaponization activities and give IAEA inspectors access to Parchin. Iran ritualistically stonewalls and uses the time to get rid of evidence of its past weaponization work. Indeed, satellite imagery shows that Iran has been busy cleaning up the facility at Parchin.[9] Not even the 2013 interim deal addressed Iran's nuclear weaponization work. Needless to say, information that Iran had actually sought to design nuclear explosives only deepened international concerns about Iranian intentions.

In February 2006, the IAEA issued the first of what would become many reports in which it declared that it could not verify that Iran's nuclear program was only intended for peaceful purposes, and it referred Iran's case to the UNSC.[10]

In the spring of 2006, Russia stepped into the diplomatic fray and made an offer that many observers sincerely believed could solve the Iranian nuclear crisis.[11] Iran's leaders trust Russia slightly more than they do the Western European powers, and Moscow made a good-faith offer to provide Iran with fuel-cycle services. If Tehran wanted enriched uranium fuel, Moscow argued, then Russia could simply provide it to them. The Russians offered to produce enriched-uranium fuel rods on Russian soil, ship them to Iran for use in Iran's (at this time still unfinished) nuclear power reactors, and then reclaim the spent fuel rods for shipment back to Russia. Iran, like the vast majority of countries on Earth with nuclear power plants, could make full use of enriched-uranium fuel without enriching the uranium itself. This deal was also rejected by Iran.

As a final effort to solve the problem diplomatically before passing a round of sanctions in the UNSC, the United States, Russia, and China joined forces with the EU-3. This group of the five permanent members of the UNSC plus Germany came to be known as the P5+1 and demonstrated the strong international support behind the proposals being offered to Iran.

In June 2006, the P5+1 made Iran an offer based on previous EU-3 packages. In exchange for the suspension of uranium enrichment and plutonium reprocessing, the great powers would offer to negotiate with Iran on the provision of light-water nuclear power reactors, a five-year supply of fuel, a guarantee to future fuel-cycle services, and cooperation on other issues. For a country genuinely interested in jump-starting a nuclear power program, this would have been a deal that was too good to refuse. But Iran rejected it out of hand, refusing to accept any restrictions on its self-proclaimed "right" to enrich uranium. It was becoming increasingly clear that Iran was interested in something other than generating electricity.

It was time to go to the Security Council. In the following month, the UNSC passed the first of what would become many resolutions against Iran's nuclear program. It demanded that Iran "suspend all enrichment and reprocessing activities" and "resolve outstanding questions" raised by the IAEA about Iran's nuclear program.[12] Before President Bush's term expired, the UNSC passed four additional resolutions, all of which reaffirmed these demands and three of which imposed UN-mandated sanctions on Iran. UNSCR 1737, passed in December 23, 2006, imposed bans on exports of nuclear technology and nuclear assistance to Iran, froze assets, and imposed travel bans on individuals working on Iran's nuclear program. UNSCR 1747, adopted on March 24, 2007, banned military exports from Iran, encouraged states to show restraint in exporting military equipment to Iran, and called on states to refrain from entering into new agreements to provide loans, grants, or financial assistance to Iran. On March 3, 2008, UNSCR 1803 was adopted and demanded that states show restraint in taking on new commitments to trade with Iran and refrain from doing business with Iranian banks; it also called for inspections of certain types of cargo going into and out of Iran.

Negotiations stalled in the two years following the first round of sanctions, but they resumed again in the summer of 2008. In May, Iran, anticipating a new proposal from the P5+1, preempted the international community by proposing its own framework for negotiations. Iran's suggestion was, however, nothing short of fantastical. The agenda included a

long list of completely unrelated issues including terrorism, poverty reduction in the developing world, and Israeli-Palestinian peace.[13] The nuclear
program was barely mentioned. This is a tactic Iran repeated in subsequent
years, attempting to broaden the scope of negotiations in an effort to distract from, and avoid talking about, the real problem.

Despite Iran's unserious proposal, the P5+1 came back with a sincere
offer of its own. It suggested a "repackaged" version of the June 2006 offer, but one that promised Iran broader incentives, including a "freeze for
freeze" provision in which the P5+1 would refrain from imposing new
sanctions on Iran if it would refrain from expanding its uranium enrichment program.[14] Once again, Iran was not receptive.

As George W. Bush's second term came to a close, therefore, the problem of Iran's nuclear program would fall to his successor.

THE OBAMA ADMINISTRATION:
ENGAGEMENT TRACK, 2009–2010

In his 2008 campaign for the presidency, then senator Barack Obama
promised to sit down for negotiations with Iran's leaders without preconditions. The Bush administration had made negotiations contingent on
Iran's suspending its enrichment activities, but Obama disagreed with this
approach, pointing out that, even during the Cold War, Washington maintained constant diplomatic contact with the Soviet Union. He argued that
diplomacy is a necessary tool of international politics and should not be
treated as a reward for good behavior. Obama's rivals for the Democratic
nomination and for the presidency criticized him as naïve, but upon taking
office, he stuck fairly close to his promises.

The Obama administration articulated a "dual-track" strategy for resolving the Iranian nuclear crisis. They vowed to keep the pressure on Iran in the form of sanctions and maintaining a credible military threat while simultaneously leaving open the option for negotiations and benefits for Iran in exchange for real curbs on its nuclear program. In many ways, this dual-track strategy of pressure and engagement was a continuation of the strategy that had begun in the second term of the George W. Bush administration.

In contrast to his predecessor, however, Obama began by leaning heavily on the engagement track. The president attempted to reach out directly to Iran's leaders. In his Cairo speech soon after taking office in June 2009, President Obama promised Iran's leaders that "we will extend a hand if you are willing to unclench your fist." In addition, the president began an annual tradition of sending a message of goodwill to the Iranian people on Nowruz, the Persian New Year.

The focus on engagement went beyond rhetoric, however. The Obama administration was determined to re-invigorate the P5+1 process. In April 2009, the P5+1 invited Iran to sit down for talks on its nuclear program without preconditions. Iran ignored the proposal for five months. In September, Iran responded with its standard stalling tactic, proposing that the two sides meet to discuss every issue under the sun, including: human rights, regional stability, sovereignty, terrorism, illicit drugs, illegal migration, organized crime, piracy, reform of the UNSC, the environment, outer space, trade and investment, poverty, and the financial crisis.[15] Iran's own nuclear program was not even mentioned.

Showing remarkable patience, the United States and the P5+1 immediately responded with a serious offer. In October 2009, they proposed a fuel-swap deal. The idea behind the deal was for Iran to ship its stockpile of low-enriched uranium (LEU) out of the country in exchange for fuel rods that could be used to fuel the Tehran Research Reactor (TRR). Iran claimed it needed LEU to produce fuel rods for reactors, and the West feared that Iran might use that LEU to fuel nuclear weapons. The fuel swap, therefore, appeared to be a win-win. The West would be reassured that Iran, depleted of its LEU stockpiles, would not be able to build nuclear weapons in short order, and Iran would receive the fuel rods that it claimed it needed for its reactors.

Specifically, the proposal called for Iran to export its entire stockpile of LEU (1,200 kilograms of 3.5 percent) in a single batch before the end of 2009; Russia to further enrich Iran's LEU to 19.75 percent, producing about 120 kilograms of enriched uranium for TRR fuel rods; France to manufacture the TRR fuel rods for delivery roughly one year after the con- clusion of the agreement and prior to the depletion of the current TRR fuel supply; the United States to work with the IAEA to improve the safety and security of the TRR; and the P5+1 to finance the entire operation. Note also that the West was making a significant concession compared to previ- ous offers: it was no longer demanding that Iran immediately suspend all enrichment activity. Rather, it was demanding simply that Iran ship out the enriched uranium it had already produced.

Iran did not summarily reject this offer as in previous cases, but Iranian officials complained publicly about the terms of the deal, including most vocally about shipping out the entire stockpile of LEU, and about its inabil- ity to trust foreign countries to be reliable custodians of its LEU stockpile.

While Iran complained about the P5+1 offer, it continued to ramp up its uranium enrichment activities. In January 2010, Iran began enriching uranium to 20 percent. Previously, it had only been enriching to 3.5 percent, and this had been a major cause for concern. Twenty percent was even more worrisome, however, because it is much closer to the 90 percent needed to produce nuclear weapons. Representatives of the P5+1 began thinking about working restrictions on Iran's 20 percent enrichment into any acceptable package.

Then in May 2010 came what some saw as a huge missed opportunity but was actually an unfortunate diplomatic sideshow. In trilateral meetings between Turkey, Brazil, and Iran that excluded the P5+1, a version of the TRR fuel-swap deal was resurrected. Turkey and Brazil are rising powers and they were eager to show that they could take on and solve one of the world's most pressing problems. From Iran's point of view, Brazil and Turkey were more attractive interlocutors because they did not drive as hard a bargain as the P5+1. After days of meetings, the three sides emerged and triumphantly announced to the world that the Iranian nuclear crisis had been resolved: Iran had agreed to a diplomatic settlement similar to the P5+1's previous TRR fuel-swap deal.

The United States quickly and firmly rejected the compromise, dashing any hopes that the Iranian nuclear crisis had been resolved.

Trita Parsi, president of the National Iranian American Council, argued that this was a mistake.[16] According to Parsi, the Brazil-Turkey TRR deal could have resolved the crisis, and the United States rejected it because it had wrongly prioritized tactics over strategy. In particular, he charges that the Obama administration, after struggling for over a year, finally convinced Russia and China to support another round of sanctions against Iran in the UNSC. This was seen as too good an opportunity to pass up. The promise of P5 unity, therefore, served as an occasion to switch from the engagement to the pressure track. Already determined to turn up the heat on Iran, Parsi argues, the Obama administration was not in a position to accept the gift of the Brazil-Turkey TRR deal that had unexpectedly been dropped in its lap. If Parsi is correct, this would be a damning critique of US policy toward Iran and would place much of the blame for the subsequent impasse squarely on Washington's shoulders.

In reality, however, the TRR was unacceptable and the United States was right to reject it. While the Brazil-Turkey offer was superficially similar to the P5+1 deal, the fine print had been altered beyond recognition, and Iran's nuclear program had advanced to the point where the deal no longer addressed Washington's core nonproliferation concerns. First, instead of transferring its LEU to Russia, under the Brazil-Turkey deal, the LEU would be transferred to Turkey, but Iran would still be in "legal possession" of the material, meaning that it could demand its return at any time. Second, Iran would, as in the P5+1 deal, ship 1,200 kgs of LEU abroad, but Iran's stockpile of LEU had nearly doubled in the intervening six months. Twelve hundred kgs was initially chosen because that was Iran's entire LEU stockpile. The purpose of the P5+1 offer was to completely eliminate Iran's LEU, but by May 2010, transferring 1,200 kgs would have still left Iran with another 1,200 kgs of LEU. Third, in the intervening months, Iran had also begun enriching to 20 percent. This was now the international community's foremost concern, but the Turkey-Brazil-Iran deal did not even mention limits on Iran's 20 percent stockpiles and activities.

In addition, as Parsi correctly points out, Russia and China were willing to support another round of sanctions in the Security Council at this point, and the Obama administration had had enough of Iranian intransigence. It was ready to switch to the pressure track.

OBAMA ADMINISTRATION:
PRESSURE TRACK, 2010–2013

On June 9, 2010, the UNSC voted on UNSCR 1929, reaffirming its previous demand that Iran halt all enrichment and heavy-water nuclear-reactor activity and fully cooperate with the IAEA. In addition, the UNSCR levied a new, fourth round of UN sanctions against Iran.[17] Turkey and Brazil, in part out of bitterness from their TRR experience, voted against the resolution, and Lebanon abstained. Nevertheless, the resolution passed. The new round of sanctions focused on restricting military purchases and financial transactions of the Iranian Revolutionary Guard Corps (IRGC), an elite praetorian guard that runs the nuclear program and is a central player in Iran's economy.

It was at about this time, in May 2010, that I re-entered government as an advisor on Iran policy in the Office of the Secretary of Defense. I did not spend much time, however, working on diplomacy. After all, this is not the Pentagon's bailiwick. We will return to the subjects on which I worked more directly in subsequent chapters.

In tandem with Obama's switch to the pressure track, the European Union (EU) began to pile on sanctions of its own that went beyond the sanctions called for in the UNSCRs and over time came close to matching the tough unilateral sanctions that the United States had imposed on Iran over the years. Other US allies, including Australia, Japan, and South Korea, added sanctions of their own. Perhaps the toughest, and to many the most surprising, of all these sanctions, was the EU embargo on Iranian oil, which began in July 2012. Oil made up a large portion of Iranian exports (~80 percent) and Iranian government revenue (~50–60 percent), and the

EU was one of Iran's largest customers, accounting for roughly 34 percent of all Iranian oil exports in 2010.[18] An EU oil embargo, therefore, promised to drastically increase the economic pressure on Iran.

Even though they knew it would hit Iran where it hurt, the West had resisted imposing comprehensive oil and gas sanctions against Iran for some time. From Europe's perspective this was in part due to a concern that an embargo could cause economic dislocation to the European national economies, which were heavily dependent on Iranian oil imports at a time when they were still reeling from the global financial crisis.

In addition, and more fundamentally, however, there was a fear that an embargo of Iranian oil could be a self-inflicted wound on the entire global economy. The market price for oil, like all markets, depends on supply and demand. Iranian exports accounted for roughly 4.6 percent of the world's global oil supply. A complete embargo on Iranian oil, therefore, would have removed 4.6 percent of global supply from the market, leading to a reduction in supply and an increase in oil prices, which would hurt the global economy and possibly send it back into a recession.

Furthermore, it is conceivable that sanctions against Iranian oil could, paradoxically, actually increase the revenues flowing into Iran's coffers. If sanctions pushed oil prices higher, Iran would earn more for every barrel of oil it was able to sell. It would be possible, therefore, that Iran could increase revenues under tough oil sanctions by selling fewer barrels at higher prices to its remaining customers.

Nevertheless, by July 2012, the EU decided that the possibility of solving the Iranian nuclear crisis short of war outweighed these and other risks and joined the United States in implementing an oil embargo on Iran.

In an attempt to keep the pressure on Iran and close any loopholes, the United States also stepped up its use of third-party sanctions on Iran. The United States had already cut off virtually all direct economic relations with Iran, so it could not do anything more to turn up the heat through its own unilateral sanctions. The idea of a third-party sanction, therefore, is for the United States to sanction other countries that continue to do business in Iran. For example, the United States threatened to levy sanctions against South Korea if South Korea continued to buy large quantities of Iranian oil. In essence, this would force other countries to choose between doing business with either Iran or the United States, the largest national economy on Earth. Given such a choice, most countries selected the United States.

In addition, Iran was virtually cut off from the international financial system. In January 2012, the United States placed third-party sanctions on foreign financial institutions that do business with Iran's central bank.[19] Later, in March 2012, the EU expelled Iranian banks from the Society for Worldwide Interbank Financial Telecommunication, or SWIFT, a global communications network used to settle almost all international financial transactions.[20] These and other sanctions made it incredibly difficult for Iran to do business in the international economy.

Countries that continued to import Iranian oil and gas paid in what essentially amounted to a barter system. Turkey paid in gold.[21] Others deposited funds denominated in their own national currency into Iranian accounts in local banks that Iran then used to buy local goods.[22] For example, China purchased Iranian oil and then deposited Chinese yuan into Iranian accounts in Chinese banks. Due to international sanctions, Iran could not repatriate these funds. It had to spend these funds locally, purchasing Chinese-manufactured consumer goods that were then shipped back to Iran. India, Japan, South Korea, and other countries all made similar arrangements.

The UN, US, EU, and other national sanctions combined to devastate the Iranian economy. By the summer of 2013, Iran's oil exports had been slashed by two thirds from roughly two million barrels of oil per day (mb/d) to 0.7 mb/d.[23] Oil prices did not increase as had been feared, meaning that this resulted in a significant reduction of Iranian revenue.[24] Iran's currency, the rial, also collapsed, losing roughly half its value. The rial traded at 16,900 to 1 US dollar in January 2010, but by 2013, the exchange rate had ballooned to 37,000 to 1.[25] There were also signs that the sanctions were affecting the quality of life of the average Iranian and contributed to rising political discontent.[26]

By early 2012, Western leaders believed that they had Iran's leaders right where they wanted them. They hoped that Iran might finally be willing to negotiate to get out from under its growing economic hardship. In April, May, and June 2012, the P5+1 and Iran met for the first face-to-face negotiations in over two years in a series of meetings in Baghdad, Istanbul, and Moscow.

These were odd locations for international talks. Generally, diplomats prefer luxe European locales, like Geneva or Vienna, but Iran forced the West to negotiate hard over the simple matter of where the meetings would be held. Presumably seeking to score cheap symbolic points, Iran insisted on locations that symbolized the limits of US power. The United States was drawing down from a difficult ten-year war in Iraq, Turkey was charting a new foreign policy course independent from its traditional NATO allies, and Moscow had been America's Cold War rival for a half century. The Obama administration was nonplussed by Iran's bizarre suggestions, however, and would probably have been willing to negotiate on the moon if it held out the hope of resolving the Iranian nuclear crisis.

In this series of meetings held in 2012, the P5+1 pursued a new "stop-shut-ship" deal. Under the terms of this proposal, Iran would need to: stop enriching to 20 percent, shut down the uranium enrichment facility at Qom, and ship out its entire stockpile of 20 percent enriched uranium. This proposal would have not fundamentally resolved the Iranian nuclear crisis and was meant merely as an incremental step to buy time. The window for diplomacy closes if and when Iran has a nuclear weapons capability, but if it had stopped enriching to 20 percent and shipped out its existing stockpile of 20 percent, then its dash time to a bomb would have been greatly lengthened. This would have provided more time to negotiate a final bargain. The third demand, to shut down Qom, was an effort to pacify Israel and prevent it from conducting a premature bombing raid. As we will discuss in chapter 6, Israel's best bunker-busting bombs cannot reach the facility at Qom, which is buried in the side of a mountain. Shutting down Qom, therefore, would reassure Israel that it can hold Iran's nuclear program at risk militarily and presumably give it the patience to see the diplomatic process through.

In exchange, the P5+1 offered Iran relatively little. The Western powers believed that Iran was starting to feel the pressure and there was some hope, perhaps naïve in hindsight, that Tehran's leaders were ready to cry uncle. Moreover, there was little the P5+1 could realistically offer in terms of sanctions relief. As should be apparent by now, the sanctions regime is a complicated and interwoven configuration of various unilateral and multilateral measures that required a great deal of hard work and political capital to construct. It is not something that can be easily disassembled. It is more like a game of Jenga: if you try to lift one sanction out of the over-arching regime, the entire structure is at risk of collapsing. This makes it difficult to provide partial, or finely calibrated, sanctions relief. In addition, stop-shut-ship was only meant to be an interim deal. The P5+1 needed to keep the pressure on Iran if it wanted to get a more comprehensive deal later. In return for stop-shut-ship, therefore, the P5+1 was only prepared to offer Iran spare parts for its aging civilian aircraft.

As might be expected, Iran rejected the deal and didn't offer a constructive alternative.

Ignoring the first rule of diplomacy, never negotiate against yourself, the P5+1 came back in April 2013 in Kazakhstan and proposed a watered-down version of the previous deal. In this formulation, the great powers again asked Iran to stop enriching to 20 percent, but this time they offered to allow Iran to keep part of its 20 percent LEU stockpile and to keep Qom open.

Iranian representatives were pleased that the P5+1 was moving in the right direction, but they still rejected the deal. And, once again, Iran floated a proposal of its own that senior US officials described as unreasonable.[27]

As another round of negotiations fell apart, US officials decided to wait for the outcome of the Iranian election, scheduled for summer 2013, before pursuing a new round of negotiations. The results of the election were about as good as US officials could have hoped for.

ROUHANI AND THE INTERIM NUCLEAR DEAL, 2013–PRESENT

Among the narrow slate of candidates pre-approved by Iran's supreme leader, the Iranian people plumped for Hassan Rouhani, the most moderate candidate of the bunch and a candidate who campaigned on a less confrontational foreign policy and the goal of seeking relief from international sanctions.

Shortly after he assumed office in August 2013, Rouhani launched a charm offensive against the West. He appointed more moderate and technocratic personnel to his government, made public speeches about his desire to improve relations with the West, and even started a Twitter account that he used to tweet holiday greetings to the Jewish people—this was quite a change in tone from Ahmadinejad, who talked about wiping Israel off the map.

As part of this charm offensive, Rouhani made a trip to the UN General Assembly's annual meeting in New York where he gave a well-received public address, met with many American journalists, academics, and former government officials on the sidelines of the conference, and took a telephone call from President Obama, the first direct communication between US and Iranian leaders since 1979.

Opinion on Rouhani's visit was sharply divided with many commentators expressing optimism that the nuclear issue might soon be resolved and that this could even pave the way to a broader and long-lasting rapprochement between the United States and Iran. Others, including Israeli Prime Minister Benjamin Netanyahu, dismissed Rouhani as a "wolf in sheep's clothing." He argued that the public relations campaign was a gambit intended to release the pressure on Iran to give it more time to build nuclear weapons. Or, in Netanyahu's words, Rouhani intends to "smile all the way to the bomb."

During the New York visit, I was part of an invitation-only meeting with Rouhani on the sidelines of the UN General Assembly attended by

American academics and journalists who frequently write on Iran. At the end of the meeting, I came away believing that we should test the diplomatic opening presented by Rouhani—not because I thought Rouhani is a nice guy. We know that he is not. For example, as a top national security official, he responded to student protests in Tehran in 1999 by following through on his threat to "crush mercilessly and monumentally" those who "dare to show their faces." Rather, I thought the change of orientation in Iran's foreign policy might be evidence that the international sanctions were finally starting to hit hard and that Iran might be willing to make meaningful concessions on the nuclear program.

During the fall of 2013, the P5+1 and Iran returned to the negotiating table in a series of meetings held in Geneva, Switzerland. In October, the first set of negotiations closed without an agreement and many people began to suspect that President Rouhani wouldn't be able to follow through on his promises to deliver a diplomatic accord. Then, on November 24, 2013, the two sides emerged from their conference room with a major announcement: there had been a diplomatic breakthrough.

According to the terms of the "interim" deal announced late that night in Geneva, Iran would freeze or roll back all elements of its nuclear program in exchange for modest sanctions relief.[28] The deal would remain in place for six months to give diplomats time to negotiate a more "comprehensive" accord. If that six-month time frame expired without a deal, the two sides could agree to renew the terms of the interim deal by "mutual consent" for an additional six months.

Proponents of the deal lauded it as a "historic breakthrough," while critics, like Israel's Benjamin Netanyahu, slammed it as a "historic mistake." I thought both perspectives were exaggerated. The interim deal was not intended to end the Iranian nuclear crisis once and for all. Rather it was designed to do limited things for a limited time. Writing on foreign-policy.com the day the deal was announced, I argued that the interim deal was a step in the right direction, but that getting a comprehensive deal would still be incredibly difficult. Or, as the title of my article had it: "Now for the Hard Part."[29]

The deal had several advantages. For nearly a decade, since I had first worked on Iran's nuclear program at the CIA in the summer of 2004, I watched Iran's estimated dash time to a nuclear weapons capability slowly drop from several years to barely more than one month. By mid-2013, I feared that we had nearly run out of time, but the interim deal finally stopped the bleeding. Iran agreed to: limit its enrichment to no more than 5 percent; eliminate its existing stockpile of 20 percent LEU by diluting it to less than 5 percent, or converting it to oxide for use in fuel plates; reduce its stockpile of 5 percent LEU by converting the excess to oxide; cap the number of installed centrifuges and refrain from installing more advanced IR2 centrifuges; and cease major construction on the Arak reactor, including the installation of the reactor's control panel. In addition, Iran agreed that these measures would be verified by more intrusive inspections from the IAEA, including daily access to the enrichment facilities and Natanz and Qom, and unprecedented, first-time access to the Arak reactor, the centrifuge assembly workshops, and uranium mines and mills. In short, the deal stopped Iran's march to a nuclear weapons capability, added about an extra month to the time it would take Iran to dash to a nuclear weapons capability, and gave us a wider window into Iran's nuclear operations.[30]

In exchange, the P5+1 offered modest sanctions relief. The deal freed up about $4 billion of Iranian funds frozen in foreign bank accounts and lifted sanctions on trade in the automobile, precious metals, and petro-chemical industries. The P5+1 estimated that the deal provided Iran with about $7 billion in sanctions relief. Outside experts countered that the actual amount of relief depends on how one calculates the benefits to be had from the newly freed-up trade opportunities and that the grand total could eventually come to as much as $20 billion. In either case, the deal left in place the toughest sanctions on Iran, including those on the oil and banking sectors, meaning that the economic noose on Iran would continue to tighten even with the interim deal in place.

As President Obama acknowledged, however, the interim agreement was only a "first step." Significant problems remained. The interim deal froze Iran's nuclear program in place, but it was still only an estimated two to three months away from a nuclear weapons breakout capability. This was much too close for comfort. The next phase of diplomacy, therefore, must achieve a significant rolling back of Iran's nuclear capabilities to ensure that Iran cannot build nuclear weapons on short order. The true test of the interim deal, therefore, will be in whether it eventually results in the successful conclusion of a more comprehensive pact.

The implementation agreement for the accord went into effect on January 20, 2014. This gives the two sides until July 20, 2014 before the agreed-upon six-month window to negotiate a comprehensive accord expires. At this point, the deal will either fall through, the two sides will agree to a comprehensive accord, or they can agree to renew the terms of the interim deal for an additional six months.

The Obama administration is under no illusions about the difficulties that lie ahead. President Obama has admitted that "huge challenges remain" and that "if you ask me what is the likelihood that we're able to arrive at the end state . . . I wouldn't say that it's more than 50–50." Gary Samore, President Obama's top nuclear advisor on WMD issues from 2009 to 2013, is even more pessimistic. He assesses that there is virtually no chance that we can get a final deal with Iran.[31] Moreover, as I will explain below, even a comprehensive nuclear deal might not mean the end of the Iranian nuclear threat. In other words, there is still a very good chance that the Iranian nuclear crisis will end somewhere other than at the negotiating table.

To better understand why and what we can do to increase our chances of a breakthrough, let us consider the fundamental interests at stake for both sides.

WHAT CAN THE UNITED STATES ACCEPT?

What does the United States and the rest of the international community want from Iran? At the end of the day, we want only one thing: to prevent Iran from building nuclear weapons. But, more specifically, what are the kinds of curbs that Iran could put on its nuclear program that would convince us that Iran is no longer a nuclear-weapons proliferation threat? In short, the answer is that the United States would need two things for a deal to be acceptable. First, we would need strict limits on Iran's uranium enrichment and plutonium-producing capability that would prevent it from accumulating enough weapons-grade fissile material to build nuclear weapons. Second, we would require an intrusive monitoring and inspections regime that would reassure us that Iran is abiding by the limits agreed to in point one. There are a variety of forms that such a deal could take, however, and this section will consider the contours of two possible deals and their respective advantages and disadvantages from the West's point of view.

THE IDEAL DEAL

The ideal deal would involve Iran's giving up all uranium enrichment and heavy-water reactor activities in a verifiable manner. This would mean dismantling the uranium enrichment facilities at Natanz and Qom, the uranium-conversion facility at Isfahan, and the heavy-water reactor under construction at Arak. In addition, Iran would promise to forswear the future development of uranium enrichment or heavy-water reactor capabilities. Furthermore, Iran would need to clear up any unresolved issues with its IAEA safeguards agreements, including allowing IAEA inspectors access to the Parchin military base. Finally, to make all of the above credible, Iran would need to implement the IAEA Additional Protocol. This would greatly limit Iran's ability to cheat on the agreement and enhance our ability to detect cheating should it do so.

This would be asking a lot of Iran. What could we offer in return? Iran says it wants nuclear technology for peaceful purposes. If that is truly what Tehran wants, then we are, and have always been, prepared to offer it to them. The United States, or other nuclear-capable states, such as France or Russia, would be willing to provide Iran with light-water reactors and the enriched-uranium fuel needed to operate them. We would be prepared to lift all of the US and multilateral nuclear-related sanctions on Iran. This would mean significant sanctions relief. Note, however, that the United States also has in place various sanctions on Iran related to its support of terrorist groups and its human-rights violations; these sanctions would likely remain in effect. Even the "ideal" nuclear deal, therefore, would not resolve all of the outstanding sources of tension between the two countries, but it would eliminate our biggest concern: the nuclear threat. Since Iran would voluntarily shut down its nuclear facilities in this scenario, we would no longer need to threaten to do the job for them with military force. We could therefore rescind our military threats related to their nuclear program, but it is unlikely that we would be willing to offer a more comprehensive security assurance given the likelihood of other conflicts related to Iran's ties to terrorist groups and its repeated naval threats in the Persian Gulf. It is of course possible that an ideal deal could go even further, leading to a grand bargain between the two sides that clears up all major conflicts of interest, but at this point, that seems to be a bridge—or two—too far.

This ideal deal would be a godsend for the United States. We would eliminate one of the greatest emerging threats to our national security without going to war.

The problem is that it is unlikely that we can get a deal this good. As we will discuss below, there are many reasons why Iran might want to avoid any comprehensive deal, but the ideal deal is the hardest of the bunch. First, by completely eliminating Iran's enrichment capabilities, it is the deal that would place Tehran farthest from its goal of having a nuclear weapons capability. In addition, this deal forces Iran to give up its "right to enrich." Iran does not actually have this right; Article IV of the NPT grants Iran the "inalienable right" to "peaceful nuclear technology." It does not say anything about enrichment specifically. Nevertheless, Iran has made the claim so often and so vigorously that it would be a humiliating retreat for them to accept a zero-enrichment deal. Moreover, the P5+1 may have already conceded this issue. The text of the interim agreement states that a "comprehensive solution would involve a mutually defined (uranium) enrichment program with practical limits and transparency measures to ensure the peaceful nature of the program." Iran's negotiators claim that this text recognizes its right to enrich. The P5+1 insists that it does not, although one can see how Iran was able to interpret the agreement in this way.

It might be possible to square this circle through a clever diplomatic compromise. We could pursue a deal in which we get zero domestic enrichment in Iran in exchange for Iranian participation, or even part ownership, of an international uranium enrichment facility located on foreign soil. This would allow Iran to save face and claim that its "right to enrich" was being respected. It would also advance the P5+1's nonproliferation objectives. Since the sensitive nuclear activity would take place outside of Iran, it would be nearly impossible for Iran to use this material to build nuclear weapons. Similar proposals were floated, and rejected, in the past, but Iran has never been this willing to compromise before, so it is worth reviving such proposals in the new, more cooperative, environment.

Alternatively, the international community might be able to recognize Iran's "right to enrich" in exchange for Iran's promise never to exercise that right under the verifiable conditions set out above. After all, the US Bill of Rights gives me the right to peacefully protest against the US government in front of the White House, but I have never exercised that right. Splitting Iran's right to enrich from whether it actually enriches could be the recipe for a diplomatic breakthrough. Certainly the history of diplomacy has seen zanier compromises. Assuming for a moment, however, that it will be difficult to strike a zero-enrichment deal, what are other, less-than-ideal options?

THE LIMITED-ENRICHMENT DEAL

If we can't get a zero-enrichment deal, what would a deal that allowed some Iranian enrichment look like? As billed, this deal would allow Iran to enrich, but put strict limits on its ability to do so, including hard ceilings on the number of facilities, the numbers and types of centrifuges, the levels of enrichment, and the sizes of stockpiles of LEU.

One possibility would be to simply settle for making the interim deal permanent. The text of the interim deal states that it is "renewable by mutual consent." This clause was intended to buy an additional six months, if necessary, for diplomats to negotiate a comprehensive pact, but some fear that this might become a loophole that will eventually turn the temporary agreement into a permanent one. It might make sense to renew the interim pact a single time in pursuit of a stronger comprehensive deal, but any additional extensions would be unwise. Continually renewing the current deal would leave Iran's nuclear program perpetually two or three months away from a breakout capability—a very thin margin of error for US policymakers.

Rather, any "comprehensive" limited-enrichment deal would need to impose much tougher terms on Iran. Such an agreement could obviously take a variety of forms, but one package commonly suggested by DC-based experts is as follows: Iran would be allowed to maintain only one uranium-enrichment facility. This would most likely mean maintaining the enrichment facility at Natanz and shutting down Qom. The deal would place more stringent restrictions on the number of first-generation centrifuges Iran could operate and on the amount of 3.5 percent LEU it is permitted to stockpile. The nuclear reactor at Arak would also need to be dismantled in order to block Iran's possible plutonium path to the bomb, and Iran would have to clear up all remaining questions with the IAEA surrounding its nuclear weapons design work. To give the West confidence that Iran was keeping its word on all of this, these measures would have to be verified by intrusive international inspections. At a minimum, Iran would need to implement the Additional Protocol, but given the significant capabilities that Iran would be permitted to maintain in this scenario, the West should also insist on a special inspections regime for Iran's enrichment facilities.

In exchange for these concessions, the United States would be prepared to offer Iran a number of benefits in return. We would allow Iran to enrich and perhaps even recognize its "right" to do so. We could offer Iran peaceful nuclear technology, including light-water reactors and fuel-cycle services, to compensate for the curbs imposed on its domestic nuclear program. Finally, as in the above package, we could offer a complete lifting of nuclear-related sanctions and remove from the table the threat to use force against Iran's nuclear facilities so long as Iran abides by the terms of the agreement.

This limited-enrichment deal would have a number of possible benefits for the United States. First, many experts believe that Iran might be more willing to accept this deal. We must be careful, however, not to overstate this possibility. As we will discuss below, Tehran will be reluctant to accept such severe curbs on its nuclear program.

Second, and more importantly, a limited-enrichment deal could address the Iranian nuclear challenge short of going to war. So long as Iran never goes beyond the negotiated limits, Iran would never acquire the materials necessary to build nuclear weapons. Furthermore, with strict international safeguards in place, we would likely have timely warning if Iran were to try to cheat on the agreement or tear it up altogether.

The primary downside of a limited-enrichment deal from Washington's point of view, however, is that it might not solve the problems it was intended to solve. It allows Iran to maintain and, over time, to perfect, its uranium enrichment capability. Moreover, a limited-enrichment deal would add some time to Iran's nuclear weapons breakout clock, but not much. According to one expert assessment, a deal that allows limited enrichment would only extend Iran's dash time to a nuclear weapons capability from the current two to three months to about six months. This would only put us back to where we were in January 2012 when "Time to Attack Iran" was first published.

Leaving such formidable nuclear capabilities in place in Iran, even under strict limits, means that there are several different ways that even a successfully-negotiated comprehensive deal could break down and result in a nuclear-armed Iran. Intact enrichment capabilities greatly increase Iran's ability to build a secret parallel program away from the watchful eyes of inspectors. While a strict inspections and verification regime should allow us to catch Iran if it tries to cheat on the deal, it might not.

Moreover, Iran's leaders might calculate, perhaps correctly, that even if the international community catches them cheating on the agreement, it won't have the stomach to stop them. At present, the US government and the international community are laser-focused on Iran, but once the United States formally declares an end to the Iranian nuclear crisis, its gaze will wander. Relations will be normalized, trade will resume, and global leaders will forget about Iran and start worrying about other issues. Iran may calculate that it would be difficult for the United States to rally support for new international sanctions if Iran cheats on its agreements, making this a tempting path for Iran.

In addition, even if Iran fully abides by the terms of a deal, it would only be for a limited time. The text of the interim agreement promises that the comprehensive agreement would hold for a "specified long-term duration." Early reports suggest that Iranian officials envision a three- to five-year timeframe for a comprehensive accord, whereas the P5+1 will press for ten to twenty years. At the end of that specified time period, however long that might be, all bets would be off and Iran could resume its march to a nuclear weapons capability without violating the agreement.

Revisiting the case of North Korea's nuclear program should curb our enthusiasm about what a successful nuclear deal with Iran might look like in a few years' time. In 1994, we celebrated the end of the North Korean nuclear crisis with a much-heralded negotiated settlement. We now know, however, that Pyongyang was cheating on the agreement from day one, building up a secret enrichment capability.[32] North Korea then pulled out of the agreement altogether in 2003. Since that time it has tested three nuclear weapons, and at present it is believed to maintain an arsenal of roughly one dozen nuclear weapons.[33] A bad deal, therefore, can be worse than no deal at all.

If that were not worrying enough, a limited-enrichment deal has another major downside: it sets a very dangerous precedent. Since the 1970s, the United States has enforced a strict policy of prohibiting the spread of enrichment and reprocessing technologies to states that do not already possess them. If we approve of uranium enrichment in Iran, however, it becomes very difficult for us to tell other countries that they cannot enrich or reprocess. This problem is compounded by the fact that Iran is not just any other country, but a rogue state that has violated its NPT commitments, sponsors terrorism, and is America's geopolitical foe. How do we tell our friends and allies that we cannot trust them with enrichment and reprocessing if we can trust Iran? Indeed, at present, South Korea is expressing interest in developing plutonium-reprocessing technologies for peaceful purposes, and Washington is putting its foot down hard on the idea. In addition, Washington recently signed a nuclear cooperation agreement with the United Arab Emirates (UAE) in which the emir forswore the option of ever developing enrichment or reprocessing capabilities. At the time, Washington touted this deal as setting a new "gold standard" for peaceful nuclear cooperation. If we grant Iran the right to enrich, however, the UAE might want to claw back that "right," and other countries in the Middle East and around the world might also demand it. They might do so in order to produce energy, but they might also do it as a hedge against Iranian proliferation or the broader collapse of the nonproliferation regime.

Since there is such a tight correspondence between the ability to enrich or reprocess and the ability to build nuclear weapons, the spread of these sensitive nuclear technologies would likely mean an increased risk of the spread of nuclear weapons.[34] One of the reasons we are so determined to stop Iran's nuclear program is to prevent a nuclear arms race in the Middle East and around the world.[35] But a deal that allows Iran a limited enrichment capability might spur nearly as much nuclear proliferation as Iranian nuclear weapons.

There are things we could do to mitigate this risk, however, and it relates to how we explain a limited-enrichment deal to the rest of the world. Some nuclear experts have argued that the United States must be prepared to extend the same deal we offer Iran to other countries. They argue that we should be prepared to allow any country on Earth the right to enrich to low levels under strict international safeguards. It would be hypocritical to do otherwise. As was stated above, there are currently ambiguities in what the NPT means by "peaceful nuclear technology," but these experts argue that we can clear up this confusion for good by simply declaring that whatever deal we come to in Iran counts as "peaceful" and is thus available to any other NPT members.

The problem with such a proposal, however, is obvious. We would be announcing to the world that any country on Earth can acquire dangerous nuclear technologies and push right up to the edge of having nuclear weapons. Not only that, but the United States will condone it. I argue, in contrast, that if we happen to get a comprehensive deal with Iran that allows limited enrichment we should emphasize that this is a special case, agreed to under duress, to prevent a new war in the Middle East. It is not a generalizable model available to all comers. To the degree that other countries want to make it a model, we can threaten that they can expect to receive the exact same treatment Iran received: years of international pressure, economic sanctions, and threats of military strikes. It is simply not in America's interest to generalize an Iran deal. It is better to be accused of hypocrisy than to encourage the spread of the world's most dangerous weapons.

Yet, there is an additional obstacle to a limited-enrichment deal: the US Congress holds an effective veto over negotiations and it might decide to scuttle them. Congress has always pushed a harder line than the Obama administration and it might object to a limited-enrichment deal, understanding the many downsides I mention above. Any comprehensive deal would promise sanctions relief to Iran, so Congress could simply kill diplomacy through its unilateral ability to pass sanctions. This outcome is easy to imagine. Indeed, shortly after the interim deal was passed, Congress drafted a sanctions bill that threatened to slap tough new penalties on Iran unless it accepts a zero-enrichment comprehensive deal within the interim deal's six-month deadline. President Obama, therefore, is playing what political scientist Robert Putnam called a "two-level game." He needs to find a solution to this standoff that satisfies both his domestic and international negotiating partners, each of whom hold an effective veto over the deal.

Despite these serious downsides to a limited-enrichment deal, many experts in Washington would prefer such a deal to the alternatives discussed in chapters 5 and 6. It might even be possible to design a deal with even more severe restrictions on Iran's enrichment capabilities that would extend its nuclear dash time line beyond the current six-month estimates. Certainly the delay imposed on a possible Iranian nuclear breakout would be a central criterion by which to judge the value of any limited-enrichment deal. We should not delude ourselves, however, about what a limited-enrichment deal achieves. A "comprehensive" deal that allows enrichment in Iran might be preferable to a military strike, but it will be unlikely to provide a "comprehensive" resolution to this crisis. Rather, it is more likely that the deal would just kick the can down the road and force us to address this issue again at a later date. To better understand this point, we need to next evaluate what might be acceptable to Iran and its supreme leader.

WHAT CAN IRAN ACCEPT?

It takes two to tango. If we hope to resolve this issue diplomatically, we must come up with a deal that not only satisfies American concerns but also meets the approval of Iran's supreme leader. Unfortunately, many (if not most) experts in the United States begin by proposing deals that would be attractive to the United States and then make unfounded assumptions about what Iran might or might not be willing to accept. This will not do.

In chapter 2, we asked what Iran wants. In this section, we will consider how that translates into what type of deal Iran might be willing to accept.

Iran's leaders would like sanctions relief and nuclear weapons too. One does not need to impugn the integrity of Iran's leaders to make this statement, but rather one can simply assume that they, like leaders of most countries, would like to have an economically vibrant and secure country.

As we discussed above, international sanctions have devastated Iran's economy. Many international relations scholars argue that sanctions never work, but the set of economic penalties put in place against Iran might just be the most effective international sanctions regime in world history. There is little doubt that without these tough sanctions: President Rouhani would not have been elected on a platform of seeking improved relations with the outside world and sanctions relief, Iran would not have signed up to the interim nuclear deal, and Iran would not be willing to seriously negotiate a comprehensive nuclear accord. Iran desperately wants economic relief, especially from the toughest penalties on its oil and banking sectors.

In addition, as we discussed in chapter 2, Iran would like to possess nuclear weapons. Nuclear weapons help Iran achieve its primary goals of deterring foreign attack and becoming the most dominant state in the Middle East. It has been building its nuclear capabilities for decades and is now only months from joining the nuclear club. Therefore, a nuclear deal that put serious limits on its nuclear program (the kind of limits that would satisfy the international community) would mean throwing away the ultimate security guarantee when it was nearly close enough to grab. That is a steep price to pay.

The international community has made it clear, however, that Iran needs to choose. The sanctions will remain in place and might even intensify if Iran refuses to put strict curbs on its nuclear program. So, Iran can have an advanced nuclear program or a healthy economy, but not both. How can Iran's leaders navigate this dilemma?

There are four possible strategies. First, Iran could decide to prioritize the nuclear program over the national economy. It could choose to damage, if not destroy, its economic well-being in order to acquire nuclear weapons. This might sound crazy, but there is a logic to it. International relations theorists believe that states must prioritize core security concerns over economic interests and it is always possible that Iran could pursue this approach.

Second, Iran could prioritize the national economy over the nuclear program. Iran could put permanent and verifiable limits on its nuclear program, or even give it up all together, in order to get comprehensive sanctions relief and revive its national economy. Some observers appear to believe that Iran made this strategic shift in the summer of 2013 and that Tehran is now willing to do whatever it takes to get out from under sanctions. Given Iran's strong reasons for wanting nuclear weapons that we discussed in chapter 2 and its extreme reluctance to dismantle any nuclear infrastructure in the interim nuclear deal, however, I am doubtful that Iran has decided to abandon its nuclear weapons ambitions. It would be much better to have your cake and eat it too, and this is the possibility that the remaining two strategies provide.

Strategy three would be for Iran to attempt to muddle through the economic sanctions until it can acquire nuclear weapons and then hope that, over time, the international pressure would begin to subside. Countries that enforce sanctions, not just the sanctioned state, suffer economic pain too and they will inevitably desire a return to business as normal at some point. Moreover, once Iran becomes a declared nuclear power the international community might realize it is impossible to put the genie back in the bottle and decide to give up and recognize Iran as a de facto nuclear power. There is precedent for this nuclear-pariah-to-nuclear-power approach working for other countries, including India and Pakistan, and this appears to be the strategy that Iran's supreme leader was pursuing until the summer of 2013. By the summer of 2013, however, the economic pain was too great and Khamenei changed tack. He could always reverse course, however, especially if he judged that the sanctions were unraveling and the economic pain to muddling through was once again perceived as bearable.

The fourth strategy would be to seek sanctions relief through a negotiated settlement first and then resume one's march to nuclear weapons later in the hope that the international community will not be able to bring systematic pressure to bear a repeated number of times. A variant of this strategy helped North Korea secure entrance to the nuclear club. In order to pursue this strategy, Iran would have to negotiate sanctions relief while maintaining as much of its nuclear program in place as possible to allow a future nuclear weapons bid. This is the strategy that is most consistent with Iran's recent behavior and I believe this is the path that Iran is pursuing. After all, Rouhani has bragged about how he has used negotiations to temporarily relieve pressure as a means to advance Iran's nuclear program in the past. And Iran's nuclear chief boasted in January 2014 that the "iceberg of sanctions is melting while our centrifuges are also still working." In order to believe that this is not Iran's strategy, one would have to conclude that Iran has definitely abandoned any and all nuclear weapons ambitions, but this interpretation borders on implausibility.

Moreover, it also bears noting that, even if Iran's leaders have temporarily decided to suspend their hopes of acquiring nuclear weapons, they
could always change their minds at a later date as long as the enrichment
program remains in place. Many observers optimistic about an impending
nuclear breakthrough place their hopes in the person of President Rouhani, but his term as president will end in four years. If Rouhani alone can
make a nuclear deal stick, what happens if a new hard-line president is
elected in 2017?

In sum, Iran's goals in the negotiations are to maintain as advanced a
nuclear program as possible with the least intrusive international inspections possible and to receive a complete lifting of international sanctions.
The United States and the P5+1, on the other hand, would prefer that Iran
maintain the most severely restricted nuclear program possible, the most
intrusive inspections regime possible, and to retain its sources of economic
leverage—a subject to which we will return below. In short, these are zero-
sum negotiations. It is hard to imagine any overlap between what Iran's
leaders might agree to and what would simultaneously reassure the international community that Iran's nuclear program is no longer a problem.

Yet there is still another complicating factor: Iran is also playing a
two-level game. Many influential hardliners in Iran, including top officials
in the IRGC and the Iranian Parliament, don't want a deal and view any
cooperation with the United States as beyond the pale. The supreme leader
has temporarily given a long leash to Rouhani and his government to attempt to negotiate an easing of sanctions, but his sympathies are clearly
with the hard-liners. Iran's theocratic government was founded on opposition to the United States and resistance to the West. Iran's leaders delight
in poking their fingers in Uncle Sam's eye. Many prefer confrontation to

cooperation. To be sure, they don't want a war with the greatest super-power on Earth and they would like sanctions relief, but they don't benefit from harmonious relations with us either. Since the Iranian Revolution in 1979, Iran took captive and held hostage fifty-two Americans for 444 days, we fought a major naval battle in 1988, and, over the past decade, Iran has sponsored terrorist and proxy attacks killing countless American service personnel. "Death to America" is a chant commonly heard at public gatherings on the streets of Tehran. Indeed, when Rouhani returned from his September 2013 trip to New York (which was widely celebrated in the West), he was greeted in Tehran by protestors throwing shoes and received a public rebuke from the supreme leader for his "inappropriate" behavior. Perhaps the single best example of the enmity between the two countries, however, is the Iranian supreme leader's penchant for referring to the United States as "The Great Satan." For Ayatollah Khamenei, therefore, a comprehensive nuclear agreement with the United States would very much be like making a deal with the devil.

All else being equal, therefore, many in Iran's elite would prefer not to resolve this dispute diplomatically. From their point of view, it is simply not in the supreme leader's interest to sit down, shake hands, and sign a formal international agreement with representatives of the United States. In extreme circumstances in the past, Iran's leaders have been willing to make peace with bitter enemies. For example, after years of brutal fighting in the Iran-Iraq War, Ayatollah Ruhollah Khomeini reluctantly made peace with Saddam Hussein, likening it to drinking from the "poisoned chalice." It is possible, therefore, that under duress, Ayatollah Khamenei could do something similar. But make no mistake about it, he views a deal with the United States as a slug of hemlock, not a sip of *doogh*.

In sum, there are still many ways that negotiations could break down. Iranian hard-liners might do their part to undermine them; Iran's supreme leader, Ayatollah Ali Khamenei, might be unwilling to make necessary concessions; or the diplomats might simply fail to come to mutually acceptable terms. We can see why Obama is not optimistic. Moreover, as discussed above, even the successful negotiation of a "comprehensive" accord may not be long lasting and Iran would have strong incentives to try to break out of the agreement.

How, then, can the P5+1 keep negotiations on track and retain leverage after the conclusion of a comprehensive deal? How should we respond if the diplomatic track breaks down altogether, either now or in the future?

SOURCES OF LEVERAGE

The key to keeping diplomacy on track, or getting it back on track if it breaks down, is convincing Tehran that it will be better off with a deal than without one. As we discussed above, acquiring nuclear weapons in a no-deal scenario would be highly attractive to Iran's leaders, so successful diplomacy hinges on being able to provide Tehran with either large benefits as part of a deal, or to threaten high costs without a deal, or both.

Let's first consider possible benefits. The United States could offer a kind of rapprochement, a grand bargain to resolve all the conflicts of interest between Tehran and Washington.[36] But as I pointed out above, many of Iran's leaders would view this as a threat, not a promise. A good relationship with the United States is something to be avoided, not pursued. Moreover, the nuclear issue is difficult enough. Tossing into the negotiations problematic issues such as Syria, human rights, international terrorism,

Israeli-Palestinian peace, and the many other points of contention between our two countries would only complicate matters further.

The United States and the international community could promise to provide Iran with peaceful nuclear technology and this would likely have to be part of any final pact to help Iran save face, but this is not a large enough carrot on its own to seal the deal. All signs suggest that Iran would like a nuclear weapons capability, and a nuclear energy program does not in any way compensate for giving up the ultimate security guarantee. Indeed, the international community has offered Iran peaceful nuclear technology in the past in exchange for giving up uranium enrichment, and these offers have all been rejected.

In short, there is really nothing (not détente, not peaceful nuclear technology, not anything else) we can offer Tehran that is more valuable than a nuclear weapons capability.

Since there are no benefits we can offer Iran's leaders that would outweigh a nuclear weapons capability, our only hope is to threaten that without a deal, we will impose costs that will be worse than swallowing hard for a nuclear deal they don't want. The two arrows that remain in our quiver, therefore, are threats of sanctions and military action.

SANCTIONS

Without the tough international sanctions regime imposed on Iran from 2006 to 2013, it is highly unlikely that Iran would have come to the negotiating table and agreed to the November 2013 interim deal. If we are able to get a comprehensive deal, it will only be because Iran is desperate to get out from under the tough sanctions that remain. Some sanctions experts fear that the successful conclusion of the interim deal will signal that Iran is open for business and that trade and investment will start flowing in despite the sanctions that remain in place. This would be disastrous for diplomacy. In order to get a comprehensive deal, therefore, it is critical that the P5+1 continue to enforce the existing sanctions regime.

What happens if we get a comprehensive deal that results in the complete lifting of sanctions in return for curbs on Iran's nuclear program? This is something that worries me. Iran only agreed to limits on its nuclear program in the interim deal because it wanted to get out from under the sanctions. If the sanctions are lifted in a comprehensive deal, therefore, it will be tempting for Iran to simply resume its disturbing nuclear activities. One might argue that the P5+1 could simply re-impose sanctions on Iran at that point, but that is easier said than done. It took a decade to build the existing sanctions regime and completely reconstructing it once it has been dismantled will be incredibly difficult. Trade with Iran will resume and countries and firms will have narrow economic reasons to resist new sanctions. It will be much easier for Iran to crank up its level of enrichment in its already spinning centrifuges than it will be for the P5+1 to resurrect a dead sanctions regime.

For this reason, the P5+1 should not dismantle the sanctions architecture as part of a comprehensive deal. Rather, the interim deal should serve as a template for what can be done. The interim deal lifted some sanctions on Iran, but it did not suspend them altogether. Rather, the sanctions were designed to "snap back" into place at the end of the six-month deal or if the agreement broke down. The sanctions relief provided as part of a comprehensive deal should include similar "snap-back" provisions. Otherwise, we will be forfeiting our most important source of leverage over Iran and make a nuclear-armed Iran more likely. Iran will be reluctant to agree to these terms, but we should be reluctant to accept a deal that does not include them.

In addition, if diplomacy breaks down in the negotiation of a comprehensive deal, or after one is struck, then the P5+1 needs to be prepared to place even tougher economic penalties on Iran. The sanctions regime is already amazingly comprehensive and there is very little blood left to squeeze from that stone, but there are additional steps we could take. Indeed, in early 2014, the US Congress was drawing up a new sanctions bill that would aim to reduce Iran's remaining oil sales and place additional limitations on Iranian financial transactions.

A TRULY CREDIBLE MILITARY THREAT

The second source of leverage we have over Iran is the threat of military force. Some may find it odd to discuss armed conflict in a chapter on diplomacy, but as Frederick the Great said, "Diplomacy without arms is like music without instruments." President Obama has always argued that he "won't take any options off the table, including military action" to keep Tehran from the bomb. While sanctions were probably the more immediate source of pressure working on Iran's leaders in 2013, the fear of military action may have also encouraged them to come to the negotiating table. After all, the prospect of muddling through the economic sanctions only to get bombed would not be a very attractive outcome for Ayatollah Khamenei. If he truly believes his choice is between a deal with the Great Satan and war with the Great Satan, he might very well choose the deal.

Indeed, many knowledgeable observers have remarked that my own writing may have contributed to diplomacy's success by convincing Iran's leaders that the United States had a viable military option that was being advocated by thoughtful experts in Washington, DC. I haven't seen any evidence that that is the case, but my hope has always been that we would never have to use the military option that I have spent so many years thinking and writing about. As the Romans said, "If you want peace, prepare for war."

Just as with economic sanctions, the military option is a source of leverage that the P5+1 will need to retain even after the conclusion of any successful comprehensive deal. The P5+1 should negotiate terms that would make a potential military strike on Iran's nuclear facilities easier in the event that diplomacy breaks down. For example, we could limit Iranian enrichment to a single, above-ground facility, such as the pilot-plant facility at Natanz. As we will discuss in more detail in the next chapter, a single above-ground facility would be easier to destroy than the current set of targets presented by Iran's nuclear program, and could reassure Israel and other nervous partners in the region that the military option remains on the table as a last resort.

Otherwise, as long as the Iranians are engaged in constructive negotiations and abiding by their agreements, the military option should be placed on the back burner. But, if diplomacy breaks down, it must once again come front and center.

Many people outside the Washington, DC beltway are skeptical that Obama is prepared to use force if necessary to keep Tehran from the bomb. Obama's failure to follow through on his threats to use force in response to President Assad's use of chemical weapons in the Syrian civil war in the fall of 2013 may have exacerbated this problem. Many conclude (I believe wrongly) that President Obama is simply not willing to use force in any situation and that he will ultimately back down in a final confrontation over Iran's nuclear program just as he caved in Syria.

Obama's closest advisers, however, including those who have worked with him in the White House on this issue, insist that the president is ready to use force if necessary to prevent a nuclear arms race in the Middle East. As Dennis Ross, former Special Assistant to President Obama and Senior Director at the White House for the Central Region, said, "When President Obama says 'I don't bluff,' I think he means what he says. If diplomacy doesn't work, we have to be prepared to use force, and I think we will be." Similarly, Gary Samore has stated that "If [the Iranians] move to high-enrichment, I think President Obama would have to act. It's a casus belli. It's a blatant move. I think that would lead to the use of force."

If President Obama is willing to use force, but other people, especially Iran's leaders don't believe him, we might be in for trouble. Indeed, this is the worst possible combination because Obama's threats will fail to deter Iran, and we will end up in what might have been an avoidable war.

If diplomacy breaks down, therefore, we must somehow find a way to convince Iran's supreme leader that we are committed to using force as a last resort. In order to get diplomacy back on track we must take steps to increase the credibility of our military threat.

In a speech before the UN General Assembly in November 2012, Israeli Prime Minister Benjamin Netanyahu called for setting a clear "red line" for the use of military force against Iran's nuclear program.[37] He illustrated his point by literally drawing a red line across an image of a bomb. In the days that followed, journalists and pundits lampooned Netanyahu's behavior and his "cartoonish" drawing. The Obama administration responded by arguing that they have already set one red line, the development of nuclear weapons, and that setting more specific red lines would have a number of other downside consequences, including unduly constraining the president's options. In subsequent months, policy analysts wrote detailed reports purporting to show that it does not make sense to set more specific red lines on Iran's nuclear program.[38] Israeli leaders in general and Netanyahu in particular have always been forward leaning on the Iranian nuclear issue, so it is understandable that some people would be skeptical of calls for military red lines emanating from Israel. But it is important to separate the message from the messenger. In this instance, Netanyahu was right.

A careful analysis demonstrates that if diplomacy breaks down there are a number of significant benefits and, on closer inspection, no real costs to setting more specific red lines on Iran's nuclear program.

As was discussed in chapter 2, practical matters make preventing Iran from acquiring one bomb's worth of WEU our de facto red line. What are the advantages and disadvantages in being absolutely clear about this to Iran and the rest of the world?

There are a number of upsides to being clear about our red lines. First, it increases the credibility of the military option by helping to demonstrate that we are serious about using force if necessary to stop Iran from acquiring nuclear weapons. This would be central to any effort to convince Iran to give up its sensitive nuclear work.

Second, and related, setting clear red lines might actually deter Iran from crossing them. If Iran's leaders fear that enriching to higher levels might trigger a US attack, they might stop short. But, if they think our red line is the construction of a nuclear weapon, there would be no reason why they wouldn't continue to inch their enrichment program forward and eventually cross our true red lines. A vague red line, therefore, is a recipe for a nuclear-armed Iran or a potentially avoidable war.

Third, if our other efforts at prevention fail and if the United States decides to go to war over Iran's nuclear program, we would want the full support of the American public and of as much of the international community as possible. Certainly that support will be easier to come by if it is clear to everyone in advance that it was Iran, not the United States, that made the fateful decision to cross the Rubicon.

In short, there are real benefits to setting red lines. What about the costs? Critics have voiced two major objections to setting more specific red lines, but neither stands up to scrutiny. First, they argue that if we set a red line, we will merely encourage Iran to race right up to it. If Washington says, for example, that Iran must not enrich to 60 percent, they fear that Iran will feel free to ramp up from current levels to 59 percent. But that is not a problem; that is the point. As long as the red line is set in the right place, we don't need to be concerned whether Iran races up to it, so long as it doesn't cross it.

Second, some have argued that setting a specific red line would place unnecessary constraints on the president. But again, this is precisely the point. Indeed, it is the reason why setting red lines increases the credibility of the military option. Since time immemorial, wise generals have understood that burning bridges behind them was the best way to signal to an adversary that the armies under their command wouldn't, and indeed couldn't, retreat if attacked. So it is true that setting red lines will reduce the president's flexibility. But this is only a problem if the president wants to keep open the option of going back on his word and acquiescing to Iranian nuclear weapons. After all, if he truly wants to keep this option open, then Iran shouldn't believe his threats. Setting red lines, therefore, demonstrates his resolve and helps solve the credibility problem.

In sum, setting red lines would be in the national interest of the United States if we fail to get a comprehensive deal or if Iran begins to cheat on that deal, but what should these red lines be? First, and most importantly, Washington should set a red line related to Iran's efforts to enrich uranium to ever-higher levels of purity. The exact line doesn't really matter (20 percent, 30 percent, 40 percent) as long as it is well below the 90 percent purity that would be required to build nuclear weapons.

Second, we should be clear that Iran will not be allowed to throw out International Atomic Energy Agency (IAEA) inspectors. It is through the IAEA's presence that we can best assess whether Iran has crossed our proposed enrichment red line. If inspectors were kicked out, we would have no idea what Iran was up to and we would have to assume that they planned to cross our stated red lines.

Third, the United States could set a red line related to the "undetectable breakout" scenario. As explained above, if Iran's program advances beyond this point, we will be in practice acquiescing to a nuclear-armed Iran.

In a 2012 interview with *The Atlantic*'s Jeffrey Goldberg, President Obama said that his policy was to prevent a nuclear Iran and that he "doesn't bluff."[39] But if he refuses to set a clear red line related specifically to Iran's enrichment efforts when the time comes, Iran's leaders might force him to show his hand, with potentially disastrous consequences.

There are additional steps the United States could take to increase the credibility of its military threat. First, the president could ask for, and Congress could grant, a congressional authorization for the use of military force (AUMF). The US Constitution gives Congress the power to declare war. While the president can conduct some limited military actions without congressional approval, there are fewer constraints when he acts with Congress's consent. Following the terrorist attacks of September 11, 2001, Congress authorized the president to take whatever means necessary to defeat Al Qaeda, paving the way for the war in Afghanistan. In addition, Congress authorized the war against Iraq in 2003. In September 2013, President Obama sought Congress's support for a strike on Syria, but he called off the vote when it seemed unlikely that he would get such support and after Russia intervened with a diplomatic proposal. If we must attack Iran, any president would prefer to have the authorization of Congress. The benefit of seeking it sooner rather than later is that it would aid our coercive diplomacy. It sends a clear signal to Iran that the country is fully behind the president and supports the use of force if necessary to stop Iran from joining the nuclear club. Some may doubt that, given its unwillingness to back a limited strike against Syria, Congress would authorize the use of force against Iran, but Congress has always been more hawkish than the Obama administration on Iran, and it has always been more concerned about Iran than about Syria. By 2013, some Republicans on the Hill were already calling for an authorization for the use of military force against Iran and, in my judgment, a presidential request for an AUMF for Iran would succeed. In May 2013, by a 99–0 vote, the US Senate passed a resolution declaring that "the policy of the United States is to prevent Iran from acquiring a nuclear weapon capability and to take such action as may be necessary to implement this policy." Indeed, given Congress's reluctance to endorse a strike on Syria, an early AUMF would send a particularly strong message to Iran.

In addition, the United States can also increase the credibility of our military threats against Iran if necessary by engaging in more visible international outreach to our friends and partners overseas. Again, if the United

States needs to use force in Iran, we would want to build a broad international coalition in order to increase the legitimacy of the military action and to ensure international and domestic support. We could therefore immediately begin high-level diplomacy with NATO and non-NATO allies and partners to discuss possible military action on Iran. We could conduct joint threat assessments and explain to them why we assess the risks of a nuclear Iran to be greater than the risks of a strike. We could work to build an international consensus on the appropriate red lines for military action. And, most importantly, we could ask for formal assurances that these countries will support us, if necessary, in a military conflict with Iran over its nuclear program.

Much like setting clear red lines and seeking a congressional authorization for the use of force, this step would be doubly helpful because it helps to enhance the credibility of the military threat for last-ditch efforts to solve this issue diplomatically, and it is an action we will have to take anyway if we eventually need to strike Iran.

NEXT STEPS

So what should we do now?[40] A lasting negotiated settlement to this crisis remains the best possible outcome and, following the election of President Rouhani and the conclusion of an interim accord in November 2013, the prospects for a diplomatic resolution have never been higher. The United States should therefore continue to pursue diplomacy while maintaining a healthy dose of realism about all the ways that things can still go wrong.

We should keep the pressure on Tehran by continuing to enforce existing sanctions and making it clear that the military option remains on the table. We must also insist on tough terms for any final agreement. This means working hard to convince Iran to give up its enrichment program altogether. This could be paired with concessions on other less sensitive nuclear matters to help Iran save face. Proponents of a weak deal will protest that Iran will never give up its "right to enrich" but we should set our position according to US interests, not Tehran's desires.

If a zero-enrichment deal proves impossible, we should consider a limited-enrichment deal only if it can be designed to put many months, if not years, back on Iran's nuclear breakout clock; will remain in place for over a decade; and limits enrichment to a single above-ground (read: easily targetable) facility. We must also keep the existing sanctions architecture in place in order to retain this key source of leverage.

If diplomacy breaks down, either because we fail to get a comprehensive accord or because Iran attempts to cheat on its agreements, then we need to immediately switch back to the pressure track. At that point, Congress should pass the toughest possible remaining sanctions. We would also need to take a number of immediate steps to increase the credibility of the military threat: setting clear red lines, passing an AUMF against Iran, and engaging in visible international outreach with our allies and partners on the military option for Iran.

Having set our clear red lines, we can then vigorously work to persuade Iran to halt its nuclear program and return to the negotiating table.

If Iran approaches the red lines we set out, however, we will at some point be forced to issue an ultimatum: either Iran accepts the deal we are prepared to offer or the bombs begin to fall. Even under those conditions, it is possible that Iran will refuse. At that point, the diplomatic window will have shut.

But it won't be all for naught. Even failed diplomacy serves a purpose. By seriously pursuing negotiations until the bitter end, we will have shown that we did our best to avoid conflict and that Iran, not the United States, was the intransigent party. As US Secretary of State John Kerry said, "If you, ultimately, have to hold them accountable because they're not doing it [abiding by their agreements], you have to be able to show that you've gone through all of the diplomatic avenues available before considering other alternatives." This will help to build domestic and international support for the possible conflict to come.

That is, unless you would prefer to roll over and simply allow Iran to have nuclear weapons.

CHAPTER FIVE

IRAN WITH
THE BOMB

IRAN'S LEADERS WOULD NEVER USE NUCLEAR WEAP-
ons because they know that if they ever did, the United States would totally
obliterate them. Therefore, we don't really have anything to fear from a
nuclear-armed Iran. This is an opinion I frequently hear expressed, and
it is certainly comforting. Unfortunately, it is also profoundly misguided.

A nuclear-armed Iran would pose a grave threat to international peace
and security. This is true even if Iran never uses its nuclear weapons. A
nuclear Iran would increase the risk of nuclear proliferation to other states
and terrorist groups, constrain the United States, strengthen the current
theocratic regime in Tehran, damage the global economy, and embolden
Iran to step up support to terrorist groups and otherwise throw its weight
around in the region.

In addition, there is a real risk that nuclear weapons in Iran will lead
to nuclear war. Iran's leaders might calculate that nuclear use makes sense

under certain circumstances, and even if Iran's leaders are terrified by the consequences of any nuclear exchange, a catastrophic nuclear war could still occur due to accident or inadvertent escalation in a high-stakes crisis. Moreover, there is always the risk that Iran's nuclear weapons could fall into the hands of terrorists who would be less constrained by fears of nuclear retaliation or taboos against nuclear use. In short, no amount of wishful thinking can get around the fact that a nuclear-armed Iran would present a severe threat to US national interests.

To manage these threats, the United States would put in place a strategy to deter and contain a nuclear-armed Iran. But deterrence and containment would not be easy. It would mean a major increase in US political and military commitments to the Middle East. These measures would need to remain in place as long as Iran has nuclear weapons and is hostile to US interests, which could be decades or longer. Moreover, even with the best-designed strategy, we still could not prevent many of the threats that would emanate from a nuclear-armed Iran. It is for these reasons that President Obama has repeatedly said that his policy is to prevent, not to contain, a nuclear-armed Iran.

Nevertheless, it is possible that the president might not follow through on his threat to attack Iran if an attack is necessary to stop it from building nuclear weapons. We might be too late. Or when the time comes, we might simply lose our courage and acquiesce. If this happens, our options will have narrowed, and we will have no choice but to attempt to deter and contain a nuclear Iran. Moreover, as one of the plausible options for dealing with Iran's nuclear program and one that many national security analysts prefer over a strike, a deterrence and containment strategy deserves serious consideration. It will receive it in this chapter. I will explain the possible negative consequences of a nuclear-armed Iran and propose a strategy for deterring and containing the Iranian nuclear threat.

Before I do, however, I must first consider what a nuclear-armed Iran might look like.

WHAT WILL IRAN'S NUCLEAR ARSENAL LOOK LIKE?

To fully appreciate the threat posed by a nuclear-armed Iran, we must evaluate the possible forms that Iran's nuclear arsenal might take. This is because some of the possible negative consequences of a nuclear Iran, such as whether it could attack the United States with nuclear weapons, will depend on Iran's nuclear capabilities. In particular, this section will focus on the numbers of warheads and types and ranges of delivery vehicles that Iran might plausibly possess in the coming years as these are among the most important elements of a country's nuclear posture.

How many nuclear weapons will a nuclear Iran possess? For a point of comparison, let's begin by considering the nuclear arsenal sizes of other states. At present, the United States and Russia have agreed to deploy 1,550 strategic, nuclear warheads under the terms of the New START treaty, signed in 2010; China possesses roughly 350 warheads; Britain, France, and Israel are thought to have around 200 each; India and Pakistan have roughly 100 each; and North Korea has roughly 12 nuclear warheads.[1]

Studying the arsenals of the existing nuclear powers reveals a couple of patterns. First, countries' nuclear arsenals tend to grow over time. The states that developed nuclear weapons earliest (the United States in 1945, Russia in 1949) also possess the largest arsenals. The second largest arsenals can be found in the second wave of countries to acquire nuclear weapons: Britain (1952), France (1960), China (1964), and Israel (1967). And, finally, the countries with the smallest nuclear arsenals are those that developed nuclear weapons most recently: India (1998), Pakistan (1998), and North Korea (2006). Second, we see that (apart from the superpowers, which have developed massive nuclear arsenals) most states seem to be content with a couple hundred nuclear weapons, but countries below that level seek to expand their arsenals. Britain, France, Israel, and China appear to have decided to cap their arsenals at 200 to 300 warheads, but India, Pakistan, and North Korea are rapidly increasing their arsenal sizes.

I predict, therefore, that, if Iran acquires nuclear weapons, it will begin with a small nuclear arsenal and then seek, over the course of the coming years, to build to an arsenal of a couple hundred nuclear warheads.

It is of course possible that Iran might decide to stop with a latent nuclear capability, but as we have discussed in previous chapters, the "Japan model" as a sustainable model for Iran seems highly unlikely. For the purposes of this chapter, therefore, we will assume that if the US policy of prevention fails, Iran will have a handful of nuclear weapons in a few years and the arsenal will steadily grow to 200 or so warheads in the next ten to twenty years.

What parts of the globe will Iran be able to threaten with these nuclear weapons? In other words, what are its primary means of delivering nuclear weapons to an intended target? We will again begin by considering delivery vehicles in the established nuclear powers. The advanced nuclear weapon states have three primary means of delivery: bomber and fighter aircraft, ballistic missiles, and submarine-launched ballistic missiles (SLBMs). In addition, it is always possible that a state could use an unconventional means of delivery. It could, for example, sneak a nuclear weapon to its intended target in a cargo container, a truck, or a backpack. Or it could pass nuclear weapons to a terrorist group, which could conduct an attack on the state's behalf.

Immediately upon becoming a nuclear power, Iran could deliver nuclear weapons to countries within range of its fighter and bomber aircraft. This would not be a very strong option, however, because Iran's air force is weak.[2] Many of its aircraft were provided by the United States in the 1970s while the shah was still in power, and they have been decaying ever since. Indeed, Iran's birds are in such bad shape that they sometimes fall from the sky in routine training missions.[3] If Iran tried to use aircraft to carry out a nuclear mission, it is likely that they would crash or be blown out of the sky by enemy air defenses before they reached their intended target.

Submarines are not a strong option either. Iran does not at present have submarines capable of delivering ballistic missiles, and it does not have plans to build any. Iran has threatened to build nuclear-powered submarines, but this appears to be merely an excuse to enrich uranium to ever higher levels.[4] US nuclear-powered submarines, for example, require uranium fuel enriched to 93 percent.[5] It does not seem feasible for Iran to develop SLBMs anytime soon. Indeed, of the nine nuclear powers, only the most powerful and earliest entrants to the nuclear club (the United States, Russia, France, and Britain) have operational SLBMs.

Rather, Iran's strongest delivery option would be ballistic missiles. Tehran currently has an advanced program with short-range ballistic missiles (SRBMs) and medium-range ballistic missiles (MRBMs) capable of reaching the entire Middle East and parts of southern Europe.[6] It is also working on an Intercontinental Ballistic Missile (ICBM) that would be capable of reaching almost any point on the globe. Indeed, the US Department of Defense (DoD) estimates that Iran could have a ballistic missile capable of reaching the East Coast of the United States by 2015.[7]

It is difficult to build a nuclear weapon small enough to fit on the nose cone of a ballistic missile, but it is likely that Iran could figure this out in a few short years.[8] According to the Defense Intelligence Agency (DIA), North Korea, a country much less technologically sophisticated than Iran, has already mastered this capability.[9]

It seems rather obvious, therefore, that Iran's nuclear delivery vehicle of choice would be ballistic missiles.

Iran could also choose unconventional means of delivery. Sneaking a nuke into an opponent's territory would not be sufficient to fight a major nuclear war, but it could be used to deal a single, devastating (and perhaps unidentifiable) blow to an enemy anywhere on the planet.

In sum, for the purpose of this chapter, I will assume that a nuclear Iran will begin with a small undeliverable nuclear arsenal, but that over the course of several years, this would grow into a larger arsenal (eventually a couple hundred weapons) that could be delivered to almost any spot on the globe, including the US homeland, via ballistic missile or unconventional means.

What kind of threats would this capability pose to international peace and security?

THREATS

Nuclear weapons in Iran would have a number of negative consequences for US national security. It would lead to the spread of nuclear weapons around the world, constrained US freedom of action, weakened US credibility, accommodation by regional states, the locking of the current theocratic regime in power for years to come, an emboldened and more dangerous Iran, spikes in oil prices that damage the global economy, and an increased risk of nuclear war. This section will consider each of those threats in turn.

FURTHER PROLIFERATION

A nuclear-armed Iran would cause the spread of nuclear weapons in the Middle East and around the world and a weakening of the global nuclear nonproliferation regime. Many analysts have predicted a "cascade" or "chain reaction" of nuclear proliferation in the Middle East if Iran gets the bomb. Egypt, Saudi Arabia, and Turkey are among the states that will be more likely to go nuclear if Tehran joins the atomic club. In addition, nearly a dozen other countries in the region, including Jordan, Morocco, and the United Arab Emirates (UAE), have expressed interest in a nuclear power program and might one day seek to join the ranks of the nuclear powers.[10] Officials in Riyadh are already talking openly about their plans to develop nuclear weapons to counter the Iranian nuclear threat.[11] As President Obama has said clearly, if Iran develops nuclear weapons, "It is almost certain that other players in the region would feel it necessary to get their own nuclear weapons. So now you have the prospect of a nuclear arms race in the most volatile region in the world."[12]

The future is, of course, unknowable, and some analysts dispute this widely held view. Philipp Bleek, my first PhD student at Georgetown University and now a professor at the Monterey Institute of International

Studies, for example, argues that predictions of nuclear dominoes falling in the Middle East are greatly exaggerated.[13] Bleek and other experts claim that many of the supply-side and demand-side factors associated with nuclear proliferation are simply absent in many of these Middle Eastern cases. First, on the supply side, they point out that none of these countries possess an advanced nuclear program at present. Therefore, they argue, these countries could not simply snap their fingers and build the bomb. Rather, they would need outside help and/or a lot of time. Second, on the demand side, they argue that these countries might not even want independent nuclear arsenals. To be sure, they would be threatened by Iran's nuclear weapons, but Bleek and others argue that these countries might still decide not to build nuclear weapons and will look for other ways to protect themselves against Iran's bombs. Turkey, a formal NATO ally, might prefer to lounge in the shade of America's massive nuclear umbrella rather than risk building its own nuclear weapons. Similarly, even states that lack a formal alliance with the United States but still value highly their relationship with Washington, like Saudi Arabia, might not want to undermine their close relationship with the United States by building a bomb despite warnings from Washington. After all, the United States has always opposed the spread of nuclear weapons and would certainly try to stop nuclear proliferation to Iran's neighbors.

Those skeptical of a coming nuclear arms race in the Middle East also point out that history has something to teach us. They argue that US-based analysts have vastly overpredicted the rate of reactive nuclear proliferation in the past. For example, when China was pursuing nuclear weapons in the early 1960s, many American policymakers argued that this would set off a chain reaction of nuclear proliferation in East Asia. They argued that

Japan, Taiwan, India, and Pakistan would automatically acquire nuclear weapons in response.[14] With the benefit of hindsight, however, we know that not all of these countries went nuclear.

In sum, Bleek and other nuclear-cascade skeptics argue that predictions of a half dozen Middle Eastern states going nuclear in response to a nuclear-armed Iran are probably overblown.

These skeptics do a service by reining in the worst-case scenarios of a tidal wave of nuclear bombs rolling across the region, but they risk going too far. It would be a mistake to argue that reactive nuclear proliferation is not a serious problem. After all, nuclear dominoes do sometimes fall and proliferation to even one additional state is a real problem.

To understand why, let's take another look at the history of reactive proliferation. Skeptics are correct that not all of the identified countries proliferated in response to China's bomb. We must not forget, however, that some did. India and Pakistan acquired nuclear weapons as part of a process set off by the bomb in Beijing. Moreover, world history has not yet stopped. It is still possible that Japan, South Korea, Taiwan, and other countries in Asia will one day build nuclear weapons, and, if they do, it is likely that China's nuclear arsenal will be a contributing cause.

Applying this lesson to the present, it is unlikely that all of the countries we identify as potential reactive proliferators in the Middle East will build nuclear weapons, but it is likely that at least some will. So perhaps Egypt will steer clear of the bomb while Turkey and Saudi Arabia decide to go nuclear. In such a scenario, Cairo's nuclear restraint will be cold comfort when we are in the midst of a future Turkish-Iranian-Saudi-Israeli nuclear crisis.

Next, let's turn to the skeptics' point about the most at-risk countries lacking the ability to produce nuclear weapons. This is undoubtedly true at present, but there are two things to keep in mind. First, these countries might get outside help. Some analysts fear that with its deep pockets and ties to Pakistan, Riyadh might be able to simply buy nuclear weapons or pay Islamabad to station its nuclear weapons on Saudi territory.[15] In the 1970s, Saudi Arabia and Pakistan established a formal understanding in which Riyadh agreed to help finance Islamabad in building the first "Islamic bomb" in exchange for a Pakistani pledge to one day funnel sensitive nuclear technology back to Saudi Arabia.[16] If this nuclear quid pro quo remains in place, an Iranian sprint to the bomb might mean nuclear weapons materializing in Saudi Arabia overnight. To be sure, this scenario is unlikely. No country has ever provided a fully functioning nuclear weapon to another state, and it is hard to see what Pakistan could possibly gain from simply handing over the most powerful weapons on Earth to Saudi Arabia. As I explain in *Exporting the Bomb,* if Pakistan wanted to help the Saudis' nuclear program (and this is still a fairly big if), it would be much more likely to transfer sensitive nuclear technology, such as uranium enrichment equipment. So, again, we are likely looking at a decade or more for Riyadh to join the nuclear club, even with Pakistan's help. Nevertheless, the possibility of rapid proliferation due to outside assistance is something that we should keep in mind.

There is, however, a second and more important point about timing: just because nuclear proliferation is slow doesn't mean that it is not a problem. As even the skeptics point out, while none of these countries could instantly produce nuclear weapons, any one of them could plausibly have nuclear weapons within a decade or so. This should be a major cause of concern. A Middle East armed to the teeth with nuclear weapons in 2024 is a frightening prospect. After all, I, and presumably many of my readers, hope to be alive and kicking in 2024.

In sum, Iran's nuclear acquisition will likely mean one or two additional nuclear-armed states in the Middle East over the next ten to twenty years. When combined with a region that already contains two nuclear-armed states (Israel and, in this scenario, Iran), this is the recipe for a poly-nuclear and highly unstable Middle East.

The spread of nuclear weapons would not, however, be confined to the region. An Iranian bomb would also lead to the further spread of nuclear weapons around the world.

Iran would be likely to become a nuclear supplier transferring dangerous nuclear technology to countries in other regions. In *Exporting the Bomb*, I study the history of sensitive nuclear technology transfer and identify the conditions associated with the export of uranium enrichment and plutonium-reprocessing technology and nuclear weapons design.[17] I argue that the spread of nuclear weapons threatens powerful states more than weak states and, for this reason, weak states can benefit strategically by exporting sensitive nuclear material and technology outside of their own sphere of influence. In this way, the spread of nuclear weapons in a distant region does not threaten the supplier. It does, however, constrain the supplier's more powerful enemies that can project power in that region. In addition, nuclear-capable states that have poor relations with the superpowers are also at an increased risk of transferring sensitive nuclear technology.

Applying these insights to Iran, we see that Iran is a country that is at risk of becoming a nuclear supplier. It could transfer uranium enrichment technology, enriched uranium, or a nuclear weapon design to countries in Asia or Latin America. Since Iran lacks the ability to project power outside of the Middle East, a nuclear arms race in any of these regions would not directly harm Iran's national security. It would, however, create real problems for the United States. Given the hostility between these two countries, therefore, Tehran might take the opportunity to intentionally impose costs on the United States, constraining America's freedom of action and distracting its strategic attention away from Tehran.

One can easily imagine Iran's president announcing in the coming years that Venezuela is a country in good standing with the NPT and that it therefore has a right to peaceful nuclear technology. Iran's leaders could argue that, in order to help Venezuela produce fuel rods for its peaceful nuclear program, Iran will provide Venezuela with uranium enrichment technology. This could all be done—just like Iran's current nuclear program—under the patina of peaceful nuclear cooperation consistent with the principals of the NPT.

A "peaceful" uranium enrichment program in Venezuela, however, would create terrible headaches for the United States even if Caracas never acquired nuclear weapons. After all, it would essentially be a replay of the decade-long crisis we are currently experiencing with Iran's nuclear program, but this time in our own backyard.

This scenario is easy to imagine, in part because Iran has already announced its intention to export nuclear technology to Venezuela in a formal nuclear cooperation agreement.[18] The terms of the deal have not yet been finalized, but it is possible that the framework could eventually facilitate the transfer of sensitive nuclear technology, including uranium-enrichment capabilities, to Venezuela and, in the future, to other countries in the region.

In addition to transferring sensitive nuclear technology, Iran could also decide to export complete nuclear weapons to other states, but this is much less likely. As I show in *Exporting the Bomb,* nuclear-capable countries have repeatedly provided sensitive nuclear technology to nonnuclear weapon states.[19] They have never, however, given away a fully functioning nuclear weapon. There is a first time for everything, of course, and we should not dismiss this scenario out of hand, but the transfer of sensitive nuclear technology and materials is much more likely and nearly as problematic.

Finally, there is the possibility that Iran could transfer nuclear weapons, or sufficient quantities of weapons-grade fissile material, to terrorist groups. Iran already provides conventional arms to Hamas and Hezbollah, and some analysts worry that Iran's leaders might also hand off a nuclear weapon to its terrorist proxies.[20] This is a frightening scenario indeed. Unlike countries that use nuclear weapons to deter attacks on their territory, terrorist groups would be much more likely to use nuclear weapons in a mass casualty attack.

Fortunately, it is unlikely that Iran would intentionally transfer nuclear weapons to terrorist groups. Nuclear weapons and terrorist groups have both existed for nearly seventy years, and no state has ever provided nuclear capabilities to a terrorist organization. This pattern makes good sense as nuclear weapons in the hands of terrorists could cause many problems for the supplier state itself. The terrorist group could choose to use the nuclear weapons against the supplier state, blackmail the supplier state with the threat of nuclear use, or use the nuclear weapons on a third state that traces the nuclear weapon back to the supplier and hence retaliates against the supplier state. For these reasons and probably many others, it is unlikely that Iran, or any other state for that matter, will purposely give nuclear weapons to terrorists.

This judgment is further reinforced by Iran's past pattern of behavior regarding conventional arms transfers to terrorist proxies. While Iran has provided much funding and weaponry to Hamas and Hezbollah, it has never provided these groups with its most advanced technology, such as tanks, aircraft, or ballistic missiles. It is likely that Iran would show similar restraint when it comes to nuclear weapons.

Iran could conceivably provide nuclear technology to terrorist groups, but this wouldn't do the terrorists much good. Building nuclear weapons is complicated, and even the most sophisticated terrorist group would have no hope of constructing and operating a nuclear weapons production complex on its own.

Iran might also provide terrorist groups with radioactive material that terrorists could use in a dirty bomb attack, but dirty bombs are not a major cause of concern. A dirty bomb is simply a conventional explosive packed with radioactive material. A dirty bomb does not create a nuclear chain reaction; it merely spreads radioactive material in the vicinity of the conventional explosion. People might die from the conventional explosive blast, but the radioactive material would not do much, if any, additional damage. Indeed, the most serious effect from a dirty bomb attack might be the mayhem resulting from unwarranted panic if officials or the general public mistake the radioactivity from a dirty bomb to mean that a real nuclear attack had occurred. For this reason, dirty bombs are sometimes referred to as "weapons of mass disruption." They should not be confused, however, with real weapons of mass destruction.

When it comes to nuclear terrorist incidents, therefore, the biggest concern would be the transfer of an actual nuclear weapon, or at least sufficient quantities of WGU, to a terrorist group. Fortunately, as we discussed above, it is unlikely that Iran would intentionally transfer these capabilities to a terrorist group.

Still, it is possible that Iran might transfer nuclear weapons unintentionally. As a new nuclear state, it is unlikely that Iran will have sophisticated security measures in place to protect its nuclear weapons.[21] It is possible, therefore, that Iran's weapons could be vulnerable to theft or that a low-level commander in the Iranian military could decide to transfer a nuclear weapon or two to a terrorist group without authorization from the national leadership. We often see IRGC naval commanders freelancing in the Persian Gulf, taking provocative measures, such as hotdogging with fast attack craft near US warships, that could not possibly have been ordered by the country's top political leadership.[22] So, the idea that Iran's supreme leader might not have an ironclad grip on Iran's military and, in the future, on nuclear command and control seems at least plausible.

In addition, while not likely in the short term, it is always possible that the Iranian government could simply collapse, leading to a loose nukes problem. Iran is a country with a history of revolutions and the current theocratic government probably cannot sustain itself indefinitely. The US government has made no secret about the fact that it would prefer to see a different, more democratic regime in place in Tehran. If a new Iranian revolution toppled the mullahs after Iran entered the nuclear club, however, this would create real problems. In the chaos of such a political revolution, there is no telling who would have control of the nuclear weapons, and there is a real risk that nuclear weapons could fall into the wrong hands. Presently, this is one of the US government's major concerns with Pakistan's and North Korea's nuclear weapons. This will continue to be a problem whenever nuclear weapons spread to countries like Iran with less than consolidated political institutions.

Nuclear weapons in Iran would thus create a genuine dilemma for US foreign policy toward the current regime. We could choose to prioritize the security of the nuclear arsenal at the cost of accepting an authoritarian and anti-American regime in power in Tehran. Alternatively, we could promote democracy and encourage a regime transition only at the risk of potentially causing a very serious loose nukes problem.

In addition to nuclear proliferation to specific states or terrorist groups, nuclear weapons in Iran will also lead to a general weakening of the global nuclear nonproliferation regime. One of the grand bargains of the NPT is the pact among the nonnuclear weapon states. In this pact, nonnuclear weapon states agree not to develop nuclear weapons so long as other non-nuclear-weapon states do not develop nuclear weapons either. In this way, countries can refrain from building nuclear weapons and remain relatively secure in the knowledge that their neighbors are not pursuing the bomb. If Iran (and potentially other countries) joins the nuclear club, however, then leaders around the world will be more likely to conclude that this central pillar of the NPT is unraveling. In addition, seeing Iran overcome international resistance on its path to the bomb, leaders of other countries might assess that the great powers no longer have the capability or the will to enforce the NPT. For these reasons and others, leaders around the world might begin to reconsider their nuclear options. It is difficult to predict who the next proliferators will be, but this group could plausibly include many countries in Asia, the Middle East, Latin America, Africa, and even Europe.

In the 1950s, the nuclear strategist Albert Wohlstetter predicted that the spread of nuclear weapons to one state would cause other states to seek nuclear weapons in response. He therefore criticized US decision makers for calculating the pros and cons of nuclear proliferation to an "Nth" state without also figuring in the potential negative consequences of what he called the "N+1 problem."[23] We must not make that same mistake today. Nuclear proliferation in Iran is not only about the threat posed by nuclear weapons in Iran. Rather, it is about the threats posed by the spread of the most dangerous weapons on Earth to Iran and to other states and potentially even to terrorist groups.

CONSTRAINED FREEDOM OF ACTION

Nuclear proliferation in Iran would also disadvantage US national security by constraining America's political and military freedom of action in the Middle East. As the most powerful country on the planet, with the ability to project power to every corner of the globe, the United States has the capacity to threaten or protect every other state in the international system. This is a significant source of strategic leverage, and maintaining freedom of action is an important objective of US national security policy.[24]

As nuclear weapons spread, however, America's military freedom of action is constrained. At present, the United States can use, or credibly threaten to use, force against Iran. In January 2012, for example, Iran threatened to close the Strait of Hormuz, a narrow Persian Gulf waterway through which roughly 20 percent of the world's oil flows, and the United States issued a counterthreat, confidently declaring that the US Navy's Fifth Fleet would use force to reopen the strait if necessary.[25] If Iran acquired nuclear weapons, however, the use of, or threats to use, force in the region contrary to Iran's interests would be much more difficult. A nuclear-armed Iran could seek to deter US military action, or counter US coercive threats, by issuing a counterthreat of devastating nuclear retaliation against US bases, forces, or allies in the region, or against the US homeland. This would give Iran the option of attempting to veto any major future political or military initiative that the United States seeks to undertake in the Middle East. We might not fully believe such threats, but we couldn't laugh them off either. Indeed, any US president would have to think long and hard about using force in the region if it entailed a risk of nuclear war. While the United States might not be deterred in every contingency against a nuclear-armed Iran, it is clear that, at a minimum, the spread of nuclear weapons to Iran greatly complicates US decisions to use, or threaten to use, force in the Middle East.

Constraints on freedom of action certainly sound less devastating than thermonuclear war, but freedom of action is an important source of national strength in a dangerous world and it would be foolish not to recognize it as such. Moreover, not only is the maintenance of US freedom of action good in and of itself, but American military power also underwrites the security and stability of the Middle East and the entire world. Increasing constraints on American military power, therefore, directly unleash other, more visceral security threats, as we will discuss in more detail below.

LOST CREDIBILITY

Allowing Iran to build nuclear weapons would also damage US credibility. Three consecutive American presidents have declared a nuclear-armed Iran to be "unacceptable." If Iran acquires nuclear weapons, therefore, we will have gone back on our word. We will have decided to simply stand by without taking action while Iran acquires nuclear weapons. Leaders around the world will come to think that US foreign policy pronouncements are a bunch of hot air and will begin to doubt the credibility of our commitments elsewhere. American threats will lose some of their ability to intimidate and American promises their capacity to reassure.

Lost credibility will be a real problem if Iran acquires nuclear weapons because, as we will see below, our ability to deter and contain a nuclear-armed Iran will hinge almost entirely on our credibility. Iran's leaders will need to believe that we are willing to retaliate against them if they take certain provocative steps, like launching a nuclear attack against our allies. This means we will have to be willing to go to war. And those very allies will need to believe that we have their backs. But will anyone really believe that we are willing to go to war with a nuclear-armed Iran if we were unwilling to go to war with a nonnuclear Iran to prevent it from acquiring nuclear weapons in the first place? It is doubtful.

Recent academic research suggests that a reputation for following through on past threats isn't important in international politics, but I have never met a senior US policymaker, the people who are actually responsible for formulating and implementing American foreign policy, who believes that credibility is unimportant.[26]

If we do not keep Tehran out of the nuclear club, America's reputation for resolve will be tarnished and, as a result, our national security will be weakened.

ACCOMMODATION

Another way American power could be constrained in the region is through the accommodation of a nuclear-armed Iran by neighboring states. A nuclear-armed Iran could lead other states to loosen their ties to the United States and bend to Tehran's will. These states would be threatened by Iran's nuclear capabilities and would therefore have incentives to balance against Tehran. On the other hand, Iran also lives in the same neighborhood and is not going anywhere; given the damage to America's credibility in this scenario, regional states might come to doubt America's will to project force in the region to protect them. For this reason, some of these states might decide to bandwagon with Iran or, at a minimum, to keep their options open by playing Washington and Tehran off against each other to a greater degree than they do at present. We have already seen this dynamic in play in Qatar, for example.[27] As these states aim to keep a safe distance from Washington, countries like Bahrain, Kuwait, and Qatar might refuse to renew leases for US bases on their territory under pressure from Iran. Losing basing, access, and overflight rights would greatly complicate America's ability to project force in the region.

REGIME STRENGTHENED

Although regime change is not the stated US government policy toward Iran, there is no secret that many US officials would prefer to see a different, more pro-American, government in power. Under the shah, Iran was a fairly close strategic partner and, geopolitically, the countries shared many interests. Yet, since the Iranian Revolution in 1979, Iran has pursued a foreign policy—most notably its support of terrorist organizations and its pursuit of WMD—that threatens the United States. There is, of course, no way to predict what a successor regime in Tehran might look like, but it is hard to imagine that it could be any more hostile to American interests.

At present, the regime is strong, but there are also reasons to believe that the unpopular and autocratic theocracy in Iran cannot remain in power forever. And from Washington's point of view, the sooner it goes, the better.

The successful acquisition of nuclear weapons, however, could help lock this regime in place for years to come. Nuclear weapons would provide Iran with the ultimate security guarantee, protecting it from foreign threats. In addition, nuclear acquisition could improve the regime's legitimacy and shore up domestic political support among certain segments of the population. Iranian nationalists, supporters and opponents of the current regime alike, will undoubtedly feel pride in being only the tenth country on Earth to join the nuclear club. Moreover, the regime will likely get credit for competence, refusing to give up on the country's right to enrich, steering the ship of state through intense international pressure, and ultimately achieving an important national objective.

Nuclear weapons are probably not among the most important determinants of whether or not this current government can hang on to power. But, to the degree that they matter, they serve to extend the clerics' reign, and each additional day that they are in power is one day too many.

EMBOLDENED IRAN

A nuclear-armed Iran would be emboldened, destabilizing the Middle East and threatening US interests. Iran harbors ambitious geopolitical goals. After national survival, its primary objective is to become the most dominant state in the Middle East. In terms of international relations theory, Iran is a revisionist power. Its leaders believe that Iran is a glorious nation with a storied past and that it has been cheated out of its rightful place as a leading nation: like pre–World War I Germany, it is determined to reclaim its place in the sun. In support of that goal, Iran currently supports terrorists and militants throughout the Middle East as a counterbalance to American power. Currently, however, Iran restrains its hegemonic ambitions because it is wary of provoking a US military response.

But if Iran obtained nuclear weapons, it could push harder. Washington would be forced to treat it with kid gloves even in the face of provocative acts because Iran would raise the stakes of any conflict against it to the nuclear level. As such, nuclear weapons would provide Iran with a cover under which to implement its regional ambitions with diminished fear of a US military reprisal. A nuclear-armed Iran would be likely to step up its support for terrorist and proxy groups attacking Israeli and American interests in the greater Middle East and around the world. Specifically, it might provide such groups with longer-range and more accurate conventional weaponry and encourage them to use it rather than hold it in reserve.[28] In addition, it might increase the scope, frequency, and location of terrorist attacks conducted by Hezbollah and the Quds Force, the covert arm of Iran's IRGC. Moreover, Iran might encourage its navy to be more assertive in its harassment of and threats and attacks against naval vessels and commercial shipping in and near the Persian Gulf. Finally, Iran would probably be more aggressive in its coercive diplomacy, possibly brandishing nuclear weapons in an attempt to deter actions contrary to its interests and to intimidate more powerful adversaries and weaker neighbors alike.

Nuclear weapons would embolden Iran to seek to fulfill its expansive foreign policy ambitions. This would lead to enhanced Iranian influence, an increase in terrorism and low-level conflict, and an even more crisis-prone Middle East. All of these developments would be highly damaging to American interests.

HIGHER OIL PRICES AND DAMAGE
TO THE GLOBAL ECONOMY[29]

As policymakers formulate strategies to curb Iran's nuclear ambitions, the oil market has loomed large, and with good reason. Iran is the third largest producer in the Organization of the Petroleum Exporting Countries (OPEC), and its location and military capabilities enable it to disrupt up to 17 million barrels of oil a day (mb/d)—roughly 30 percent of the global oil trade—produced in and exported from the Persian Gulf. Iran holds a knife to the jugular of the world economy.

The Obama administration's dual-track pressure-and-negotiate strategy was crafted with the risk of oil price spikes in mind. As was pointed out in the last chapter, a complete embargo on Iranian oil as part of the sanctions and diplomacy approach would take 4.6 percent of traded oil off the market, contributing to a rise in oil prices. In addition, critics of a military strike on Iran's nuclear facilities argue that a strike might cause spikes in oil prices. This is correct; we will consider this threat in more detail in the next chapter.

Much less obvious, and far less studied, however, are the longer-term oil market and economic consequences if nonproliferation policies fail and Iran arms itself with nuclear weapons. Whatever else it would portend, an Iranian nuclear breakout would pose first-order challenges to the stability of the entire global economic order via its impact on energy prices, a concern with obvious broad strategic implications.

After acquiring nuclear weapons, Iran might remain under sanctions from an international community intent on rolling back its nuclear capability. As noted in chapter 4, Western sanctions have already led to a drop of about 1.3 mb/d in Iranian production, a nontrivial amount given that OPEC spare capacity is only 2.5 mb/d at best. New sanctions measures could cut further into Iran's production and exports, contributing to upward pressure on oil prices.

But the impact of sanctions on future Iranian production pales in comparison with the other geoeconomic implications of nuclear weapons in Iran. As was pointed out above, a nuclear Iran would be likely to increase the frequency and scope of geopolitical conflict in the Middle East, which bears jarring consequences for global oil prices. Conflict in the Middle East tends to result in oil price spikes. This is because conflict can cut off oil supplies coming out of the region and, due to the laws of supply and demand, increase oil prices. Even if supplies are not disrupted, however, conflict leads to oil price spikes because oil traders must factor in the possibility that supplies could be disrupted. The price increase resulting from fears of supply disruptions is known as a "risk premium."

Recent history shows that even without nuclear weapons, Iran-related events in the Middle East have affected oil prices through such a risk premium. Traders bid up oil prices in January 2006 when the IAEA referred Iran to the UN Security Council. In subsequent months, news reports about heated Iranian rhetoric and military exercises helped to drive crude prices up further. The surprise outbreak of the Israel-Hezbollah War in 2006, which was related to concerns about Iran, triggered a $4 per barrel spike on contagion fears. The Iran risk premium subsided after 2007, but a roughly $10–$15 per barrel (10 percent) risk premium returned in early

2012 after the United States and the European Union put in place tougher sanctions, and hawkish rhetoric heated up on both sides.

Were Tehran to acquire nuclear weapons, the risk premium built into oil prices would be much higher for a variety of reasons. First, if Iran becomes emboldened, the types of Middle Eastern crises that we have seen in the past would become even more common.

Second, oil price spikes would be exacerbated by a prospective diminished US ability to act as guarantor of stability in the Persian Gulf. American military presence and intervention have been critical to resolving past geopolitical crises in the region and calming oil markets. Examples include the destruction of much of Iran's surface fleet in response to Iran's mining of the gulf in 1988 and the leading of a coalition to repel Saddam Hussein's short-lived invasion of Kuwait in August 1990. Currently, the United States can use, and threaten to use, force to ensure the free flow of oil out of the region, but, as I argued above, Iranian nukes would constrain American military freedom of action in the region, making market participants jittery.

Third, and most importantly, nuclear weapons in Iran increase the risk of nuclear war, and a nuclear war in the Middle East could destroy much of the world's oil supply, spelling unprecedented economic calamity. A nuclear war in the region could destroy or render inoperable up to 23 mb/d of crude oil production and 17 mb/d of exports. A conflict that destroyed even one-third of this supply would quickly settle the debate over when peak oil production will occur: it will have arrived, at least for many years. Even a single nuclear attack on the Saudi oil-processing facility at Abqaiq, which accounts for some 6 mb/d of production, would in one fell swoop remove 7 percent of global oil production and nearly all spare capacity, triggering a price shock that would cause a severe, protracted global recession.

With oil supplies wiped out, oil prices would rise to whatever levels were necessary to ration demand by the amount of diminished oil supply. Since oil demand is less responsive to price than economic activity, the oil price spike would likely trigger a major recession first by crushing gasoline consumption and auto sales. Consumer confidence would subsequently fall off, and investment would ratchet back as productivity dropped in a chain reaction rippling through the economy. This could destabilize credit markets and perpetuate a self-reinforcing cycle of destruction to growth and employment, quickly metastasizing into general institutional failure throughout the real and financial economy. During the years-to-decade-long recovery, political concerns about pollution and global warming would likely be subordinated to the overarching necessity to increase energy production as fast as possible.

Depending on the amount and duration of oil supply destroyed in a nuclear conflict, oil prices themselves might even become irrelevant. In the wake of a massive supply shock and resulting oil price spike on traded futures exchanges, the global oil trade could collapse altogether, giving way to bilateral deals between desperate producers and consumers. Market mechanisms could even be suspended as governments invoke emergency powers to commandeer resources, impose rationing, ban exports, and ensure that energy supplies are directed to critical infrastructure, national security, and food production and distribution.

While all countries and regions would suffer economic damage, those that depend on food and energy imports would suffer most. Food prices are linked to oil and gas prices due to the energy-intensive nature of modern agriculture and food distribution. Relatively self-sufficient states in the Americas, Russia, and Australia would not fare as badly as would Europe, seaboard Asia, and non–oil-producing Middle Eastern countries. However, all countries, including the relatively self-sufficient United States, would be exposed to new geopolitical uncertainty as sudden shifts in the balance of power upend global geopolitics.

Even if this nightmare scenario never comes to pass, however, oil prices will permanently rise because oil traders will need to factor this possibility into the prices they pay for every barrel of oil. Robert McNally, a leading expert on energy markets, and I calculate, therefore, that a nuclear-armed Iran would likely embed a risk premium of at least $20–$30 per barrel and spikes of $30–$100 per barrel in the event of actual conflict.[30]

Hydraulic fracturing technology is unlocking new oil resources and reducing US and North American dependence on imported oil, but reduced imports will not insulate our economy from global oil price spikes. The price of oil is set in a global market. As Daniel Yergin writes, "There is only one world oil market, so the United States—like other countries—still will be vulnerable to disruptions, and the sheer size of the oil resources in the Persian Gulf will continue to make the region strategically important for the world economy."[31] Even if North American oil imports fell to zero, our businesses and consumers would still be hit with volatile and spiking oil prices emanating from elsewhere on the globe. In economic terms, it's not the supply itself to any given group of consumers that matters most but the price.

In sum, even if North American energy independence is achieved, a nuclear-armed Iran would embed a large risk premium in oil prices that would be extremely harmful for economic growth and employment in the United States and the global economy.

NUCLEAR WAR

Nuclear weapons in Iran could lead to a nuclear war against the United States or Israel or Iran's other regional competitors such as Saudi Arabia. Former Iranian president Ahmadinejad has threatened to "wipe Israel off the map," leading some to fear that if Iran acquired nuclear weapons, it would immediately use them against Israel.[32] It is incredibly unlikely, however, that Iran's supreme leader would ever wake up and decide that that is a good day to start an unprovoked nuclear war. Despite their inflammatory rhetoric, Iran's leaders have pursued a fairly pragmatic foreign policy since 1979; they value highly the survival of the regime, and it is hard to imagine them intentionally launching what could be a suicidal nuclear war.

To be sure, Iran's government does contain some leaders who genuinely hold millenarian religious worldviews and who could one day ascend to power and have a finger on the nuclear trigger. Or the current regime in Iran might one day fall, and a less pragmatic one could arise in its place. Therefore, we cannot completely rule out the possibility that some future leader will choose to launch a nuclear war, knowing full well that it could result in self-destruction, but this scenario seems highly unlikely.

Irrationality, however, is not a necessary precondition for nuclear war. There are many other more likely scenarios under which nuclear weapons might be used, even if Iran's leaders don't have a death wish. To understand this point, let's reconsider how Washington and Moscow were able to avoid nuclear war during the Cold War. The success of nuclear deterrence during the Cold War resulted in part because the nuclear balance between the two sides was so stable. Both countries possessed secure second-strike capabilities, meaning that they were both confident that they could absorb a nuclear attack from their opponent and still respond with a devastating nuclear counterattack of their own. Both sides knew, therefore, that they would suffer greatly in any nuclear war, so there was little to gain from striking first. Analysts have referred to this situation as mutually assured destruction, or MAD.

Other conditions also contributed to Cold War nuclear stability. The long geographic distance between the two superpowers meant that it would take roughly thirty minutes for nuclear-armed ballistic missiles to travel from one country to the other. This meant that if Washington had received warning of a Russian nuclear launch, it would have had thirty minutes to be doubly sure that it wasn't a false alarm. Washington's leaders would have had a half hour before their nuclear weapons would be destroyed to carefully think through whether they should launch a nuclear salvo of their own. In other words, the distances involved reassured both sides that they didn't have to launch nuclear weapons immediately upon warning in a crisis. Moreover, US and Soviet leaders established a "hotline" between the two capitals to maintain open communications to reduce the possibility of misperception or miscalculation in a crisis.

When we think of the likely nuclear balances of power between Iran and its probable adversaries, such as Israel and the United States, however, we see that those sources of stability are completely absent and, as a result, the likelihood of a nuclear exchange would be much higher. Iran and Israel would not be operating in the stable MAD environment because neither state would have a secure, second-strike capability. Even though it is believed to have a large arsenal, Israel might not be confident that it could absorb a nuclear strike and respond with a devastating counterstrike of its own. Its land-based bomber and missile forces might be vulnerable to a nuclear first strike; Israel does not have SLBMs; and it is unclear whether it has nuclear-armed cruise missiles that it could fire from submarines.[33] Even if its nuclear weapons survived an Iranian first strike, given Israel's small size and lack of strategic depth, Israel's leaders might not be confident of their nuclear retaliatory capability. Its leadership might be completely wiped out in a nuclear attack, preventing them from ordering a nuclear response. Moreover, even if Israel's leadership and nuclear warheads survived, it would be small comfort if the entire country had already been destroyed. Indeed, even former Iranian president Ayatollah Ali Akbar Hashemi Rafsanjani knows that Israel is exceptionally vulnerable to nuclear attack. Rafsanjani once said that "an atomic bomb would not leave anything in Israel but the same thing would just produce damages in the Muslim world."[34]

Iran would also be vulnerable. Over time, Iran might eventually be able to build a large and survivable nuclear arsenal, but, when it first crosses the nuclear threshold, it will initially have a small and vulnerable nuclear force. Leaders in Tehran, therefore, could not be fully confident that they could absorb an Israeli nuclear strike and still hit back hard.

This situation greatly increases the risk of nuclear war because, in the event of a crisis, both sides would have an incentive to strike first. Israel might decide to strike first, hoping that it could completely disarm Iran. Iran might launch first with the intention of completely decapitating Israel and preventing a retaliatory response. Or either side might go first, hoping to prevent these things from happening, a "use 'em or lose 'em" scenario. Finally, if it is better to strike first than second, then either side might decide to strike first even if it doesn't want to out of fear that the other side is about to strike. Nobel Prize–winning nuclear strategist Thomas Schelling dubbed this nuclear war out of "reciprocal fear of surprise attack."[35]

Unlike in the Cold War situation, the other strategic factors only exacerbate this danger. There are no clear lines of communication between the various parties. Not only is there not a hotline, Iran does not even have formal diplomatic relations with either Israel or the United States. Instead of a half hour to think through one's next move, Iran and Israel would only have a few minutes for ballistic missiles to travel between their two countries. If this weren't bad enough, Israel's strategic culture has always emphasized preemptive action rather than waiting for threats to gather, and there is no reason to believe that Israel's leaders will be more relaxed about the prospect of nuclear conflict with Iran.

Given these realities, leaders in Tehran and Jerusalem would have incentives to take steps to make sure that they were able to get their nuclear weapons off in a crisis: they could adopt preemptive nuclear war doctrines, place their nuclear weapons on continuous alert, adopt launch-on-warning policies, and delegate nuclear-launch authority to low-level commanders. While these procedures would greatly decrease the risk that one's nuclear arsenal would be wiped out in a first strike, they have one major drawback: they greatly increase the risk of accidental or inadvertent nuclear war.

Even if, over time, Iran and Israel could develop secure second-strike capabilities and enter a more stable MAD environment, there would still be a very real risk of nuclear war. Now pay attention here because this is a point that is lost on the vast majority of international relations scholars and military planners: rational states might still find themselves fighting a nuclear war in situations of MAD. Let me explain.

International politics doesn't end when states acquire nuclear weapons. Nuclear-armed states still have geopolitical conflicts of interest, and they still seek to coerce nuclear-armed opponents. They can't, however, credibly threaten to intentionally start a suicidal nuclear war, but they can, according to Schelling, "make a threat that leaves something to chance."[36] In other words, they play games of nuclear brinkmanship.[37] They enter high-stakes nuclear crises, like the Cuban Missile Crisis. These are competitions in which both sides take steps to raise the risk of nuclear war in the hope that their opponent will be less resolved and will back down. When playing these games of nuclear chicken, however, there is always the chance that neither side will swerve in time and there will be a devastating crash. Indeed, nuclear crises create coercive leverage precisely because there is a genuine risk that things might spin out of control and result in nuclear war.

Yes, you might be saying, but wouldn't both sides have strong incentives to avoid nuclear war? Therefore, won't they both do their utmost to avoid these nuclear crises and even if they find themselves in one, wouldn't they immediately pull back from the brink? The answer is yes and no. Yes, no "rational" leader would want to fight a nuclear war against a country with an assured retaliatory capability. But no, because there are other important incentives working at cross-purposes. If the stakes in the crisis are high enough, then rational leaders will be willing to run some risk of nuclear war rather than immediately conceding the contested issue to their opponent. Indeed, we have seen over the past seventy years that time and time again, nuclear-armed states have been willing to risk nuclear war in order to achieve their geopolitical outcomes.[38] In addition, while leaders might have incentives to prevent nuclear weapons from being used, they also have incentives to make their opponents believe they could be used. Therefore, leaders take steps to purposely increase the risk of war in these games of nuclear chicken, like using conventional force against a nuclear-armed state or putting nuclear weapons on high alert. These steps have coercive value only because they increase the possibility that the crisis will escalate and result in disaster.

After all, I doubt many readers of this book would characterize US presidents during the Cold War as "irrational," yet they were willing to risk nuclear war with the Soviet Union time and time again in high-stakes nuclear crises in Berlin, Cuba, and elsewhere. Even though the US-USSR balance was characterized by relative stability, both sides did things during crises to increase the risk of nuclear war, and any one of these crises could have escalated into a devastating nuclear exchange. Indeed, President Kennedy estimated that the probability of nuclear war in the Cuban Missile Crisis alone was as high as 50 percent. The lesson we must take from the Cold War, therefore, should not be that nuclear deterrence worked, but that we were incredibly lucky to avoid a nuclear attack.

Iran and its adversaries, including Israel and the United States, will all face similar, if not more dangerous incentives. Over the coming years, Iran will almost certainly have geopolitical conflicts of interest with its adversaries. Some of these conflicts will become high-stakes crises. As nuclear powers, both sides will have incentives to raise the risk of nuclear war in order to force the other side to submit. It would be naïve to assume otherwise. And, in these high-stakes nuclear crises, there is a genuine risk—a much greater risk than during the Cold War, given the inherent instabilities in the region and in the nuclear balance of power—that things will spiral out of control and result in a catastrophic nuclear exchange.

Given Israel's small size, a nuclear attack might very well threaten the country's existence. Israel's leaders are correct, therefore, not hyperbolic, when they warn that a nuclear-armed Iran poses an existential threat. As was pointed out above, a nuclear attack against Saudi Arabia, in addition to destroying the country, could wipe out global oil supplies and cause an unprecedented worldwide economic depression. Finally, once Iran has ballistic missiles capable of reaching the East Coast of the United States, a future confrontation between Washington and Tehran could even result in nuclear war on the US homeland.

Granted, on any given day, the probability of nuclear war is low. But it is not zero. Moreover, to accurately calculate the threat, this nonzero risk must be aggregated day after day, week after week, month after month, year after year, decade after decade, as long as Iran possesses nuclear weapons. Given enough time, the probability of a nuclear exchange becomes much more likely. Indeed, I for one will be surprised if nuclear weapons are not used in my lifetime, and a Middle East with multiple nuclear powers would be among the most likely candidates for the world's next nuclear war.

DETERRENCE AND CONTAINMENT

If Iran acquired nuclear weapons, the United States could not simply accept the grave threats emanating from a nuclear-armed Iran. Rather, we would put in place a strategy to deter and contain them. A comprehensive strategy could attempt to address all of the potential threats listed above. We could seek to deter Iran from taking actions contrary to our interest, to contain Iran's malign influence and other negative consequences of an Iranian bomb, and over time seek to undermine Iran's theocratic government so that a new, less threatening regime can come to power. In addition to deterring and containing Iran, we could seek to assure our allies to prevent them from doing things contrary to our interests, like developing nuclear weapons, or starting a nuclear war. This section explains how we could try to do it.

DETERRENCE

"Deterrence" is often defined in the world of defense policy as a strategy designed to prevent an adversary from taking a threatening course of action by convincing the adversary that the costs of taking that course of action outweigh any possible benefit. To affect an adversary's cost-benefit calculation, one can threaten to raise costs or deny benefits. Deterrence by punishment is a strategy in which one threatens devastating military retaliation in response to an adversary's taking a particular course of action. In other words, it threatens to raise costs. During the Cold War, for example, we attempted to deter the Soviet Union from invading Western Europe or using nuclear weapons against the United States by threatening a massive nuclear war in response.

Deterrence by denial is a strategy based on threats to deny an adversary the benefits of a specific course of action. It denies benefits. For example, one can deter a conventional military invasion by building fortifications and massing defensive troops on the border. The adversary will see the defenses, understand that an invasion is unlikely to succeed, and decide that the attack is not worth the effort.

While "deterrence" is often used as an all-encompassing strategic concept, a little bit of thought reveals that by necessity it can only cover a narrow range of contingencies. One can try to deter a specific adversary from taking a specific course of action, but one cannot deter an adversary from doing anything whatsoever. After all, we can't deter Iran from existing.

Rather, we must select a few specific actions that Iran could take that would be so terrifying that we truly could not accept them and that we would be willing to go to war over. These are the actions that we could credibly seek to deter. We would warn Iran that if it took these actions, we would respond with a devastating use of force. Then we would essentially be making a strategic decision to accept other types of malign actions that Iran might take that fall outside of this deterrence strategy. A deterrence policy, therefore, is always paired, explicitly or implicitly, with a corresponding reassurance policy. After all, if we threatened a massive military response no matter what action Iran took, it would have no reason to show restraint.

I teach my undergraduates at Georgetown University that there are four C's of deterrence: capability, credibility, communication, and calculation. In order to deter an adversary, one must have the *capability* to carry out the threat. You can't deter an adversary by threatening to do something you physically cannot do. Next, the threat must be *credible*. Even if one has the ability to carry out a threat, an adversary still might not be deterred if he doesn't believe that you will actually carry it out. We must also clearly *communicate* the threat to our adversary. After all, an adversary can't be deterred by the threat of a tough response if he doesn't know that his action might elicit that tough response. And, finally, the adversary has to be rational enough to carefully *calculate* costs and benefits before taking major strategic actions. If you are dealing with a madman, he might not care whether his actions provoke overwhelming retaliation. Or, if he is exceptionally crazy, he might actually welcome it.

The fourth C, calculation, has already been addressed in Iran's case. Although a change of government could one day bring a madman to power, it is my assessment that the current Iranian regime is fairly pragmatic and calculates costs and benefits as we might expect from a "rational" state. The rest of this section, therefore, will address the other 3 C's.

Communication

A policy for deterring Iran must begin with a declaratory policy in which we clearly communicate to Iran and the rest of the international community which actions a nuclear-armed Iran could take that we would find unacceptable. Then we would threaten that if Iran ever took those actions, we would respond with a devastating use of military force.

I argue that the actions we must deter a nuclear-armed Iran from taking are: an armed attack (nuclear or conventional) against the United States or our allies; the sponsorship of a major terrorist attack against the United States or our allies; and the transfer of nuclear weapons or sensitive nuclear material and technology to state or non-state actors. In other words, we would like to deter Iran from starting a war, promoting terrorism, or purposely proliferating nuclear weapons.

Shortly after Iran acquires nuclear weapons, therefore, an American president should give a major foreign policy address in which he clearly states that the United States will reserve the right to respond with overwhelming force—including potentially with nuclear weapons—should Iran launch a nuclear or conventional attack on the United States or our allies, sponsor a terrorist attack against the United States or our allies, or support or enable another state or terrorist group in its efforts to obtain nuclear weapons.

To be crystal clear, our declaratory policy must not include only what types of action we intend to deter, but also against whom. We should declare that we would respond to attacks against ourselves and our allies. But which states count as US allies? If this is not clear to Iran, it is possible that the Iranian leadership would miscalculate and attack a country that we consider to be within our defensive perimeter. In other words, they might not be deterred.

The concept of "extended deterrence" was developed during the Cold War as the United States used its massive nuclear arsenal not only to deter Soviet attacks against the US homeland, but also to extend its nuclear umbrella over the heads of its allies in Europe. This threat to Moscow and promise to leaders in European capitals was made crystal clear by the terms of the NATO alliance that legally obligated the United States to come to the defense of all NATO members.

At present, the United States does not have a similar alliance arrangement in the Middle East, meaning that our threats and promises to respond to Iranian attacks on our regional allies would be vague. Our only formal treaty ally in the Middle East is Turkey, which has been a member of NATO since 1952.

The United States certainly has other partners in the region, however, and these are the states we would want to defend against Iranian aggression. The United States and Israel have a close and continuing security relationship that dates back to the 1960s. Few doubt that the United States would come to Israel's defense in a crisis and many US policymakers have announced that Washington will guarantee Israel's security. Yet the two countries do not share a formal military alliance. In addition, the United States has close partnerships with many other states in the Middle East. Egypt is one of the world's largest recipients of US foreign aid, and the United States and Egypt have close military-to-military contacts. King Abdullah of Jordan is a friend of Washington who supports the Middle East peace process and works to combat terrorism. The United States fought a war to oust Saddam Hussein and spent ten years rebuilding Iraq. Although the United States does not maintain military forces in Iraq, it would like to continue to have influence in the country and prevent it from becoming an Iranian client state. Perhaps Washington's closest security relationships in the region besides that with Israel are with the countries of the Gulf Cooperation Council (GCC). Despite sources of friction, Saudi Arabia and the United States have strong bilateral relations that included in 2010 the largest arms sales package in history, totaling $60 billion.[39] The US Navy's Fifth Fleet is stationed at a major naval base in the tiny gulf nation of Bahrain. The United States maintains a major air base in Kuwait and a smaller air base in Qatar.[40] Washington also engages in security cooperation with the United Arab Emirates.

In short, there are at least nine countries in the region that fear Iran's nuclear capabilities to various degrees and might find promises of American military protection attractive. They are also countries that Washington might be able and willing to defend from Iranian threats. To be sure, Israel and the GCC states are the most likely contenders for a more formal security guarantee from Washington at present, but, over the longer term, any of these states could plausibly ally themselves with Washington.

To deter Iranian attacks against these countries, therefore, we have to make it abundantly clear that these states are allies that we would be obligated to defend. As part of its deterrence strategy, therefore, Washington might need to sign formal military alliances with Israel, the gulf states (either individually or with the GCC as a group), and potentially other states in the region.

If we could deter Iran from intentionally taking the proscribed actions listed above against us and our allies and partners in the Middle East, we would greatly reduce many of the threats posed by a nuclear-armed Iran.

But do we have the capability and the credibility to follow through on these threats?

Capability

The United States is the world's only superpower and has far and away the most formidable array of conventional and nuclear forces on the planet. There is little doubt, therefore, that Washington would be capable of following through on its threats to impose unacceptable costs on Iran should it cross the stated red lines in our declaratory policy. Still, to remove any doubt, there are measures the United States should take to augment its capabilities in a deterrence and containment scenario. Fundamental to nuclear deterrence is maintaining the forces to launch a devastating nuclear strike and to be able to limit to the greatest extent possible damage to US and allied homelands in the event of nuclear war. The United States must therefore maintain a large enough nuclear arsenal to inflict unacceptable damage on Tehran. It must also maintain a nuclear arsenal capable of conducting a "counterforce" strike on Iran's nuclear forces. By attacking Iran's nuclear weapons, Washington could blunt Iran's nuclear capability and therefore limit damage to the United States and our allies.

At present, the United States possesses such a nuclear capability, but President Obama has announced his intention to slash the size of the US nuclear arsenal as part of achieving his vision of a world without nuclear weapons. While I don't believe that further cuts to the US nuclear arsenal are a good idea in any scenario, deeper nuclear cuts will make even less sense if we need to deter and contain a nuclear-armed Iran.[41] Nuclear cuts might call into question our ability to extend deterrence to our allies. It is a truism that it is easier to deter our enemies than it is to reassure our allies. But our allies might not believe that we can deter attacks against more than thirty allies (twenty-seven members of NATO and other treaty allies) if we continue to cut the size of our nuclear arsenal. Indeed, it would be incongruous for us to extend our nuclear umbrella to additional countries in the Middle East at the same time that the umbrella is shrinking; somebody is bound to get wet. This could force our allies in the Middle East, Asia, and Europe to reconsider their nuclear options. We cannot allow this to happen. The United States must therefore maintain, and perhaps even augment, its nuclear counterforce capabilities if we hope to deter and contain a nuclear-armed Iran.[42] If, on the other hand, we are committed to cutting the size of the nuclear arsenal and de-emphasizing nuclear weapons in our foreign policy, then we will have an even harder time dealing with a nuclear-armed Iran.

Missile defenses will also be useful in limiting damage if Iran decides to launch a nuclear attack, reducing Tehran's expected benefits from conducting it in the first place, and contributing to deterrence. In a deterrence and containment scenario, therefore, the United States must continue to develop a national missile defense system and theater ballistic missile systems for the protection of our homeland and our forces and allies in the region.

The United States also needs to maintain a robust conventional force in the Middle East to ensure that we maintain clear escalation dominance over Iran. Escalation dominance is the idea that if one side has clear military superiority at each level of conflict, from a low-level skirmish to a nuclear war, then it will be harder for that state's adversary to escalate the conflict. When the United States and a nuclear-armed Iran find themselves in inevitable geopolitical conflicts of interest and begin to play games of nuclear brinkmanship, US escalation dominance will help to persuade Iran to back down. The United States must therefore maintain a large, diverse, and capable military presence in the region.

With these military capabilities, the United States will maintain the ability to inflict unacceptable damage on Iran if it crosses our stated red lines. In order to deter Iran from transferring nuclear weapons to other states or terrorist groups, however, we need additional capabilities. First, we need to improve intelligence-collection efforts on Iran to quickly detect the transfer of sensitive nuclear material or technology to other actors. Second, we need to enhance our Proliferation Security Initiative efforts (PSI) in the region to ensure that we have the ability to interdict any Iranian nuclear transfers before they reach their intended target. Finally, we must continue to improve our nuclear forensics capabilities. Similar to criminal forensics procedures popularized by shows like *CSI: Miami,* nuclear forensics is the science of studying interdicted nuclear material to determine its origin. This analysis can be performed on smuggled nuclear material that might be intended for use in a bomb or, god forbid, on radioactive debris after a nuclear explosion. Strong nuclear forensics capabilities announce to Tehran that if they give nuclear weapons to terrorists or other states, we will know about it and will hold them fully accountable. Taken together, intelligence, interdiction, and forensics capabilities will help to deter Iran from transferring sensitive nuclear material and technology to terrorists or to other countries.

Credibility

In order for our deterrent threats to be effective, they must be credible. Iran and our regional allies and partners must believe that we are really willing to use force if Iran crosses the red lines set out in our declaratory policy. After all, if Iran's leaders don't think that we will follow through on these threats, they won't be deterred and they will be more likely to take actions harmful to American interests. Similarly, if our allies and partners in the region don't believe that we will follow through on these threats, they won't be reassured, and they will be more likely to take their national security into their own hands and do things to protect themselves that simultaneously imperil US national security, like building indigenous nuclear weapons arsenals. The success of this deterrence and containment regime therefore hinges on credibility. So, would Iran and our allies and partners in the region believe that we would really be willing to use force if Iran takes those threatening actions?

Threats to use force in the event that the US homeland is attacked are inherently credible. Indeed, as the attacks on Pearl Harbor in 1941 and on New York and Washington in 2001 might illustrate, it is hard to imagine the United States refraining from military action after suffering a direct attack. For this reason, it is likely that we can deter Iran from attacking the US homeland.

But what about threats to respond to attacks against our allies? These so-called "extended deterrent" threats are much less credible. After all, let's call a spade a spade: these are nothing less than threats to go to war with a nuclear-armed Iran. Once Iran has acquired ballistic missiles capable of reaching the East Coast of the United States, promises to extend deterrence means risking a nuclear attack on the US homeland in defense of our allies.

As French president Charles de Gaulle famously asked about extended deterrence to NATO during the Cold War, would the United States really be willing to trade New York for Paris? In this new Middle Eastern context the operative question is: Would the United States really be willing to trade New York for Riyadh? Would the American public support a policy based on threats to fight a nuclear war on Saudi Arabia's behalf?

This credibility problem would be exacerbated by the tarnished US reputation for resolve. As was stated above, in this scenario, the United States, after repeated threats to use force to keep Tehran from the bomb, will have simply stood by while Iran built nuclear weapons. Why would anyone believe that we would fight a nuclear war with Iran if we didn't even have the stomach for a conventional war with a nonnuclear Iran?

In short, the credibility problem would be severe.

There are, however, things that the United States could do to increase the credibility of its threats. During the Cold War, we deployed US troops on the territory of our allies in Europe and East Asia. As Schelling argued, the purpose of these troops wasn't to defend territory; their purpose was to die. He argued that these troops served as "trip wires" that if kicked would guarantee a major US military response. It is hard to imagine a US president sitting on his hands if the Soviet Union had attacked Western Europe and killed American soldiers in the process. The deployment of these forces, therefore, tied our own hands and made it harder for us not to follow through on our threats even if, when the time came, we would have preferred to avoid a war with the Soviet Union. By tying our own hands, we increased the credibility of our threats.

In addition to deploying forces, the United States deployed nuclear weapons on the territory of our allies in Europe and East Asia. Indeed, to this day, the United States maintains forward-deployed nuclear weapons on the territory of Belgium, Germany, Italy, the Netherlands, and Turkey.[43] These weapons serve a similar function. If they had come under attack from an enemy's forces, it would have greatly increased the risk that the conflict would go nuclear, again increasing the credibility of the threat. Moreover, in addition to deterring enemies, these forces also reassured our allies as a constant reminder of our nuclear protection. Indeed, some nuclear strategists have even compared the United States' forward-deployed nuclear weapons as a wedding ring to Europe, symbolizing our commitment to our NATO allies in good times and bad.

In order to increase the credibility of our extended deterrent threats against a nuclear-armed Iran, therefore, the United States would need to forward-deploy troops and nuclear weapons on the territory of our Middle Eastern partners and allies. We currently have forces in Turkey, Kuwait, Bahrain, and Qatar. We also have, as mentioned above, nuclear weapons in Turkey. In addition to our current posture, therefore, we might need to build US military bases in Israel and Saudi Arabia. We also might need to station US nuclear weapons in Israel and the GCC countries. Taken together, these measures would help to improve the credibility of US extended deterrent threats.

CONTAINMENT

In addition to deterring the threatening actions that Iran's leaders could decide to take, a strategy for dealing with a nuclear Iran must also have a component to contain other contingencies that could arise. Like deterrence, the concept of containment has an illustrious pedigree in US strategic culture. George Kennan, as a young State Department officer stationed in Moscow in the early days of the Cold War, coined the concept of "containment" as a strategy for dealing with Soviet Russia. He argued that the Marxist-Leninist ideology on which the Soviet system was based depended on the continuous expansion of communism to new countries, which meant that if the United States could contain increases in Soviet influence long enough, the internal contradictions in the Soviet system would eventually lead the system to collapse. The term has been expanded beyond its original Cold War and Soviet-specific context to mean a strategy of checking the expansion of a hostile state.

ROLL BACK IRAN'S NUCLEAR CAPABILITIES

A containment strategy would seek to contain, if not roll back, Iran's nuclear capabilities. The most harrowing consequence of a nuclear-armed Iran from America's point of view would be the threat of nuclear war against the US homeland. To mitigate against this threat, the United States would seek to contain the expansion of the quantity and quality of Iran's nuclear forces. Through the use of international economic sanctions, technology denial, cyberattacks, sabotage, and perhaps other measures, Washington could attempt to prevent Iran from expanding the size of its arsenal and from increasing the range, accuracy, and survivability of its ballistic missiles. In this way, we could seek to contain the threat of nuclear war against the US homeland. Furthermore, over time we could, through continued pressure and negotiation, seek to roll back Iran's nuclear capabilities. While difficult to achieve, the ultimate goal of this strategy should be the complete and verifiable nuclear disarmament of Iran.

DISSUADE NUCLEAR PROLIFERATION

A major objective of a containment strategy would also be to contain the nuclear proliferation cascade that would inevitably result from Iran's nuclear acquisition. This objective would partly be achieved by attempting to deter Iranian transfers of sensitive nuclear material and technology. Also, as stated above, we would seek to assure partner and allied states in the region that we can provide for their security. In addition to the steps listed above, we could provide advanced conventional military capabilities to these states so that they could feel capable of defending themselves without nuclear weapons. This aid could come in the form of arms sales to wealthier states and military aid to others.

To prevent the broader collapse of the nuclear nonproliferation regime, we would want to bolster nuclear nonproliferation by, if possible, closing loopholes in the regime that Iran was able to exploit.[44] We could, for example, seek reforms that make clear that uranium enrichment and plutonium-reprocessing capabilities do not quality as peaceful nuclear technology under Article IV of the NPT and that, therefore, nonnuclear weapon states do not have a right to them. We could eliminate, or greatly restrict, the Article X provision that allows states to withdraw from the NPT with ninety days' notice. We could also develop more automatic enforcement mechanisms to convince the next Iran that it can't simply violate its NPT commitments with relative impunity.

PREVENT ACCIDENTAL NUCLEAR WAR

Preventing an inadvertent or accidental nuclear war between Iran and Israel (a war that could potentially involve the United States) would be another threat to be contained, and there are a number of steps the United States could take to help stabilize the Iranian-Israeli nuclear balance.

As was stated above, the fear of a nuclear first-strike advantage is thought to increase the risk of nuclear war, so Washington could reduce the risk by making sure that both sides possess secure second-strike capabilities. Of course, the idea that the United States would help Iran, a sworn enemy, enhance its nuclear capabilities is out of the question, but there are things we could do to enhance Israel's second-strike capabilities. This could reduce the risk of nuclear war by convincing Iran's leaders that they cannot hope to launch a successful nuclear first strike against Israel and by reassuring Israel's leaders that they could absorb an Iranian nuclear attack and still retaliate, obviating the need to go first. To improve Israel's second-strike capability, we could help them develop a more advanced nuclear posture similar to the postures maintained by the United States and the Soviet Union during the Cold War. We could help them build hardened ballistic missile silos, SLBMs, and a second submarine base on the Red Sea to disperse their submarine fleet and make it less vulnerable to attack. In addition, we could help them with arrangements for continuity of government and nuclear command and control to ensure that their national leadership would survive and would be able to execute nuclear war plans even after suffering an Iranian nuclear attack.

We must be careful, however, as efforts to aid Israel's nuclear capabilities could actually make the situation less stable by convincing Israel's leaders that they have a splendid nuclear first-strike option against Iran. To make sure this doesn't happen, we must only provide assistance that improves the survivability of the nuclear arsenal. We must avoid transferring assets like more accurate missiles or detailed intelligence on the number and location of Iranian nuclear forces that could improve Israel's ability to conduct a nuclear first strike.

In addition, we could work to establish a "hotline" between Tehran, Jerusalem, and Washington to ensure that the nations' leaders could communicate in a crisis and cut through the fog of war. Washington and Moscow set up a hotline between the American president and the Soviet premier, and it was thought to have reduced the risk of inadvertent nuclear escalation during crises. Establishing such a hotline could be incredibly difficult, however, given the lack of trust between all parties. Still, improving communications and the survivability of Israel's nuclear forces could help to reduce the risk of nuclear war.

REGIME CHANGE

The final, and perhaps most important, piece of a deterrence and containment strategy would be a long-term policy to undermine the current theocratic government in Iran and bring to power a more friendly regime. This will be difficult, but it is a necessary component to the strategy if we are ever to free ourselves from the threats posed by a hostile nuclear-armed Iran.

The United States should therefore make regime change of a nuclear-armed Iran our official policy. Much as with the Communist Soviet Union during the Cold War, we should maintain constant diplomatic contact with the country while explicitly stating that our goal is to bring down the theocracy and to one day see it replaced by a more representative government that abides by international norms. After our experiences in Iraq and Afghanistan, military regime change is no longer a serious option, nor should it be. There are, however, other, more subtle things we can do to weaken the government and strengthen opposition movements. We should keep the pressure on the current regime as much as possible by, for example, seeking to maintain the robust international sanctions currently in place, continuing to isolate the country diplomatically, and always speaking out against its autocratic form of rule and its gross human rights violations.

To support the opposition in Iran, we can disseminate information technologies that will allow anti-government forces to organize and communicate. Nongovernmental organizations can also provide policy advice on sustaining an opposition movement in an oppressive environment and on lessons learned from democratic transitions in other countries.

The theocratic regime in Iran has a firm grip on power, and it does not look as if it is in danger of falling anytime soon. Moreover, the acquisition of nuclear weapons will only strengthen its hand. Nevertheless, there are inherent weaknesses in the regime's model of governance, and there are reasons to believe that sooner or later, it will lose its hold on power. An explicit regime change policy from the United States and the rest of the international community could hasten that day and should, therefore, be an essential element of a deterrence and containment policy.

AN EVALUATION: CAN WE DETER AND CONTAIN A NUCLEAR-ARMED IRAN?

The above discussion suggests that some of the threats emanating from a nuclear-armed Iran can be deterred or contained. It is likely that we could deter Iran from intentionally launching a suicidal nuclear war. We could likely deter Iran from directly attacking us and our allies. It is also likely that we could deter Iran from intentionally transferring nuclear weapons to terrorist groups.

There are many other threats posed by a nuclear-armed Iran, however, that we simply could not address in a deterrence and containment regime. It is unlikely that we will ever be able to roll back Iran's nuclear capabilities. It is tough to put the genie back in the bottle. Historically, there has only been one country, South Africa, that has gone through the trouble of building nuclear weapons only to voluntarily give them up. And this required a near-perfect storm of factors, including the collapse of the Soviet Union and the threat it posed in sub-Saharan Africa and the end of the apartheid regime in South Africa, that might not ever be repeatable. It is likely that Iran's leaders, no matter who they are, will find clinging to nuclear weapons more useful than disarming.

Similarly, the United States will not be able to prevent every state in the Middle East from building nuclear weapons in response to Iran. By extending our nuclear umbrella, we might be able to dissuade some states from exploring the nuclear option, but others will likely decide to build indigenous arsenals anyway. After all, during the Cold War, the United States extended deterrence to Western Europe, but Great Britain and France were not satisfied with US nuclear weapons alone and chose to construct independent nuclear arsenals. Over the next ten to twenty years, therefore, it is my best estimate that, if Iran acquires nuclear weapons, then, despite America's best efforts, one or two additional Middle Eastern powers will also join the nuclear club.

It is unlikely that we will be able to deter Iran from transferring sensitive nuclear material and technology to other states. If Iran were to transfer uranium enrichment technology to Venezuela, for example, would the

United States be willing to fight a nuclear war to stop it? It is doubtful. Indeed, from the beginning of the nuclear era, countries have transferred sensitive nuclear technology at least fourteen times and in none of those instances did the United States take military action in response.[45] If Iran calculates that it can get away with transferring sensitive nuclear technology (and this is the correct calculation in my view), it won't be deterred.

In addition, pushing tough reforms through in order to strengthen the broader nonproliferation regime will be all but impossible. The NPT works on consensus, so any changes to it would require unanimity. Getting 189 countries to see eye to eye on anything, not to mention on issues dealing with national security, is an insurmountable challenge. The broader proliferation regime will inevitably be weakened.

We will also be forced to live with Iran's stepping up support to terror or proxy groups. It is simply not credible for the United States or Israel to threaten to fight a war with a nuclear-armed Iran over small terror attacks. If an Iranian-sponsored group carried out an attack on the scale of 9/11, things might be different. But there is a lot of room for Iran to turn up the intensity of its asymmetric attacks in the Middle East and around the world before it would need to fear a major American military retaliation.

In the short to medium term, there is little we can do to mitigate the risk of higher oil prices resulting from a nuclear-armed Iran. Weaning ourselves off Middle Eastern oil won't do the trick because oil is traded in a global market, and what matters is not the source of the supply but the price. Over the longer term, it is possible that we could make our economy less vulnerable to Middle Eastern supply disruptions by switching away from fossil fuels toward alternative energy sources. But that day is a long way off.

We also cannot deter Iran from engaging in nuclear coercion or from playing games of nuclear brinkmanship. Indeed, nuclear brinkmanship is an unfortunate consequence of successful nuclear deterrence. Since Iran cannot credibly threaten to launch a nuclear war against Israel or the United States, it will be forced to "make threats that leave something to chance."[46] In other words, in a high-stakes crisis, Iran will intentionally take steps to increase the risk of nuclear war in an effort to force its adversaries to back down. And in these high-stakes crises, there is always a risk that things can spin out of control and result in a nuclear exchange.

This is why it is so utterly stupid when analysts ask whether Iran (or any other state for that matter) can be deterred. Deterrence is not binary. It does not have an *on* or *off* switch. A country is not either deterrable or not deterrable. Rather, the better question to ask is what risk of nuclear war Iran (or any other state) would be willing to run against a particular adversary in a particular crisis. The answer to the question is never zero. The answer is never that the state would always completely capitulate to its adversary regardless of the terms. Rather, the answer is that any state would be willing to run some risk of nuclear war under certain circumstances. Indeed, in twenty separate instances since 1945, we have seen states from the Soviet Union and the United States in the Cold War to India and Pakistan today engage in nuclear crises.[47] From Iran, a revisionist and risk-acceptant state, we can expect similar, if not more reckless, behavior. Iran will almost certainly be willing to risk nuclear war in future geopolitical conflicts, and this will mean that it will be able on occasion to engage in successful nuclear coercion. It also means that, in playing these games of brinkmanship, it will increase the risk of a nuclear exchange.

This brings us to our last and most important point. We cannot deter an accidental or inadvertent nuclear war. This is true by definition. Given the tumult in the region and the instabilities in the American-Iranian-Israeli nuclear balance, there is a real risk of an absolutely catastrophic outcome.

At this point, some readers might object and say, "Wait a minute. We have dealt with nuclear-armed rogue states in the past. Pakistan and North Korea have both acquired nuclear weapons in recent years and the world hasn't ended. Why are we so worried about a nuclear-armed Iran?" This is a good question, and the answer only reinforces my point. Let's take a moment to review the record. Pakistan tested nuclear weapons in the late 1990s. Since that time, it has transferred sensitive nuclear technology to Iran, Libya, and North Korea. Indeed, we have Pakistan to thank for our current Iran problem. Emboldened by nuclear weapons, Pakistan has stepped up its support of terrorist and proxy groups, conducting cross-border attacks on neighboring India. American officials are constantly concerned that Pakistan could collapse and that its nuclear weapons could fall into the hands of terrorists operating inside the country. Moreover, India and Pakistan have engaged in several high-stakes nuclear crises, including the 1999 Kargil War and the 2001 India Parliament Attacks, that US officials genuinely feared could result in nuclear war.

Pyongyang's record is no better. Since conducting its first nuclear test in 2006, North Korea has transferred sensitive nuclear technology to Syria and perhaps to other states. With nuclear weapons serving as a shield, North Korea has thrown its weight around more in East Asia, attacking a South Korean warship and shelling a South Korean island. Indeed, North Korea has even gone so far as to threaten nuclear war against the US homeland.

Moreover, these two countries have only possessed nuclear weapons for roughly a decade. These are early days. We haven't even begun to witness the full range of negative consequences that will result from nuclear weapons in these states. Indeed, we might very well one day suffer a nuclear war involving Pakistan's or North Korea's nuclear weapons.

These are exactly the kinds of consequences we can look forward to if Iran acquires nuclear weapons: sensitive nuclear technology transfers leading to nuclear proliferation in other countries, an emboldened and more aggressive Iran, the constant possibility of a state collapse with nuclear weapons falling into the hands of terrorists, a nuclear scare every few years, and an increased risk of nuclear war. Indeed, if Pakistan and North Korea are models for what a nuclear-armed Iran might look like, we should all be very concerned.

Finally, as if this were not bad enough, not only can a deterrence and containment regime not manage all the threats posed by a nuclear-armed Iran, it is also costly in and of itself. A deterrence and containment regime would mean a massive increase in US political and military commitments to the region that would need to remain in place as long as Iran exists as a state and has nuclear weapons. This could be decades or longer. A deterrence and containment regime, therefore, would be costly in economic terms. It would also mean new military expenditures in the Middle East in a time of budget austerity. In addition, it would complicate the United States' stated goal of "rebalancing" US strategic attention away from the Middle East and toward East Asia. Rather, a nuclear-armed Iran would force us to devote much more attention to the Middle East for decades to come. It would require us to maintain or perhaps even develop new nuclear forces at a time when President Obama would like to cut the size of the nuclear arsenal. In addition, there would be other second-order negative consequences from a deterrence and containment regime. For example, we removed US forces from Saudi Arabia after 9/11 because we believed that a heavy US military footprint in the region contributed to anti-American sentiment and terrorism against the United States. A deterrence and containment regime against a nuclear-armed Iran, however, would mean that not only would we be stepping back into the region, but doing so while wearing even bigger shoes.

CONCLUSION

This chapter demonstrates that deterring and containing a nuclear-armed Iran would be a costly decades-long endeavor that could not begin to address many of the challenges posed by a nuclear-armed Iran. It is for this reason that President Obama has said "a nuclear-armed Iran is not a challenge that can be contained." Indeed, President Bush and President Obama don't agree on much, but they do agree that a nuclear-armed Iran is "unacceptable." They are correct. Reasonable people can disagree, but in my view, deterring and containing a nuclear-armed Iran is not only a bad option, it is the worst.[48]

In the past two chapters we have learned that deterrence and containment of a nuclear Iran won't work and that diplomacy might not succeed. If diplomacy fails, then how can we resolve the Iranian nuclear challenge?

By process of elimination, we are left with only one option.

CHAPTER SIX

BOMBING IRAN

A YOUTUBE SEARCH FOR THE "MASSIVE ORDNANCE Penetrator" (MOP) turns up video footage of the United States' newest bunker-busting bomb slicing through thick walls of concrete like a knife through warm butter.[1] This 30,000-pound bomb is capable of penetrating up to 200 feet before exploding and was designed with Iran's deeply buried and hardened nuclear facilities in mind.[2]

With capabilities like these, the US military could destroy Iran's key nuclear facilities, setting back Iran's nuclear program by years and creating a significant probability that Iran would never acquire nuclear weapons.

There are, however, significant downside risks to a US attack on Iran, including Iranian military retaliation, spikes in global oil prices, and anti-American sentiment. Many analysts exaggerate these risks, however, and ignore the fact that the United States could put in place a strategy to manage them.

The Israeli military option, on the other hand, would be an unmitigated disaster. Israel simply lacks the capability to inflict sufficient damage on Iran's nuclear program and would not be in a position to handle the fallout of a strike.

This chapter will analyze the American and Israeli military options. In addition to considering the possible costs and benefits of a strike, it will provide a strategy for how to best maximize the chances of success and minimize the downside risks. Before we can understand the costs and benefits of taking military action against Iran's nuclear facilities, however, we must first better understand the various military options.

TYPES OF ATTACKS

There are three major forms that an attack on Iran's nuclear facilities could take: Israel could conduct a limited strike on Iran's key nuclear facilities, the United States could conduct a limited strike, or the United States, with its more formidable array of firepower, could conduct a more massive attack that also targets Iran's conventional military or seeks to destabilize the Iranian regime.

Before discussing the important differences between these types of attacks, however, I will begin by pointing out what they have in common. First, it is important to note that all of these options use air power and/ or sea power only. None of these force packages would put boots on the ground in Iran. This is not an Iraq- or Afghanistan-style invasion in which the United States invades Iran, overthrows the government, occupies the country, and attempts to rebuild the nation in our image over the course of a decade. Rather, those who would support striking Iran under certain conditions, including myself, are in favor of an hours- or days-long bombing campaign against Iran's key nuclear facilities. Some analysts opposed to war with Iran make disingenuous claims comparing a strike on Iran with the wars in Iraq and Afghanistan, but these kind of statements reflect either gross ignorance of our military options for Iran, a purposeful intention to deceive, or both. Even the largest force packages for Iran, therefore, are smaller than anything we've experienced in our recent history and would also, therefore, be less costly and more time-limited operations.

A second commonality to all of these options is the target set. To be successful, a strike would need to destroy Iran's four key nuclear facilities: the uranium conversion facility at Isfahan, the uranium enrichment facilities at Natanz and Qom, and the reactor under construction at Arak. There are other nuclear-related facilities in Iran that could be targeted in a strike, but, as was pointed out in chapter 2, these additional facilities are much less important to Iran's ability to build a bomb and could therefore be left off the target list with very little cost to the success of the overall mission. This expanded list could include the light-water reactor at Bushehr, the military base at Parchin, and various centrifuge-component manufacturing plants in Tehran and Natanz. If Iran has secret facilities that we do not know about, we would obviously miss them in a strike against known facilities, but as was discussed in chapter 2, it is highly unlikely that Iran has any operational nuclear facilities still unknown to Western intelligence agencies.

A LIMITED US ATTACK

Now let's turn to the differences among the various options.[3] If the president of the United States decided to attack Iran's nuclear facilities, he would have a range of options from which to choose. We will begin with the smallest force package, a limited US attack that would target the four key Iranian nuclear facilities. The nuclear facilities at Isfahan and Arak are above ground and are therefore easy military targets. We could easily destroy these facilities using air- or sea-launched cruise missiles, launched from US B-52 bombers operating outside Iranian airspace or US warships in the Persian Gulf.[4]

The uranium enrichment facilities at Natanz and Qom are both underground and represent more difficult military targets. According to open source reporting, Natanz is buried under seventy feet of earth and several meters of reinforced concrete, and Qom is built into the side of a mountain and is therefore protected by 295 feet of rock.[5] To destroy these sites we would need to use the Massive Ordnance Penetrator, or MOP. The MOP weighs 30,000 pounds and, according to open source reporting, is capable of penetrating up to 200 feet before exploding.[6] Some simple arithmetic (200 feet is greater than 70+ feet) suggests that Natanz doesn't stand a chance. It is unlikely that the MOP could penetrate into the enrichment chamber at Qom in a single shot (295 feet is greater than 200 feet), but we could simply put subsequent bombs in the crater left from a previous bomb and thus eventually tunnel our way in.[7] Putting multiple bombs in the same hole requires a fair bit of accuracy in our targeting, but we can do it.[8] In addition to destroying the chamber containing the centrifuges, we could also render the facilities unusable by destroying their entrances, exits, ventilation heating and cooling systems, and their power lines and sources.[9] The MOP can only be carried on the US B-2 stealth bomber.[10] Since it can be refueled in midair, the B-2 can be sent on a roundtrip mission from US bases in Missouri and Diego Garcia in the Indian Ocean to its targets in Iran and back home again without stopping.[11] The B-2 could also be escorted by stealthy US F-22 fighters, or F-16s, to protect it against Iranian fighter aircraft.[12]

Iran has protected these facilities, however, with air defenses, in particular surface-to-air missile (SAM) batteries that could be used to shoot down American aircraft. To limit the risk to US planes, therefore, we would first need to suppress Iran's air defenses, even in a limited attack. We could begin with standoff cruise missile attacks against Iran's SAMs, radars, and fighter aircraft.[13] Once Iranian airspace was secure, we could safely send in our bombers.

The smallest force package, therefore, would consist of a barrage of cruise missile strikes and bombing sorties that would be carried out in a very short period of time, plausibly even in a single night. Most importantly, a limited strike would almost certainly succeed in its intended mission and destroy Iran's key nuclear facilities.

The major downside to a limited strike, however, is that it leaves Iranian military capabilities in place that could be used for retaliation against the United States and our allies. Moreover, a limited strike would almost certainly mean that the clerics in Tehran would remain in power. One could attempt to also deal with these threats, however, by bringing more firepower to bear.

A MASSIVE US ATTACK

The rationale for a massive US bombing campaign against Iran would be to blunt Iran's military capabilities and/or destabilize the regime. Therefore, in addition to destroying Iran's key nuclear facilities and air defenses, a larger force package could also destroy Iran's navy, air force, ballistic missile storage sites, ballistic missile launchers, and command and control centers. Such an attack would all but neutralize Iran's ability to retaliate. If we wished to also attempt to destabilize the regime, we could target military headquarters, government offices, and the residences of Iran's top leadership. As Jamie Fly and Gary Schmitt argue in a *Foreign Affairs* online article, responding to my FA piece, if we are going to war in Iran, "we should go big—then go home."[14] Similarly, Colin Kahl, my former boss at the Pentagon and now a colleague at Georgetown University, argues that it would be easier to destroy Iran's conventional capabilities before they are dispersed in a conflict, so there are good tactical reasons to either begin with a massive military assault on Iran or not strike at all.[15] Therefore, he argues that if we get into a conflict with Iran (something he is skeptical that we should do), we should conduct a massive bombing campaign from the get-go.

There are, however, significant downsides to a larger bombing campaign. First, a massive attack would result in much more collateral damage. Second, the United States has an incentive to keep this conflict from escalating into a broader war. Our interests are best served if we can destroy Iran's nuclear facilities quickly while limiting other negative consequences. Expanding the target set and putting Iran's back to the wall in a massive bombing campaign will make it much harder to contain the conflict. A massive bombing campaign might make tactical sense as Kahl argues, but good planners understand that strategy should drive tactics, not the other way around. Third, the United States could make a compelling case that a limited strike is justified in order to enforce Iran's violations of its NPT commitments. As long as we are only destroying Iran's key nuclear facilities, our actions would be consistent with this rationale and we could garner significant international and domestic support. A massive bombing campaign, however, looks much more like full-scale war. If we completely destroy Iran's military and its government offices and inflict large numbers of civilian casualties, it would be much harder, if not impossible, to make the case that the conflict is only about Iran's nuclear program.

If the United States takes military action, therefore, we should begin with a limited strike on Iran's key nuclear facilities. We will always have the option to escalate later if necessary; this is a subject I will return to later in the chapter.

ISRAEL'S MILITARY OPTION

The final military option to consider would be an Israeli attack on Iran's nuclear facilities. It is important to distinguish between the American and the Israeli military options. They are very different options, but they are often conflated in the public discourse on this issue. Israel's leaders have been threatening to strike Iran for years; therefore, when many people think about a possible attack on Iran, they immediately think in terms of an Israeli attack. In my discussions on this issue, some experts have even suggested that an Israeli attack might be the best option for the United States because we could allow Israel to do our dirty work for us and avoid blame for the operation.

In actuality, however, an Israeli attack on Iran's nuclear facilities is the worst military option because Israel simply lacks the military capability to inflict lasting damage on Iran's nuclear program. Israel could certainly destroy the above-ground nuclear facilities at Isfahan and Arak. The underground facilities at Natanz and Qom, however, are much harder. Israel does not have the MOP. Rather, its best bunker-busting bomb is the US-provided GBU-28, capable of penetrating 100 feet of earth or 20 feet of reinforced concrete.[16] Therefore, Israel could not penetrate Natanz or Qom in a single shot. With two or three bombs in the same crater, Israel could get Natanz, but Israel couldn't even dream of destroying Qom, which is buried under 295 feet of rock.[17]

Some have suggested that the United States should give the MOP to Israel, but Israel does not have aircraft capable of carrying it.[18] Israel's air force is made up of US-provided F-15 and F-16 fighter-bombers. The 30,000-pound bomb can only be carried by the B-2 bomber; providing this bomber with its top-secret stealth technology to Israel, or to any other nation, is simply out of the question.

The second challenge for Israel would simply be getting to the targets inside Iran and back again. Compared to the United States, Israel has fewer and less capable aircraft.[19] Israel also lacks aircraft carriers and bases in the Persian Gulf. To attack Iran, Israel's jets would have to fly long distances over hostile territory, potentially contend with Iranian air defenses, bomb their intended targets, refuel at some point, and return to Israel.[20] It is not clear that this is a viable operation. In addition, since Israel's munitions are less capable, they would need to get many more bombs on target than the United States would in order to achieve the same result, but with the limits in the numbers and ranges of their aircraft, this would be incredibly difficult.

One underestimates Israel's military capabilities at one's own peril; the IDF is highly capable and has exceeded foreign military analysts' expectations many times in the past. Yet this mission is simply too hard. Israel would have a difficult time getting to Iran's targets and even if it reached all four key nuclear facilities, it might not be able to get Natanz and it would have no hope of destroying Qom.

Therefore, I estimate that a US strike would impose at least a five-year delay in Iran's nuclear progress, but an Israeli strike would only buy us two to three years.[21] An Israeli strike would, however, still unleash all of the downside risks. If we are going to suffer the costs of an attack against Iran, we might as well get the full benefits in terms of a maximum delay to the program.

Some have suggested a joint US-Israeli attack to augment Israel's capabilities, but a joint operation does not make sense. The United States gains nothing from conducting the operation with Israel (we have the capabilities to deal with this on our own), but a joint operation would entail additional costs because it would be more difficult to get international, and especially Arab, support for an attack that involved Israel.

For these reasons, the Israeli military option provides a rare opportunity for agreement among American analysts on this issue, hawks and doves alike: an Israeli attack is not a good option for addressing the Iranian nuclear threat.

This does not mean, however, that Israel won't attack. While the United States is threatened by Iranian nuclear development, Israel's leaders rightly consider it an existential issue. If Israel's leaders come to believe that they cannot rely on the United States to handle this issue for them, they might very well take matters into their own hands. For years, Israel's leaders threatened that an Israeli strike on Iran's nuclear facilities was just around the corner. Former defense minister Ehud Barak, for example, warned about a coming "zone of immunity" in which a large portion of

Iran's nuclear program would be safe from an Israeli military attack.[22] He maintained that Israel had to attack before Iran reached that point.

For now, however, the threat of an Israeli military attack has subsided for two reasons. First, Iran has already entered the zone of immunity. Since the facility at Qom became operational in February 2012, Israel's military option is no longer of much value and Israel's leaders know it. Second, the United States has launched a robust outreach effort to convince Jerusalem that Washington has its back and that we will take military action if necessary to stop Iran. This reassurance campaign has included public statements from senior military officials, including at the American Israel Public Affairs Committee (AIPAC) annual conference; private meetings with Israeli leaders; demonstrations of American military capabilities, including the MOP; and provision of military capabilities to Israel, including refueling tankers.[23] For now, therefore, the likelihood of an Israeli strike is low. If, however, Iran's nuclear program crosses certain key red lines and if Israel's leaders are convinced that the United States will not act, they might very well get desperate and destroy the parts of the nuclear program they can reach, knowing full well that they are only purchasing a minor delay in the program.

To prevent this from happening, the United States must be willing to act. The upshot of this section is that, if it comes to using force against Iran's nuclear facilities, the strike should be limited, not massive, and it should be carried out by the United States, not by Israel.

Good military analysts know that before deciding to use military force, one must make a careful means-ends assessment. One needs to ask, what are our goals and how does the use of military force help us achieve them? If one cannot clearly answer these questions, one is in danger of an open-ended military commitment that has no hope of success. While this might seem obvious, political leaders sometimes reach for military tools for intractable problems simply because nothing else is working. The US invasion and occupation of Iraq might be one example in which these questions were not clearly answered. In Iraq our goals were to overthrow Saddam Hussein and establish a stable, representative government in its place. The US military was well suited to the first mission, and we toppled Saddam Hussein in a matter of weeks. Unfortunately, it was poorly suited to the second mission, and the result was a costly, decade-long occupation that fell short of even our most modest goals.

When looking at the Iranian nuclear threat, a simple means-ends analysis suggests that military tools are very well suited to the task at hand. Iran is operating four facilities that it could use to produce nuclear weapons in short order it if decided to do so. Our goal is to get Iran to shut these facilities down. We are currently negotiating with Iran to convince them to dismantle these facilities. They are refusing. If we bomb those facilities, we will shut them down. Our operational objective would be achieved. Furthermore, as we will see in the next section, such an attack would likely provide even broader strategic benefits.

BENEFITS OF ATTACK

The primary benefit of a US attack on Iran's nuclear facilities is that it would set Iran's nuclear progress back and create a significant possibility that Iran would not acquire nuclear weapons. It is impossible to determine exactly how much time a strike would buy because the answer depends on knowing things that are simply unknowable. Will Iran decide to rebuild its nuclear program? How long will Iran's leaders wait before they decide to rebuild? (It is unlikely that if Iran is bombed on a Friday, its engineers would be back out rebuilding on Saturday morning.) Will the post-strike enforcement regime put in place by the international community to complicate Iran's reconstitution efforts be effective? Will Iran be able to get needed supplies for its centrifuges, like maraging steel, on the international marketplace? Will there be subsequent attacks or will Iran be involved in other armed conflicts? Does Iran's domestic political situation remain stable, and so forth?

Assuming, however, that Iran decides to rebuild shortly after a strike, and doesn't encounter any serious problems, I estimate that it would take a minimum of five years for Iran to rebuild its nuclear program to its present state. This is, however, a worst-case scenario from the US perspective. Also possible, and somewhat more likely in my judgment, is that a US strike would prevent Iran from acquiring nuclear weapons indefinitely. Let me explain why.

First, there is a strong possibility that Iran would simply decide not to rebuild its nuclear program. Iran's leaders might calculate that they have spent two decades and over $100 billion on a nuclear program only to invite international isolation and sanctions and an armed attack on their country, and all they have to show for it is a pile of rubble.[24] An attack would make it even clearer that the international community is determined to prevent them from acquiring nuclear weapons. They would have to ask themselves if they really want to hit *replay* on that tape. Is it worth spending additional decades, billions of dollars, all under intense international scrutiny and pressure, with the possibility that it would only lead to another attack?

Even if Iran decided, at some point, to rebuild its nuclear facilities, the five-plus-year window opened up by an attack would create space for a number of things to happen whereby Iran is prevented from acquiring nuclear weapons. First, it creates time for additional diplomacy. Diplomacy has always been our preferred means of solving this problem, and if diplomacy fails to prevent Iran's march toward a nuclear weapon this time around, a strike would give the dual-track approach an additional chance to work. Moreover, while a strike might make negotiations harder in some respects (it is not easy to sit down for negotiations with a country that has just bombed you), it increases the likelihood that Iran's supreme leader would be willing to make a deal in other ways. At present, he is loath to trade away an advanced nuclear program that is within weeks of providing him with the ultimate security guarantee. But after a strike, he would be trading away nothing more than a heap of desbris. Furthermore, in a post-strike environment he would be convinced that the United States and the international community are truly determined to keep him from the bomb, raising the prospective costs of rebuilding and increasing the attractiveness of a diplomatic settlement.

A strike also creates space for domestic political developments in Iran to play out. While a strike is likely to create a rally-around-the-flag effect in the short term, strengthening the current theocratic regime, over the medium to long term it could weaken the regime by creating an opportunity for opponents to criticize the government for mismanaging the nuclear issue to the point that they lost the nuclear program and invited an armed attack on the country.[25] The other noticeable cracks in the foundation of the regime might also come to the fore in a post-strike environment, leading to political instabilities. If the revolts that have hit the rest of the

Middle East finally make their way to Iran, Iran's nuclear program would grind to a halt as the government would be forced to focus on the insurrection. And, if a new government came to power in Iran, it is at least possible that they would be eager to engage with the international community and would be more willing than the clerics currently in power to trade away the nuclear program.

Finally, the years an American strike would buy create space for future conflict that would prevent Iran from acquiring the bomb. If Iran decided to rebuild and in a decade or so was again close to having a nuclear weapons breakout capability, Israel or the United States could always attack Iran's nuclear facilities again. Some Israelis refer to this option as "mowing the grass." They casually assert that we can just go back in every few years whenever the grass, i.e., the nuclear program, gets too high. There is certainly some bravado in that statement, but there is also a grain of truth. In addition to targeted strikes on the nuclear program, there is the possibility that the window opened by a strike would create space for a larger and more devastating conflict between Iran and some other state, again preventing Iran from building the bomb.

Indeed, when we look at the history of strikes against nuclear facilities, we see that, historically, strikes have been a decisive nonproliferation tool. They have set the targeted nuclear program back far enough that other factors were able to intervene to keep the targeted state from building the bomb. There have only been four countries that have had their nuclear facilities bombed historically: Nazi Germany during World War II, Iran during the Iran-Iraq War, Iraq several times in the 1980s, 1990s, and 2000s, and Syria in 2007. None of those countries have nuclear weapons today. Let's consider each in turn.

Following Allied strikes on Germany's nuclear plants, Germany lost World War II, and a new government came to power that joined the American-led NATO alliance and renounced nuclear weapons.

After the attacks on the Bushehr reactor, Iran's nuclear program was halted. A decade later it began slowly and methodically rebuilding, but, at present, thirty years after the attacks, it still does not have nuclear weapons.

Iraq's nuclear program was delayed by a 1981 strike by Israel. This helped to buy time until Saddam Hussein invaded Kuwait, leading the United States to completely destroy the program in the Persian Gulf War in 1991. We now know that after the devastating defeat in that war Saddam Hussein decided not to rebuild his nuclear program.

Finally, in the early 2000s, Syria was secretly building a nuclear reactor with help from North Korea, but Israel destroyed it in a preventive strike in 2007. Syria did not immediately rebuild its program. We don't know if Syria's leaders had decided to abandon the program altogether, or if it was just waiting until the dust cleared to reconstitute it, but in the end it didn't matter. In the spring of 2011, Syria became engulfed in a civil war that prevented the government from doing anything other than focus on fighting the domestic insurgency. In all four cases, therefore, military strikes created space for other events to intervene, and, in all four cases, the targeted states lack nuclear weapons to this day.

It is this logic and history, therefore, that leads me to conclude that a US strike on Iran's nuclear facilities will most likely mean that Iran will be prevented from building nuclear weapons in a politically meaningful time frame. Predictions quickly become science fiction when they go out a few decades, and it is impossible to know what might happen several decades from now. Still, my best estimate is that, when combined with the inevitable politics and geopolitics that will come into play, a strike on Iran's nuclear facilities will likely mean that Iran will not become a nuclear power for at least a decade, or perhaps never at all.

Some critics of a strike argue that an attack would actually be counterproductive and make it more likely that Iran would acquire nuclear weapons. They claim that after a strike, Iran would make a definitive decision to dash to a bomb as quickly as possible. If there is currently uncertainty inside Iran about whether the country needs nuclear weapons to protect itself, they argue, an armed attack on their country would remove all doubt. In the aftermath of a strike, they claim, Iran would declare its intention to withdraw from the NPT, kick out international inspectors, and move with full haste to build a bomb. In addition, they aver, we would not be able to stop Iran from its dash to a bomb after a strike because Iran would move its program even deeper underground, making it impossible for us to stop them with military force. Moreover, they claim that a strike would be controversial and would therefore shatter the international coalition that we put in place to pressure Iran, causing the sanctions regime to fall apart.

As evidence for the broader argument, they cite the 1981 Israeli strike on the Osiraq reactor in Iraq, claiming that the attack only hardened Saddam's resolve to get the bomb and that this is evidenced by a drastic increase in the resources he poured into the nuclear program after the bombing raid. Indeed, they claim, he was very close to having the bomb in 1991, and it took the Persian Gulf War, a major military operation, to finally destroy the nuclear program. In sum, they argue that a strike will bring about exactly that which we are trying to prevent: it will actually help Iran get the bomb.

Such claims, if accurate, should certainly make us think hard before using force, but these arguments fall apart on closer inspection. First, the argument that a strike will convince Iran to build the bomb assumes that Iran's supreme leader has not already made his decision, but as we saw in chapter 2, this is a faulty assumption. It is likely that he has already made up his mind. He fully understands that nuclear weapons would improve his nation's security, and he doesn't need a US strike to convince him of that point.

Second, even if we were concerned that a strike might backfire by convincing the supreme leader to go nuclear, this concern can be completely mitigated through the timing of a strike. No one is arguing that we should attack Iran's nuclear facilities next Tuesday. Rather, the argument is that we strike if and when Iran crosses our stated red lines. If Iran enriches uranium to 90 percent, kicks out international inspectors, or pushes its program to the point of "undetectable breakout" after we have warned them not to, it will be patently obvious that they are trying to build the bomb. Under such a scenario, we wouldn't need to worry that a strike would cause them to build the bomb because it would be clear that that is exactly what they will do unless we strike.

Third, Iran would not "dash" to build nuclear weapons after a strike because it simply would not be in a position to do so. A strike would take what had been a 100-meter dash and transform it into a marathon. Remember, its nuclear infrastructure would have just been reduced to rubble. Maybe Iran's leaders would like to sprint to a nuclear capability after a strike, but this simply wouldn't be possible. Rather, as was explained above, this would be a massive and methodical undertaking that would take five years at a minimum.

Fourth, and related, claims that Iran would kick out inspectors and withdraw from the NPT misread Iran's strategy. Iran remains in the NPT and allows inspectors to visit facilities at present, not because it trusts the international community, but because it is trying to maintain the fiction that it is building nuclear capabilities as part of a peaceful program. Iran's leaders believe correctly that this fiction will help reduce international pressure. They will only officially declare their nuclear weapons intentions if and when they have all the pieces in place to quickly dash to a small nuclear arsenal and present the international community with a fait accompli. In other words, it is Iran's limited capabilities, not its intentions, that account for its cooperation (albeit halting) with the IAEA and the nonproliferation regime. After a strike, Iran's intentions would not change, but its capabilities would be greatly set back. There is therefore no reason to believe that Iran's strategy would change. What would Iran gain by declaring that it intends to build nuclear weapons when that day is now five years or more in the future? This strategy would be counterproductive. It would only invite international scrutiny and pressure at a time when Iran was not in a position to carry out this threat. Rather, it is more likely that Iran would once again attempt to rebuild its nuclear capabilities under the guise of a peaceful program and only exit from its NPT commitments many years down the road if and when it is again at the point of being able to dash to a bomb.

Sixth, even if Iran did immediately pull out of the NPT and kick out inspectors, and if the sanctions regime fell apart, it wouldn't really matter. These things are not good in and of themselves, they are there to serve a purpose: to prevent Iran from acquiring nuclear weapons. If, however, Iran crosses our red lines and is dashing to a bomb, those tools will have outlived their usefulness. After all, what value is there in having international inspectors on the ground watching Iran turn the final screws on a nuclear device? Granted, if Iran takes these actions, it might make it harder for us to deal with Iran's nuclear program down the road, but none of these actions would change the fact that a strike would still buy us a bunch of extra time to solve the problem.

Seventh, to those who argue that Iran will simply rebuild its nuclear program, but this time even deeper underground, I say, "I'd like to see them try it." The enrichment facility at Qom is built into the side of a mountain. It is under 295 feet of rock. It doesn't get much harder or deeper than that. And it is still not enough to avoid American military power. There are real challenges to building facilities deep underground that have to do with things as simple as making sure the facility is properly ventilated. It is not easy to see how Iran could move its program even deeper. Furthermore, this possible action by Iran after a strike would not change the fact that we had still bought many additional years to solve the problem. And if they tried to build the program deeper and harder, it would be a difficult and time-consuming process, which is more good news than bad. It would mean that our strike had bought even more time than we bargained for.

Eighth, the Osiraq case is an example of a successful, not a failed, preventive strike, and those who argue otherwise don't quite understand the technology behind building nuclear weapons. In 1981 Saddam was pursuing the plutonium path to the bomb. He was building a large nuclear reactor with French help. Once he had it up and running, it would have been technically quite simple to separate the plutonium from the spent fuel rods to produce fuel for nuclear weapons. The Israeli strike, however, destroyed the reactor and with it Saddam's dreams of pursuing the plutonium path to the bomb. Instead, he was forced to pursue the much more difficult uranium enrichment path. Saddam spent more money and tried harder on his nuclear program after 1981, not because he was more resolved, but because the Israeli strike had made his job much harder. The strike forced him to flail around for a decade. He tried four or five different types of uranium enrichment technologies and never made much progress. It is true that Saddam was close to having a bomb on the eve of the 1991 Gulf War, but not because his efforts to enrich uranium during the 1990s paid off. They didn't. Rather, he decided to break apart his limited supply of foreign reactor fuel in an attempt to extract enough enriched uranium to make one or two bombs.[26] Fortunately, this effort didn't work out either, but even if it had, he was not even close to having an indigenous ability to produce weapons-grade fissile material for a larger nuclear arsenal. Finally, and most importantly, at the end of the day, the only outcome we really care about is whether a country actually acquires nuclear weapons or not. Iraq does not have nuclear weapons today. We can't be certain that the outcome would be the same if Israel hadn't conducted the 1981 Osiraq raid.

In sum, it requires quite a lot of tortured mental gymnastics to come to the conclusion that a military strike that destroys Iran's nuclear program somehow puts Iran closer to having a nuclear bomb. Careful inspection reveals that these arguments do not hold any water whatsoever. There is absolutely no doubt that a strike on Iran's nuclear facility would significantly set back Iran's nuclear progress and create a real possibility that Iran would remain non-nuclear for the foreseeable future.

Moreover, a strike would also have broader strategic benefits. Not only would it stop Iran from building nuclear weapons, it would remove the threat that is currently causing other countries in the Middle East to hedge their nuclear bets. It would also help to assuage fears among leaders around the world that the nonproliferation regime might crumble. A strike, therefore, would stem the spread of nuclear weapons in the Middle East and bolster the global nonproliferation regime around the world. To be sure, some leaders might conclude from a strike that the United States is an unpredictable superpower and that they therefore need nuclear weapons to protect themselves, but the clearer take-home message from an attack on Iran is that the United States is serious about enforcing violations of the NPT and stopping the spread of nuclear weapons. In the future, leaders who think about starting a nuclear weapons program will be dissuaded by the fear that such a course of action might be more likely to result not in acquiring the bomb, but in being bombed.

Furthermore, a US strike would also strengthen American credibility. We declared many times that we were prepared to use force if necessary to stop Iran from building nuclear weapons. A strike would demonstrate that we mean what we say and say what we mean and that other countries, friends and foes alike, would be foolish to ignore America's foreign policy pronouncements.

A US attack on Iran's nuclear facilities, therefore, would bring a number of strategic benefits. But it would not be cost free.

COSTS OF AN ATTACK

A US strike on Iran would likely unleash a number of downside consequences. While it is important to recognize the risks of a preventive strike, it is also important not to exaggerate them. It is hard to imagine how a US strike on Iran's nuclear program could lead to World War III, for example, as some pundits misleadingly claim. This section will provide a complete and frank assessment of the costs of attacking Iran's nuclear facilities.

COLLATERAL DAMAGE

Just war doctrine stipulates that in order for a war to be ethical, the military advantages of the war must be proportional to the evils it unleashes. Consistent with just war doctrine, the United States seeks to limit civilian casualties in its military campaigns. This raises the question: How many people would die in a US strike? The answer depends to a large degree on the nature of the strike. If the American president opted for a massive bombing campaign, the collateral damage could potentially be quite high. If he or she instead selected a limited strike on the key nuclear facilities and the air defenses necessary to get there, the collateral damage would be minimal.

While Iran's nuclear facilities are located near cities (Natanz, Qom, Isfahan), they are not *in* cities. Rather, they are on the outskirts of town, removed from population centers. Indeed, readers who are interested can see this for themselves with a quick Google Earth search.[27] The US military is fully capable, therefore, of destroying these facilities without doing damage to unintended targets.

If the United States decided to increase the scope of the attack by going after centrifuge manufacturing facilities in downtown Tehran or Natanz, or by attacking command and control centers or government offices located in cities, then the death toll would be higher. The accuracy of US precision-guided munitions is nothing short of remarkable, but collateral damage is unavoidable when targeting urban areas.

Some have expressed concern that a US strike on nuclear facilities could cause a nuclear explosion or disperse radioactive material that could lead to deaths and sickness from radiation poisoning, but this is simply not true.[28] Designing a functioning nuclear warhead requires careful engineering; one cannot create a nuclear explosion by simply bombing a nuclear plant. Neither would a US strike cause the dispersion of radioactive material that could lead to radiation poisoning. The materials being handled at the nuclear facilities at Isfahan, Natanz, and Qom, such as yellowcake and uranium hexafluoride, are not sources of ionizing radiation. A strike on a nuclear reactor sustaining a critical chain reaction would likely cause radioactive contamination of the surrounding area, but the Arak nuclear reactor is still under construction, and the Bushehr reactor could simply be left off the target list as light-water reactors like Bushehr do not pose a serious proliferation risk.

In a limited strike, therefore, the dead and wounded would consist almost entirely of people working at Iran's nuclear facilities and military bases, including Iranian scientists, engineers, technicians, and military personnel. It is my best estimate, therefore, that there would be hundreds, but not thousands, of Iranian casualties from a limited strike. This number could be reduced still further if the United States announced the timing of the attacks in advance and struck at night when there would be fewer employees at these facilities.

Some of my colleagues have grimly noted that these deaths are not collateral damage but are an important part of the target. After all, eliminating the personnel working on the program would reduce the number of people with the training and experience to help Iran build nuclear weapons in the future. Indeed, we should not fool ourselves about the identity of the most likely victims. These are far from innocent bystanders. Rather, they are working to build the world's most dangerous weapon for a vicious authoritarian regime. If they want to reduce the likelihood that they will die in a US strike on Iran's nuclear facilities, they have a simple option: find a more virtuous line of work.

Still, the loss of any human life is regrettable. In an anarchic international system, however, states have a moral responsibility to defend their own citizens, and sometimes this means endangering the lives of people in other nations who intend to do them harm.

IRANIAN MILITARY RETALIATION

The most obvious and, perhaps the most serious, negative consequence of an American strike on Iran would be Iranian military retaliation. Iran's supreme leader is unlikely to take an armed attack on his country lying down; he will strike back. To understand Iranian military retaliation, we must understand both what Iran could do (its military capabilities) and also what it is likely to do. These are not one and the same. This section will consider each in turn.

Iran does not have a powerful conventional military. Its regular army, navy, and air force barely deserve mention. Rather, Tehran has been investing in asymmetric military capabilities to offset the conventional military superiority of its adversaries. In particular, Iran has three primary types of asymmetric response options: ballistic missiles, terrorist attacks, and wreaking havoc in the Persian Gulf.

First, Iran could conduct ballistic missile attacks. It could choose to attack major cities in Israel such as Jerusalem or Tel Aviv. In a tit-for-tat response to an attack on its nuclear facilities, Tehran could try to return the favor and target Israel's nuclear reactor at Dimona. Tehran could strike population centers or oil facilities in Persian Gulf states if Tehran's leaders thought they had been complicit in the attack. In addition, Iran could attempt to target American forces and bases in the region.

To carry out these attacks, Iran could draw from its stockpile of 300 Shahab-3 missiles with ranges capable of reaching the greater Middle East.[29] It also maintains a larger stockpile of other shorter-range ballistic missiles and artillery that it could use against nearer targets. While it is likely that Iran would arm the ballistic missiles with conventional warheads, Tehran is also thought to maintain an arsenal of chemical and biological weapons, and Iran's leaders could potentially decide to conduct a chemical or biological weapons attack.[30]

There are important limits to Iran's missile capabilities, however. First, it only possesses ten launchers for its Shahab-3 missiles, meaning that it could only launch ten missiles at a time.[31] Second, its missiles are not very accurate. If it aimed at cities, it would likely hit something, but if it attempted more pinpoint targeting, such as against nuclear facilities, bases, or forces, it is likely that many of the missiles would fall harmlessly into the desert or the sea. In addition, even the missiles that hit population centers would be unlikely to inflict many casualties. For a point of comparison, in the 1991 Gulf War, Saddam Hussein fired dozens of Scud missiles into Israel, resulting in only two deaths. Iran's Shahab-3s are more advanced than Saddam's Scuds, but Israel is also better prepared. Its urban areas are protected by the Iron Dome missile defense system, and 75 percent of the population now has access to bomb shelters.[32]

Second, Iran could sponsor terrorist attacks in the region and around the world. It could encourage its terrorist proxies, Hamas and Hezbollah, to launch rocket attacks against Israel. It could step up its support to groups fighting US and NATO forces in Afghanistan. And Iran's own Quds Force or Hezbollah could attempt to conduct terrorist attacks against soft targets anywhere in the world including, conceivably, in the American homeland. In the past couple of years, Iran's special forces are believed to have attempted terror attacks in Thailand, Georgia (the country, not the state), India, Bulgaria, and even Washington, DC.

There are also limits, however, to Iran's ability to wage terror. Hamas and Hezbollah are supported by Iran, but they are still, at the end of the day, independent actors. They have their own interests and are unlikely to simply salute and do exactly what Iran commands. Hezbollah's leader, Hassan Nasrallah, is constantly engaged in a delicate balancing act to satisfy his two constituencies. He wants to keep Iran, his principal supplier of money and military hardware, happy, but he also wants to maintain the support of the population in southern Lebanon where Hezbollah operates. Southern Lebanon was badly damaged in the 2006 war between Israel and Hezbollah, and this greatly angered Nasrallah's base of support in Lebanon. Since this time, he has trod lightly to avoid starting a major confrontation with Israel.[33] If the United States struck Iran, therefore, it is likely that Hezbollah would engage in at least token rocket attacks against Israel, but it is also likely that he would attempt to stop short of an attack that could provoke another Israeli invasion of Lebanon. Indeed, Nasrallah even went on record saying that, in the event of an attack on Iran, Iran's leadership "would not ask Hezbollah to do anything."[34] This is hard to believe as Iran founded Hezbollah in the 1970s with the specific intention of maintaining a retaliatory option and strategic deterrent precisely for a situation like this. Nasrallah's statement, therefore, appears to be intended to downplay expectations to give Hezbollah the wiggle room to avoid a major retaliatory response.

Moreover, Hezbollah's rockets, while terrifying, are not very accurate or deadly. It is unlikely that they would cause many casualties in Israel. In the 2006 Lebanon war, for example, Hezbollah fired 4,200 Katusha rockets into Israel but only managed to inflict fifty-four casualties, or about one casualty for every eighty rockets fired.[35]

Similarly, Hamas, Iran's other terrorist proxy, would make its own calculations about what level of response best served its interests. Like Hezbollah, it would likely engage in at least token rocket fire, but it would also want to stop short of inciting a major Israeli attack against its base of operation in Gaza. Hamas's rockets are not very deadly either and would be unlikely to cause large numbers of casualties.

An additional limit on Iran's ability to wage terror is the sheer incompetence of Iran's own Quds Force. While Iran attempted to conduct many covert attacks around the world in recent years, only one, an attack on an Israeli tour bus in Bulgaria in 2012, actually succeeded. The others were all failed or thwarted attempts that made the Quds Force look more like the Keystone Cops than a fierce paramilitary organization. The Iranians plotted to assassinate Saudi Arabia's ambassador to the United States at Café Milano, his favorite restaurant in Washington, DC, in 2011.[36] Such an attack would have hit close to home as the restaurant is just around the block from my home and a place where many Washingtonians go to see and be seen. Fortunately, the plot was foiled when the bone-headed conspirators confessed their plan to an undercover Drug Enforcement Agency officer posing as a member of a Mexican drug cartel. Even more spectacularly stupid was the 2012 attempted operation in Thailand in which an Iranian covert operative hurled a grenade at a Thai police officer only to have it ricochet off of a tree, land back at his feet, and blow off his own legs.[37] In short, Iran's potential to wage terror is something short of terrifying.

The third major option for Iranian military retaliation would be to wreak havoc in the Persian Gulf. Iran could harass or attack American warships or commercial traffic in the body of water and could even attempt to close the Strait of Hormuz, a narrow waterway through which roughly 20 percent of the world's traded oil flows.[38] To conduct such attacks, Iran could lay mines, conduct attacks from the shore with anti-ship missiles, and use its irregular IRGC navy, which maintains swarming fast-attack craft armed with machine guns and rockets, and Kilo-class and midget submarines.[39] Using such capabilities, Iran could send global oil prices soaring (a subject to which we will return below), and damage, if not sink, commercial vessels or US warships. It could also close the Strait, at least for a couple of weeks, before it would be reopened by American military power.[40]

There is no doubt, however, that a large-scale use of force by Iran in the Persian Gulf would provoke a tough American response. The United States has already declared that if Iran attempts to close the Strait of Hormuz, we will use force to reopen it.[41] The most likely outcome of such a conflict would be that, after two weeks of intense fighting, the Iranian navy would be at the bottom of the Persian Gulf, and the Strait of Hormuz would once again be safe for tanker traffic.

In sum, in the worst-case scenario, Iran could launch hundreds of ballistic missiles, some armed with chemical and biological weapons, at targets in the Middle East, attempt to set off a wave of terror attacks against Israel and around the world, and close the Strait of Hormuz, leading to an intense, but short naval battle in the Persian Gulf. But, the more important question is not what *could* Iran do, but what *would* Iran do?

The answer depends in part on the size of the US military operation against it. If the United States launched a massive attack on Iran and if Iran's supreme leader believed, rightly or wrongly, that Washington was coming to downtown Tehran to overthrow his regime, he would have nothing left to lose and would therefore have no reason not to exercise his riskiest retaliatory options. If it meant the difference between losing his regime and his life, or possibly surviving to fight another day, it might even make sense to use chemical and biological weapons, close the Strait of Hormuz, and sponsor terror attacks on the US homeland. This is why it is never a good idea to put an opponent's back against the wall in international politics.

If the United States conducted only a limited strike on Iran's key nuclear facilities, however, he would face a very different set of calculations. Indeed, it is important to understand that, in the event of a limited attack, Iran's supreme leader would face his own strategic dilemma. On one hand, he would want to strike back hard at the aggressor to re-establish deterrence internationally and save face domestically. On the other hand, he would not want to strike back too hard for fear of provoking an even larger war with the United States.

Put yourself in the shoes of Iran's supreme leader. Imagine that you woke up one morning to find out that your key nuclear facilities had been destroyed in an attack. You would have to do something. You would look like a wimp if you did nothing. But your primary goal is still regime survival. In the aftermath of a limited attack, your regime and your military are still intact. The last thing you would want to do, therefore, is to pick a fight with the world's only remaining superpower, the only state on Earth that could completely eviscerate your military and bring your regime to an end. As Karim Sadjadpour at the Carnegie Endowment of International Peace put it, "If they respond too little, they could lose face, and if they respond too much, they could lose their heads."[42]

In addition, as supreme leader, you would want to save back some military capabilities to deter and defend against future contingencies. If you shot off all of your ballistic missiles and picked a major naval battle with the United States that led to the destruction of your navy, you would be left completely and utterly defenseless.

Moreover, you couldn't really afford to close the Strait of Hormuz. You could certainly threaten to do so to send oil prices soaring and even harass and attack some ships passing through the area, but actually closing the strait would be cutting off your nose to spite your face. First of all, you could only close the strait for a couple of weeks at most. Second, it would provoke a US response that would result in the destruction of your navy and coastal defenses. Third, if you closed the strait, you would be unable to export any of your own oil, so you would be cutting off a key export that contributes upward of 80 percent of all government revenues.[43] Fourth, you would be declaring war, not just on the United States, but on the entire world, which also depends on Middle Eastern oil. You would force every great power, including Russia and China, to align against you.

For these reasons and others, it is almost certain that Iran's supreme leader would aim for some kind of calibrated response. He would want to strike back, but not too hard. He would want to do enough to claim he had retaliated, but not so much that he would provoke a major war with the

United States. Of course, it is always possible that he would misjudge and strike back too hard or not hard enough, but he would do his best to get it just right.

By my estimate, therefore, Iran's most likely retaliatory response might look something like this: four to five salvos (forty to fifty missiles) of conventionally armed ballistic missiles over the course of several days against military and civilian targets in the Middle East; several days of rocket attacks from Hamas and Hezbollah into Israel; sporadic Quds Force plots against American and Israeli soft targets around the world for months or even years after the attack; and the harassment of and attacks against navy and commercial vessels in the Persian Gulf, combined with empty threats to close the strait.[44]

Israel is the country that would bear the brunt of Iranian retaliation, and their defense experts estimate that Iranian military retaliation following an attack on its nuclear facilities would result in about 300 Israeli deaths.[45] Given the limits of Iran's capabilities and its interest in restraining the conflict, the global ramifications would not be much more devastating. In sum, the consequences of Iranian military retaliation would be serious, but far from catastrophic.

REGIONAL WAR

Some analysts, such as Colin Kahl, fear that any attack on Iran could lead to a broader regional war.[46] He suggests that, in response to Iranian and Hezbollah retaliation, Israel might return fire on Iran and invade Lebanon. Then Syria could come to the aid of its allies in Iran and Lebanon, leading to a broader regional war. In addition, Kahl fully admits that Iran would aim for a calibrated response, but he fears that the war would escalate because the United States, not Iran, would be itching for a larger fight.

This outcome is conceivable, but highly unlikely. Given prevailing conditions and presuming good strategy on America's part, we would almost certainly avoid it. It is doubtful that Syria would attack Israel as it is tied down in a bloody multiyear civil war and wouldn't be looking to take on additional military obligations. Moreover, a wild Israeli response to Iranian retaliation is a near necessary condition for a broader regional war and, as I discuss below, the United States could restrain its ally to prevent this from occurring.

Finally, what about the argument that we can't trust Washington not to turn this into a major war? First, Kahl argues that it would be easier to destroy Iran's conventional capabilities before they are dispersed in a conflict, so there are good tactical reasons to either begin with a massive military assault on Iran or not go at all. Therefore, as I stated above, he argues that if we get into a conflict with Iran, we should conduct a massive bombing campaign right off the bat. But, as we also discussed above, strategy should drive tactics, not the other way around, and there are many more good strategic reasons to prefer a limited bombing campaign over a massive one.

Second, Kahl argues that the United States might not be able to accept any Iranian retaliation because if Iran got in a lucky shot that happened to sink a US warship or killed a large number of US service personnel, any American president would feel overwhelming political pressure to respond. In making this argument, however, Kahl underestimates US military planning and our political leadership. As we will discuss below, US forces would go into force-protection mode in the days following a US strike.

American service personnel, therefore, would hardly be sitting ducks for Iranian retaliation. Moreover, even if Iran happened to get in a lucky shot, the United States should show restraint. It would be in our interest to de-escalate the conflict, and the president could easily communicate this to the American people. He could make the case that through these soldiers' heroic efforts we eliminated the greatest emerging threat to our national security. This is a truthful message and one that would be accepted by the American people.

In sum, it is possible to imagine a limited US strike leading to a broader regional war, but just barely. It is much more likely that the conflict would stay limited.

SPIKES IN OIL PRICES

Any attack on Iran will lead to spikes in oil prices that could damage the global economy. Although unlikely, the worst-case scenario would involve Iran's closing the Strait of Hormuz and cutting off exports of Persian Gulf oil until the US military was able to forcibly reopen the strait. A survey of nearly two dozen traders and analysts conducted by the Rapidan Group found that a protracted conventional conflict between the United States and Iran that resulted in a three-week closure of shipping through the Strait of Hormuz would lead to a $25 per barrel rise in oil prices despite the use of the Strategic Petroleum Reserve.[47] Even if Iran didn't close the strait, oil traders would fear that possibility and other potential supply dis-ruptions and would therefore bid up the price of oil, resulting in perhaps a $4–$15 per barrel (roughly 4–15 percent at current prices) risk premium. The duration of the price spikes would depend largely on the duration of the fighting, and prices would be likely to return quickly to their pre-conflict levels in the conflict's aftermath.

COMPLICATIONS FOR CONTAINMENT

Joshua Rovner, a professor at Southern Methodist University, has argued that a strike on Iran's nuclear facilities is a bad idea because, in his view, it is inevitable that Iran will get nuclear weapons at some point in the future and when it does, deterrence and containment will be much more difficult after a strike. He reasons that if we strike Iran and it rebuilds and acquires nuclear weapons anyway, then it will be angrier, more aggressive, and therefore harder to contain.[48] Therefore, to avoid this outcome, he argues that we should simply acquiesce to a nuclear-armed Iran and not try to prevent it through the use of force. This argument, like a house of cards, stands for a while if you look at it, but it collapses instantaneously when poked. First, as we discussed earlier in this chapter, it is highly unlikely that Iran will join the nuclear club any time soon if the United States strikes. Second, in the many years that would pass from a US strike to the earliest feasible point at which Iran could join the nuclear club, there will have been much water under the bridge, and it is a stretch to imagine that a limited US strike will be the defining feature of Iranian foreign policy that far into the future. Third, deterring and containing a nuclear-armed Iran will be difficult because, as discussed above, they will be emboldened by their capabilities. This is true regardless of their emotional state.

Fourth and most importantly, if anything, a US strike would, on balance, make deterring and containing a nuclear-armed Iran *easier*, not harder. This is because, as we discussed above, our lack of credibility will be a major obstacle to our ability to deter and contain a nuclear-armed Iran. If we were unwilling to go to war with a non-nuclear Iran, despite repeated threats to do so, who on Earth is going to believe our threats to go to war with a nuclear Iran? If, however, we hit Iran's nuclear facilities hard, and they still somehow manage to get nuclear weapons, our threats to hit them again will carry much more weight.

If anything, therefore, the effect of a strike on our ability to deter and contain a nuclear-armed Iran in subsequent years should be tallied in the benefits, not the costs, column.

IRANIAN DOMESTIC POLITICS

An armed attack would strengthen the theocratic regime in Iran, forestalling opportunities for a near-term regime transition to a new government more friendly to American interests. Political scientists have documented a rally-around-the-flag effect.[49] When countries are attacked, the population tends to become more nationalistic and supportive of whatever government is in power. Any attack on Iran would therefore temporarily bolster the clerics in Tehran. We also know, however, that the rally-around-the-flag effect tends to be very short-lived.[50] Therefore, predictions that a strike would extend the lifespan of the Iranian regime by decades are pure hyperbole.[51] Rather, it is likely that in the medium to long term, a strike would open the space for regime opponents to criticize the regime for bringing a crisis to the country and mismanaging the issue to the point of suffering an armed attack and losing the nuclear program altogether. In the end, however, the regime's grip on power will ultimately depend on other factors.

ANTI-AMERICAN SENTIMENT

A US strike on Iran's nuclear facilities would be likely to lead to anti-American sentiment in certain corners of the world. Many Western Europeans will decry Washington as a rogue superpower operating outside the bounds of international law. The Arab street will protest against American imperialism and what they perceive as poor treatment of Muslims (after Iraq, Afghanistan, and Libya, this would, after all, be the fourth American war against a Muslim country in fifteen years). US relations with other great powers would temporarily sour. Moscow and Beijing would certainly protest America's muscle flexing without an explicit UNSCR.

The response would not be as severe as many observers might fear, however. While Arab governments might lodge formal diplomatic protests to satisfy their populations, behind closed doors they would be congratulating American officials for eliminating the Iranian nuclear threat.

The opposition of the great powers would also be mixed. Russia would likely be a vocal opponent of a US attack, but it is incredibly unlikely that, apart from diplomatic protests, it would do anything to intervene in the conflict, to aid Iran, or to retaliate against the United States.

China would likely remain mute. I have traveled to Beijing four times over the past several years to discuss this issue with Chinese academic experts and government officials, and I have received the same message each time. First, China would prefer peace and stability in the Middle East, so that they can continue to purchase fossil fuels from the region to keep "China Inc." running smoothly. Second, China sees this as a conflict primarily between Tehran and Washington, and they have interests in maintaining good relations with both sides. Third, and related, they have no intention of getting into the middle of the conflict.

Finally, depending on the circumstances leading up to the attack, many countries around the world, including NATO and non-NATO allies, and other regional partners might fully support a US preventive strike and even laud the United States for taking necessary steps to defend international peace and security. In this and other areas, therefore, the American strategy for conducting the attack will help to shape the magnitude of the downside risks.

COST-MITIGATION STRATEGY

The United States would not simply accept the risks of a strike on Iran, however. Rather, we would rather put in place a strategy to manage and mitigate them. Just as the United States would seek to contain the threats posed by a nuclear-armed Iran if we choose to acquiesce, we would seek to contain the threats of an attack on Iran if we go down this path. In short, the strategy would involve building an international coalition in the run-up to the attack, conducting a limited military strike on Iran's key nuclear facilities, and then pulling back to quickly de-escalate the conflict. In this way, we can trade Iran's nuclear program, the greatest emerging threat to the country, for limited Iranian military retaliation.

The first element of the strategy would be to deter the worst forms of Iranian retaliation. Iran's leaders are afraid of a full-scale war with the United States, and we can play these fears to our advantage. We can clearly communicate that we are only interested in destroying Iran's nuclear facilities, not in obliterating the military or overthrowing the regime. We would threaten that, if Iran crossed certain red lines in its retaliation, we would be forced to follow up our limited initial strike with a more massive military response. In this way, we can deter Iran from exercising its riskiest retaliatory options.

The forms of retaliation that we would find unacceptable would include closing the Strait of Hormuz, using chemical or biological weapons, sponsoring terror attacks on the US homeland, or launching massive missile barrages on our allies or against US bases and forces in the region. While we lack formal diplomatic ties, we could clearly communicate this message to the Iranians through presidential speeches, backchannel communications, and trusted intermediaries.

In this way, we should be able to deter Iran's worst forms of retaliation. In the unlikely event that Iran decides to cross these red lines, however, the United States must be prepared to escalate the conflict. In this case, we could expand the bombing campaign to include the targets in the more expansive military option listed above. In so doing, we would also degrade Iran's military capabilities and their ability to do further harm to us and our allies. Indeed, if Iran's leaders want to take the gloves off, the inevitable outcome will be that the United States wins a decisive victory and Iran's military will be completely destroyed in a matter of weeks. As even Colin Kahl, a skeptic regarding American military action against Iran, admits, "there is no doubt that Washington will win in the narrow operational sense. Indeed, with the impressive array of US naval and air forces already deployed in the Gulf, the United States could probably knock Iran's military capabilities back 20 years in a matter of weeks." Tehran's leaders understand this full well, however, and this will likely deter them from crossing our stated red lines in the first place.

This strategy of deterring Iran's worst forms of retaliation, however, also means that the United States must be prepared to absorb Iranian retaliation that falls short of these red lines. It is unlikely that Iran's supreme leader would simply do nothing, but it is also not worth starting a full-scale war in response to small-scale Iranian reprisals. This means that Washington must turn the other cheek to limited Iranian retaliation, such as several salvos of ballistic missiles that taper off after a few days, minor terror attacks in the Middle East and around the world, and the harassment of and attacks against American ships in the Persian Gulf.

To give Iran a face-saving path out of the conflict, we should also refrain from correcting inevitable Iranian exaggerations about the damage caused by their limited military reprisal. Giving them a propaganda victory, at least to domestic audiences, might help quell the crisis.

To further prevent the conflict from widening, we must strike a bargain with Israel in which we agree to take care of the Iranian nuclear threat so long as Israel promises not to enter the fray. As we saw above, an Israeli counterstrike in response to Iranian retaliation for an American strike is one means by which this conflict could become a wider regional war; we must seek assurances from Israel that they and their capable defense forces will be willing to absorb Iranian retaliation and remain on the sidelines. We reached a similar bargain in the 1991 Gulf War in which Israel agreed to absorb Scud missile attacks from Saddam Hussein without hitting back so long as we pushed Saddam out of Kuwait. This successful example should serve as a model for any future Iran contingency.

By "absorbing" Iranian retaliation, however, I'm not arguing that the United States and our allies leave ourselves wide open to attack. Rather, we would do what we can to defend against these attacks. Our bases and forces in the region should take all necessary force-protection measures. We and our allies should also be prepared with missile defenses to counter Iran's missile salvos. Israel's population should seek cover in bomb shelters. And the United States should evacuate all non-essential diplomatic personnel from the region in the run-up to the attack. In this way, the damage caused by Iran's retaliation would be minimized.

In addition to limiting the scope of the conflict, the United States could also address the broader economic, political, and diplomatic fall-out of the strike with a carefully designed strategy. To blunt the economic consequences of a strike, we could offset any disruption of oil supplies by opening the Strategic Petroleum Reserve and by encouraging some Gulf states to increase their production in the run-up to the attack. Given that many oil-producing nations in the region, especially Saudi Arabia, have urged the United States to attack Iran, they would be likely to cooperate.

To counteract the regime-strengthening rally-around-the-flag effects, the United States, after a suitable period of time, could begin to provide support to opposition movements within Iran and maintain pressure on the regime, much as in the deter-and-contain scenario.

The United States could also greatly mitigate the international political fallout of a strike through its diplomatic approach. The United States has been working for years to build an international coalition opposed to Iran's nuclear program that has, to this point, already resulted in eight UN-SCRs against Iran. By pursuing a diplomatic resolution to the last possible moment and by setting clear red lines for developments in Iran's nuclear program that would trigger a US military response, we can make it clear to the international community that we have made every effort to solve this dispute peacefully and that the conflict is solely the result of Iran's intransigence. Through this approach, the United States should be able to win the support of much of the international community if and when it comes time to take military action.

Finally, to minimize the risk that Iran could quickly rebuild its nuclear program in the aftermath of a strike, the United States must implement a post-strike nonproliferation strategy. The centerpiece of this strategy would be an international diplomatic effort to convince the Iranian government to finally give up its right to domestic enrichment in exchange for a complete lifting of sanctions and a return to the community of nations. If Iran accepts, the Iranian nuclear crisis will be resolved. If they refuse, we must maintain various forms of pressure to maximize the delay, for years if not decades, in any Iranian efforts to rebuild the nuclear program.[52]

In sum, with a carefully designed strategy, Washington can mitigate many of the risks posed by a strike on Iran's nuclear facilities, trading the greatest threat to its national security in exchange for limited Iranian military retaliation.

CONCLUSION

Many who oppose a strike on Iran do so for moral reasons and these objections are understandable. Yet, if the rules that govern the international system, including the nuclear nonproliferation regime, are to have any meaning, they must be enforced. Some people are comfortable with military intervention for humanitarian reasons but place nuclear proliferation in a different category. But the spread of nuclear weapons poses a grave threat to international peace and security. If the United States believes that it is imperative to prevent nuclear war and stop additional countries from acquiring the world's deadliest weapons, then it must be willing, in principle, to use force to achieve that objective.

When it comes to using force to prevent nuclear proliferation, therefore, the questions are practical ones: Does the use of force have a reasonable chance of success, and is it superior to available alternatives? In some instances, such as North Korea's nuclear program today, those questions must be answered in the negative. But Iran is different.

As this chapter demonstrated, a limited American strike on Iran's key nuclear facilities is not an attractive option, but it might be better than the alternatives. By taking military action, the United States can destroy Iran's nuclear program, setting it back by many years and creating a strong possibility that Iran will remain non-nuclear for the foreseeable future. It is of course possible that Iran succeeds in immediately rebuilding its nuclear program and becoming a declared nuclear power in the years after a strike as many critics argue, but this outcome seems much less likely than the alternative. In addition, a strike also carries real risks that one should not underestimate. That said, a careful analysis reveals that these costs are not as great as many analysts might imagine and that the United States could mitigate many of these costs with a carefully designed strategy.

Nevertheless, some dedicated opponents of the military option for Iran will use any rhetorical device they can find to confuse people about the potential costs and benefits of this option. Some go so far as to compare an attack on Iran to the 2003 US invasion of Iraq.[53] They argue that in both cases advocates argued that we needed to go to war against an autocratic state in the Middle East to prevent it from obtaining WMDs. In both cases, proponents claimed that the costs of nuclear proliferation would be astronomical and that war would not be as bad as many people feared. To flesh out the analogy to the point of absurdity, they even point out that the names for both countries are four-letter words that begin with the letter "I." In conclusion, they argue that the war in Iraq was an unmitigated disaster and that Iran will be no better. Indeed, as I have heard some of them proclaim, "if you liked Iraq, you'll love Iran."[54]

This rhetorical argument is as powerful as it is misleading. In *Analogies at War,* Yuen Foong Khong, a professor at Oxford University, argued that people often reason by analogy as a way to help think through complicated foreign policy problems.[55] In trying to decide on a course of action for a current foreign policy challenge, they ask, what are the lessons of Munich, Vietnam, and Iraq? Khong argued, however, that reasoning by analogy in foreign policy leads to erroneous conclusions because people seize on superficial similarities and ignore the underlying differences. And, he argued, it is usually the underlying differences that really matter.

Iraq in 2003 and Iran today are very different cases in many ways, but I will highlight the two most important. First, Iran is much closer to having nuclear weapons than Saddam Hussein ever was, and we know that with high confidence. Saddam Hussein had kicked international inspectors out, and our intelligence estimates on Iraq's nuclear program were based largely on informed guesswork. We now know that he never attempted to reconstitute his nuclear program after the 1991 Gulf War. In Iran, in contrast, international inspectors are on the ground visiting Iran's nuclear facilities daily and writing detailed reports every three months. We know exactly how close Iran is to the point of no return, we know exactly where Iran's nuclear facilities are located, and we know that we can destroy them. Second, a strike on Iran would be much less costly than the war in Iraq. Iraq was so costly in terms of blood and treasure because we put over 100,000

US troops on the ground and stayed for ten years. Nobody is talking about that kind of operation in Iran. We are talking about a limited strike on Iran's key nuclear facilities. Iran has some ability to try to hit back, but not much. It would be foolish, therefore, to draw simple conclusions for Iran policy today based on our experience in invading Iraq over a decade ago.

Rather, we must judge our options for Iran against one another on their own merits. We will do so in the next chapter.

CHAPTER SEVEN

WHICH IS WORSE?

TO THIS POINT, WE HAVE REVIEWED OUR VARIOUS OP-
tions for resolving the Iranian nuclear threat in isolation; we are now
ready to compare them side by side. Chapter 4 demonstrated that a diplomatic resolution to this crisis would be best if we could get it. It also
showed that we might be unable to resolve this issue through negotiations. This means that at some point soon, an American president might
have to make the gut-wrenching call between acquiescing to a nuclear-
armed Iran and taking military action to keep Iran from the bomb. These
are the options we explored in chapters 5 and 6. We saw that neither option is particularly attractive. The operative question, therefore, is which
is worse?

This chapter will explore that question by examining how a few key
US national security objectives would be affected by the choice. In essence,
this chapter rearranges and compares information that has already been
presented in chapters 5 and 6. Therefore, readers interested in more detail

on any of the points raised in this chapter should refer to the previous chapters.

PROTECT THE US HOMELAND

The United States, like all nations, would like to continue to exist. It would like to defend its territorial integrity and the lives of its citizens and prevent adversaries from conducting devastating attacks against its homeland.

At present, Iran lacks the ability to directly attack the US homeland. In the event that the United States took military action against Iran's nuclear facilities, therefore, the US homeland would not be in much danger. Iran could attempt to sponsor terror attacks on US soil, but it has thus far not proved itself capable of conducting terror attacks in the United States. Most importantly, however, it would have no ability to do major damage to, or threaten the existence of, the United States of America.

A nuclear-armed Iran, however, could conduct a catastrophic nuclear attack on US soil. In addition, Iran's nuclear weapons could fall into the hands of terrorists who could conduct such an attack. As Iran's nuclear capabilities grow over time, it is even possible that a nuclear war with Iran could threaten the very existence of the United States. While the risk of nuclear war on any given day is low, it is not zero. And that risk needs to be aggregated day after day, week after week, year after year, and decade after decade as the countries go through various political conflicts of interest, crises, and possibly even wars. Given enough time, there is a real risk that something could go terribly wrong. From the point of view of protecting the US homeland, therefore, there is no doubt that a military strike is vastly preferable to acquiescing to a nuclear-armed Iran.

PREVENT NUCLEAR PROLIFERATION

The director of national intelligence (DNI) estimates that the spread of nuclear weapons to additional countries poses a threat to US national security; preventing nuclear proliferation has been a top objective of US national security policy for decades.[1]

A strike on Iran would contribute to this goal by halting the Iranian nuclear threat, removing a motivation for future nuclear proliferation in the region, eliminating a potential supplier of sensitive nuclear technology around the world, bolstering the global nonproliferation regime, and sending a message that the United States is willing to use force to stop the spread of nuclear weapons. It is possible that a strike would contribute to proliferation in some cases by making leaders believe they need nuclear weapons to defend themselves against American power, but this would almost certainly be outweighed by the nonproliferation benefits.

Acquiescing to a nuclear-armed Iran, on the other hand, greatly harms this national security objective in all the ways listed above. It allows Iran to have nuclear weapons, increases pressures on other states in the Middle East to acquire nuclear weapons, gives Iran the power to become a sensitive nuclear supplier, weakens the nonproliferation regime, and sends the message that the United States and the international community are not serious about stopping determined proliferators. From a nonproliferation standpoint, therefore, a strike is far and away the stronger option.

COMBAT TERRORISM

The American intelligence community assesses that international terrorism poses a threat to the national security of the United States, and

Washington seeks to combat terrorist groups that could harm the United States and our allies.[2] Unfortunately, both of these scenarios result in an increased risk of terrorism against the United States and our allies. (We will consider how these options would contribute to terrorists' ability to recruit new foot soldiers in the following section on America's reputation. Here we will consider the direct effect of these options on Iranian-sponsored terrorist attacks.)

If Washington takes military action, Tehran will almost certainly respond by encouraging its terrorist proxies to attack and by conducting covert operations around the world with its Quds Force. If, on the other hand, Iran acquires nuclear weapons, it will likely be emboldened to step up its support for terrorist proxies. A military strike would lead to a short-term burst of certain terrorist activity, but a nuclear-armed Iran would step up its support for terrorists and proxies for years to come. It is difficult to say which would be worse, on balance, for American interests.

PROMOTE REGIONAL STABILITY

The United States would like to prevent major conflicts in the Middle East. In addition to having a general preference for peace over war, Washington would like to protect our allies in the region and maintain the stability that fosters international economic exchange. Again, this interest is threatened under both scenarios. A US attack on Iran would undoubtedly spark Iranian retaliation and could potentially result in a wider war, destabilizing the region for the duration of the conflict. On the other hand, a nuclear-armed Iran would be emboldened to throw its weight around in the region. This would lead to future crises and conflicts and, given the instabilities in the Iranian-Israeli nuclear balance, could even result in a nuclear war. It is clear, therefore, that in the short term a strike would be worse for regional stability. At some point in the future, however, the balance of the scale would likely flip as multiple crises set off by a nuclear-armed Iran compound over time to destabilize the region.

CONTAIN MILITARY EXPENDITURES

There was a time in the not-too-distant past when the United States was willing to pay whatever it took to minimize any threat to the security of the country. Those days are gone. After the global financial crisis and the budget sequester, lawmakers are asking tough questions about military spending, raising the obvious question of which option would cost more. A strike on Iran's program would be costly in that we would expend fuel, cruise missiles, and bombs in the attack and use resources in defense, such as ballistic missiles, and potentially lose military platforms, bases, and personnel in the exchange. There would also be costs involved with any subsequent strikes or military conflicts resulting from the initial strike. A deterrence and containment regime for a nuclear-armed Iran would be costly in that we would need to provide ballistic missile defenses and conventional military capabilities to our regional allies; finance Israel's development of a secure, second-strike capability; build, maintain, and supply new military bases and deploy additional US forces in the region; and also expend resources in any contingency that results from a nuclear-armed Iran, including crises and wars in the region and beyond. In the short term, a strike would be the more costly option, but it would likely be less than the long-term costs of a deterrence and containment regime.

SECURE THE FREE FLOW OF OIL
AT REASONABLE PRICES

Modern economies run on fossil fuels, and the United States has sought for decades to secure the free flow of oil into the international market to facilitate the economic vitality of the American and global economies. Unfortunately, both options threaten supply disruptions and spikes in oil prices, but the economic consequences of a nuclear-armed Iran would likely be much worse than those resulting from military action.

Oil market analysts estimate that a US strike on Iran's nuclear facilities would lead to a $4–$15 per barrel increase in prices and, if shipping in the Strait of Hormuz were cut off, a $25 spike. These price increases would remain in effect as long as the conflict persists.

A nuclear-armed Iran would embed a much larger and longer-lasting risk premium because oil traders would have to factor the risk of nuclear war into any future Middle Eastern crisis. Experts estimate that a nuclear-armed Iran would embed a permanent risk premium of at least $20–$30 per barrel and spikes of $30–$100 per barrel in the event of actual conflict. It is likely, therefore, that a military strike would better protect this interest.

MAINTAIN FREEDOM OF ACTION

It has long been a goal of US policy to maintain military freedom of action. Freedom of action increases America's influence around the world and provides viable options for addressing threats to the national security of the country. A nuclear-armed Iran would constrain American freedom of action as Tehran could attempt to deter any major US military initiative with the threat of nuclear war. In addition, we could lose access, basing, and overflight rights if some of our partners in the region accommodated the demands of a more powerful Tehran. A strike on Iran's nuclear facilities, on the other hand, would not in any way constrain America's future freedom of action. A strike, therefore, would be the superior option for protecting this national interest.

PROMOTE REGIME CHANGE IN IRAN

The Islamic Republic is no friend of the United States, and Washington would prefer that a new government come to power in Tehran sooner rather than later. A military strike on Iran would create a rally-around-the-flag effect that would strengthen the current regime in the short term, but this effect would wear off and potentially even reverse over time as the strike created an opening for regime opponents to criticize the regime for mismanaging the crisis. Acquiescing to a nuclear-armed Iran would give the country the ultimate security guarantee and a source of domestic legitimacy that could lock it in place for years to come. It is difficult to say which option would do more to complicate our hope of regime change, but my best estimate is that acquiescing to a nuclear-armed Iran, due to the more permanent nature of its effects, would be worse. In the end, whether the regime hangs on to power will likely be determined by other factors.

BURNISH AMERICA'S REPUTATION

While not generally stated as a key goal of American foreign policy, the United States would prefer to be liked and respected by leaders and populations around the world. Joseph Nye, a professor at Harvard University, argues that being liked gives a country "soft power" with which it can influence other nations without using brute force. In addition, the United States (and other nations) would like to have a reputation for credibility. If leaders around the world believe the American president when he makes threats or promises, it is more likely that we can achieve our goals through our stated declaratory policy and not have to resort to bribes or punishments.

A US strike on Iran would likely lead to anti-American sentiment in some corners of the world as Washington will be accused of launching an imperialist war in contravention of international law. America's enemies, like Russia and China, would use this as an opportunity to drag our name through the mud. Terrorist organizations might use this, America's fourth attack on a Muslim country in a decade and a half, as a rallying cry for recruitment.

On the other hand, by acquiescing to a nuclear-armed Iran, the United States would be going back on decades of promises to prevent Iran from acquiring nuclear weapons, undermining its credibility and making it more difficult to coerce and cajole in the future. This would greatly worry our allies as they wonder whether we will similarly follow through on our promises to provide for their security when the chips are down. In addition, as part of a deterrence and containment regime, the United States would need to take on an even greater political and military role in the Middle East and would likely station more US forces on the territory of more Muslim states. This could also provoke charges of imperialism, generate anti-American sentiment, and contribute to terrorist recruitment.

It is difficult to predict which outcome would be worse for America's reputation, but, like many of the national security interests reviewed here, it seems plausible that America's reputation would suffer the most in the short term from military action, but over the longer term, its reputation would be most damaged from acquiescing to, and then attempting to deter and contain, a nuclear Iran.

A NOTE TO MY CRITICS

I will end this discussion of how these options serve US interests with a rejoinder to my critics. Some of the critics of my FA article have argued that there is a tension in my analysis.[3] They argue that the Iran in the deter-and-contain scenario seems to be very different from the Iran in the military strike scenario. They claim that I seem to assume that, after a US strike, Tehran's leaders would be rational and cautious because I argue that they would restrain any military retaliation and that they would be unwilling to provoke a major war with the United States. In sharp contrast, however, they argue that I must assume that Tehran's leaders are wildly irrational in the deter-and-contain scenario because I argue that they would throw their weight around, provoke crises, and might even cause a nuclear war. This is a clever attempt at a critique, but it is profoundly misguided.

The Iran I discuss in both scenarios is one and the same. It is a "rational," pragmatic state seeking to advance its national security goals, which include survival and becoming the most dominant state in the region. There is one minor difference that is relevant to Iran's strategic behavior in these two scenarios, however, that perhaps my critics have overlooked: in one of these scenarios Iran has nuclear weapons!

At present, Iran restrains itself because it fears major military retaliation. Therefore, as I argue in chapter 6, if we conduct a limited strike on Iran's nuclear facilities, Iran's supreme leader will have strong incentives not to escalate the conflict to avoid a major war with the world's only superpower. If Iran acquires nuclear weapons, however, it will be emboldened because, as I argue in chapter 5, it can deter a direct American attack with the threat of nuclear war and will no longer need to fear large-scale American military retaliation. This will give it the freedom to throw its weight around more in the region. And Iran, like all nuclear states, will undoubtedly play games of nuclear brinkmanship that greatly increase the risk of accidental and inadvertent nuclear war—a risk that doesn't exist at all at present. So, in sum, Iran will be more aggressive with nuclear weapons, not because I'm shading the analysis one way or the other, but because, quite simply, Iran will be more aggressive with nuclear weapons. This is an analytic judgment that some of these very same critics make in their own writings.[4] In making this criticism of my work, therefore, it is my critics, not me, who lack consistency.

CONCLUSION

The systematic comparison of the two options presented in this chapter reveals that several very important objectives—protecting the homeland, preventing nuclear proliferation, maintaining freedom of action, and securing the free flow of oil—are clearly better served by a military strike. Other objectives, such as promoting regional stability, combating terrorism, and containing military expenditures, are better served through acquiescing to a nuclear-armed Iran in the short term. Given enough time, however, the direction of these effects would be likely to shift in favor of

a strike. Still other effects, such as promoting democracy in Iran and bur-
nishing America's reputation, are pure toss-ups. There are no national
security interests that are clearly better protected in both the short and
long term by acquiescing to a nuclear Iran. There is very little doubt in
my mind, therefore, that a military strike better serves America's national
interest than does deterrence and containment.

One comes to the same conclusion when one attempts to break down
these threats even further according to their probability, duration, and
gravity. Beginning with probability, it is clear that many of the costs of
deterrence and containment, such as nuclear proliferation or nuclear war,
are unlikely on any given day and that the costs associated with a strike,
like some form of Iranian military retaliation, are almost certain. Yet the
low probabilities of the threats of a nuclear Iran aggregate over time and,
given enough time, their probabilities greatly increase. They are also longer
lasting in that we will be living with these threats for decades, if not longer,
while most of the effects of a strike will be absorbed within weeks of an
attack. Finally, the threats posed by a nuclear-armed Iran are much graver
than the threats posed by a strike. We can easily absorb the worst that Iran
can throw at us in the event of a military strike, such as ballistic missile attacks against US bases and forces in the region. We cannot simply absorb
many of the threats posed by a nuclear Iran, however, such as nuclear war
against the American homeland; they are truly unacceptable. This analysis,
therefore, leads me to the same conclusion as above, namely, that when
compared to attempting to contain a nuclear-armed Iran, a military strike
on Iran's nuclear facilities is in the best interest of the United States.

Nevertheless, the sequencing of the costs and benefits presents a problem to American foreign policymakers because the costs of a strike, such

as Iranian military retaliation, will be incurred immediately and with near certainty. In ordering a strike, therefore, a US president would be voluntarily taking action that will increase threats to our national security in the short run in order to prevent even greater threats to the country in the future. This would be a noble act, yet the four-year election cycle of American politics, and perhaps human nature, would encourage a weak leader to forgo the tough decision to strike, acquiesce to a nuclear-armed Iran, and push the costs of a nuclear-armed Iran on to his successors—even if a strike is in the long-run best interest of the nation. This is something that worries me. While a strike is the better option in my view, I fear that our political system might incentivize a leader to go weak in the knees.

Still, no president would want to go down in history as the leader who let Iran acquire nuclear weapons on his watch, especially if nuclear weapons in Iran one day result in a devastating nuclear war. And President Obama appears to comprehend full well the relative merits of these options. He has said himself that a nuclear-armed Iran is unacceptable and that he is willing to use force if necessary to stop it. In other words, he also assesses that a strike is better than simply acquiescing to Iranian nuclear weapons.

Still, this chapter is titled "Which Is Worse?" because neither of these options is attractive. Sooner or later, the Iranian nuclear challenge will be resolved some way or another. And the way in which the crisis ends will have important implications for the future of world order. What will the resolution of the Iranian nuclear challenge mean for the future of nuclear proliferation, Middle Eastern politics, and America's place in the world? We will consider these questions in the next, concluding, chapter.

CHAPTER EIGHT

CONCLUSION

IT WAS APRIL 2011 AND I WAS AT A LARGE OVAL TA-
ble surrounded by senior defense officials—top political appointees and
military brass—in a secure briefing room in the Pentagon. I was the most
junior person in the room, but I was given ninety minutes to explain
America's strategic options for Iran's nuclear program. The schedules of
senior Pentagon officials are divided into thirty- and sometimes fifteen-
minute increments. Ninety minutes is an eternity reserved for the most
important briefings on the most pressing subjects.

Pentagon officials like to receive information in PowerPoint slides, and
the final slide in my presentation was a color-coded chart showing how
the two outcomes under consideration (a nuclear-armed Iran or a military strike on Iran) would affect about a dozen key US national security
interests. National objectives that improved in a particular scenario were
colored green, those that were neutral were coded yellow, and increased
threats to the national security of the country were depicted in various
shades of orange and red, depending on their severity.

Two patterns stood out to everyone in the room. First, there was very little green and a lot of orange and red on the slides; these were not good options. Second, the "nuclear-armed Iran" side of the chart was noticeably darker than the "military strike" side of the chart, meaning that the risks of a strike paled (quite literally in this case) in comparison to the threats posed by a nuclear-armed Iran. Indeed, at the end of the briefing, the senior-most official in the room looked me straight in the eye and said, "Well, if you are right, this is a no-brainer."

Reasonable people can disagree, but in my view the senior DoD official quoted above is correct: this is a no-brainer. We should seek to resolve the Iranian nuclear crisis through diplomacy if at all possible. But, if that effort does not succeed, the United States must take military action. We should work in advance to form an international coalition, conduct a limited strike on Iran's key nuclear facilities, pull back and absorb an inevitable round of Iranian retaliation, and seek to de-escalate the crisis. This is not a good option. But when compared to the dangers of living with a nuclear-armed Iran for decades to come, it is the least bad option.

This is the central conclusion that this book comes to after systematically reviewing the background of the Iranian nuclear threat and our options for dealing with it. Chapter 1 reviewed the history of Iran's nuclear program from its beginnings under Atoms for Peace in the 1950s to the initiation of the current crisis in 2002. Chapter 2 argued that Iran is pursuing nuclear weapons, not nuclear energy, and that its program has advanced dangerously close to a nuclear weapons breakout capability. We probably have months, not years, to resolve the Iranian nuclear crisis.

Chapter 3 showed that there are no black swans that are likely to save us from the Iranian nuclear threat. We cannot sabotage, assassinate, regime-change, or cyberattack our way out of this problem. We also saw that allowing Iran to obtain a latent nuclear capability, aka the Japan Model, is unacceptable and would be tantamount to giving up and acquiescing to nuclear weapons in Iran.

In chapter 4, we learned that diplomacy offers the most desirable solution to the crisis and outlined the contours of possible negotiated settlements. Unfortunately, the chapter also explained why it is possible, if not likely, that we will fail to get a satisfactory diplomatic resolution to this crisis.

If diplomacy does not work, this means that at some point soon, it is possible that an American president will be forced to choose between letting Iran have the bomb or bombing Iran. Chapter 5 showed that simply acquiescing to a nuclear-armed Iran would be a terrible option. It would mean a nuclear arms race in the Middle East and around the world, an emboldened and more aggressive Iran, an even more crisis-prone Middle East, and an increased risk of nuclear war that could even result in a nuclear attack on the American homeland. For these reasons and others, many thoughtful observers, including President Barack Obama, declare that this outcome is simply unacceptable.

We might be left then with only one option: the military option, the subject of chapter 6. This chapter made clear that a US strike on Iran's nuclear facilities is not an attractive option either. Such a conflict would result in Iranian military retaliation, spikes in oil prices, and anti-American sentiment. Yet a military strike would also have benefits. It could destroy Iran's nuclear facilities, set back Iran's nuclear program, and create a significant possibility that Iran would never acquire nuclear weapons. If diplomacy fails, this is our only hope for keeping Tehran from the bomb. This option undoubtedly carries risks, but as I demonstrated in chapter 7 and in my DoD PowerPoint presentation three years ago, these risks are less severe than the risks of a nuclear-armed Iran.

Years from now, we can, with the benefit of hindsight, look back and know the denouement of the Iranian nuclear crisis, but for now much remains a mystery. Will we prevent Iran from going nuclear short of the use of force? Are our two countries on a collision course toward war? Must we prepare ourselves to live the rest of our lives under the fear of Iran's nuclear weapons? These are the most important unanswered and, at least at the present, unanswerable questions that remain.

Regardless of how the Iranian challenge plays out, however, its resolution will have profound implications for the future of international order. The ripple effects will be felt everywhere, but they will be most notable in the realm of nuclear nonproliferation, the Middle East, and America's place in the world.

Nuclear proliferation poses one of the greatest threats to world peace, and it is why I have decided to spend the first decade of my academic career studying it. I feel that many people, experts and the general public alike, believe that nuclear weapons are old news. They assume that nuclear war was a threat during the Cold War, but that those days are long gone. Or they assume that by fearing nuclear war with the Soviet Union, we worked ourselves up over nothing; after all, we made it through a half century of intense political competition and never had a nuclear exchange. In hindsight, therefore, they might judge that humanity learned its lesson at Hiroshima and Nagasaki: nuclear war is terrible, no sane leader would ever authorize one, and we don't really have much to worry about. Moreover, they might claim that in today's advanced, globalized, and interdependent economy, war itself is becoming obsolete, and analysts such as myself who worry about major threats to the national security of our country are dinosaurs stuck in a bygone era.

I truly wish these people were right. Unfortunately, this line of thinking is not only incorrect but profoundly dangerous because it could lull us into a false sense of security and prevent us from remaining appropriately vigilant to future security challenges.

In February 2006, I was in Singapore for a conference on international politics with journalists, government officials, and academics from Europe, North America, and Asia. The conference centered around a series of scenarios of possible future states of the world meant to stress and strain our assumptions and lead to new insights about the future of world order that we could take back with us to our day jobs. One of the scenarios dealt with a future global financial crisis. The session was a complete bust. Many participants refused to even engage in the exercise because they argued that the scenario was so preposterous as to be a complete waste of time. They were willing to stretch their minds, but this was going too far. They argued that it was unthinkable that there could be another global financial crisis. They averred that humanity had learned its lesson during the Great Depression and that we had designed enlightened policies to prevent another financial collapse. Moreover, they claimed, the global economy was so much more interconnected and robust than in previous eras and Great-Depression–like busts were a thing of the past. In the end, we didn't even finish the session because the well-educated and informed group of participants agreed that a worldwide financial crisis simply could not happen.

And then it did. The Great Recession hit the very next year. It was the world's worst financial crisis since the Great Depression. The signs that it was coming were already apparent in 2006, but none of the assembled experts in Singapore (except perhaps for the scenario's designer) could foresee this outcome. Moreover, not only did they not predict this outcome, they carefully considered it and then rejected it out of hand as completely beyond the realm of plausibility.

I fear that we (the expert community and the general public alike) are in danger of being similarly Pollyannaish about nuclear war. Are we really willing to bet the existence of our country on the argument that something has not happened in seventy years and that it will therefore never happen again? We were dead wrong about the strength of the global economy only a few years back. Applying this thinking to nuclear war would be equally naïve but much more dangerous.

In short, I fear that allowing Iran to have nuclear weapons will increase the risk that nuclear weapons will be used again someday soon, perhaps against the United States. We can take action now to prevent Iran from acquiring nuclear weapons or we can risk looking back on this moment after a future nuclear catastrophe and wonder how we could have been so complacent.

What does the resolution of the Iranian nuclear crisis mean for the future of the Middle East? Since the collapse of the Ottoman Empire in World War I, the region has lacked a dominant power that is able to impose a stable political order. A succession of outside powers, first the United Kingdom and then the United States, have attempted to exert influence over the area, but the region nevertheless continues to produce more than its fair share of dysfunctional and autocratic governments, WMD proliferation, and international terrorism. As a result, many Americans are fed up with Uncle Sam's involvement in the Middle East's problems. What's more, China is rising and, according to some predictions, it could over-take the United States as the most dominant power in the international system. The relationship between these two great powers is therefore likely to be the defining feature of the twenty-first century. For this reason, US strategists are arguing that Washington needs to "pivot" and "rebalance" its strategic attention away from the Middle East and toward East Asia to ensure that we get this relationship right. Taken to its extreme, some ad-vocates of the rebalance contend that Washington should turn its back on the Middle East and the Iranian nuclear threat. Such inaction, however, would be inadvisable not only for US national security broadly but also for America's aspirations in the Asia-Pacific region. Whether we like it or not, the Middle East will continue to throw up nasty security challenges, including international terrorism and WMD proliferation, that will re-quire sustained American attention. The idea that we can completely and quickly pivot from the Middle East to East Asia is unrealistic. Richard Haass, my former boss at and the president of the Council on Foreign Relations, paraphrased Michael Corleone's desire to escape the life of a Mafioso in the classic film *The Godfather III* to describe America's likely future role in the Middle East: "Every time I try to get out, they keep pull-ing me right back in."[1]

Indeed, there are few security threats that could do more than a nuclear-armed Iran to distract us from the "rebalance" to Asia because deterring and containing a nuclear Iran would force us to increase and maintain our political and military commitments to the Middle East for decades to come. If we truly wish to pivot to Asia (and I fully agree that the future of great power politics is likely to take place in East Asia, not the Middle East), then preventing a nuclear Iran becomes even more essential.

This discussion raises important questions about America's role in the world. Many readers might be asking, why are Iranian nuclear facilities America's problem? Or why does the United States have to be the world's policeman?

The answer is that since 1945, the United States has been the most dominant state on Earth. We have had the largest and most dynamic economy, a military that is second to none, and a vibrant and free society that serves as a model for the rest of the world. And with great power comes great responsibility. As former secretary of state Madeleine Albright proclaimed, the United States is the world's "indispensable nation."

Before the era of American dominance, competing European powers of roughly equal size dragged the world into two world wars and contributed to an economic depression. Since 1945, American military power has overawed potential competitors and provided the world with security, stability, order, and economic prosperity. America provides public goods to the world not only out of a sense of responsibility, but because the United States itself benefits from this liberal world order. While critics sometimes decry America's strong foreign policy, the alternative—a vacuum of power, and a return to the warlike international system of the nineteenth and early twentieth centuries—would be much worse.

A nuclear-armed Iran would threaten the security and economic prosperity of the Middle East and, in turn, of the entire world, weakening this US-led international order. We are the only country capable of stopping Iran from building nuclear weapons. If we do not take care of this problem, no one else will. In broader perspective, therefore, a US policy to prevent Iran from building nuclear weapons is consistent with the broad thrust of American foreign policy over the past century, dealing with tough international security challenges to the benefit of much of humanity.

Americans should be proud that our nation has contributed to making the world a safer and more prosperous place. But the test of a great nation is whether it can step up and do the right thing even when doing the right thing is difficult.

Now is not the time to shirk our responsibility.

NOTES

ACKNOWLEDGMENTS

1. Matthew Kroenig, "Time To Attack Iran: Why a Strike Is the Least Bad Option," *Foreign Affairs* 91, no. 1: January/February 2012, 76–86.

2. Matthew Kroenig, "Now for the Hard Part," *Foreign Policy online,* November 24, 2013, accessed at http://www.foreignpolicy.com/articles/2013/11/24/now_for_the_hard_part#sthash.NrkCWF2q.dpbs; Jamie Fly and Matthew Kroenig, "On Iran, It's Time for Obama to Set Clear Lines for Military Action," *Washington Post,* May 18, 2012; Matthew Kroenig and Robert McNally, "Iranian Nukes and Global Oil," *The American Interest,* March/April 2013; Matthew Kroenig, "Iran Diplomatic Window Rapidly Closing," *USA Today,* June 17, 2013.

INTRODUCTION

1. James R. Clapper, "Worldwide Threat Assessment of the US Intelligence Community," *Statement for the Record,* Senate Select Committee on Intelligence, January 29, 2014, accessed at http://www.intelligence.senate.gov/140129/clapper.pdf.

CHAPTER 1: FROM ATOMS FOR PEACE TO ATOMS FOR WAR

1. William Arkin, "The Pentagon Preps for Iran," *Washington Post,* April 19, 2006; Paul Rogers, "America's Iran War Plan Revealed," *Real Clear World,* July 2, 2012; Rowan Scarborough, "Iran Is Top 'Contingency' in Whittled U.S. War Plans," *Washington Times,* May 1, 2012.

2. David Bodansky, *Nuclear Energy: Principles, Practices, and Prospects,* 2nd ed. (New York: Springer, 2004), 32.

3. Matthew Kroenig, *Exporting the Bomb: Technology Transfer and the Spread of Nuclear Weapons* (Ithaca, NY: Cornell University Press, 2010).

4. Robin Wright, *Dreams and Shadows: The Future of the Middle East* (New York: Penguin Press, 2008), 438.

5. Ruhollah Musavi Khomeini, "Letter from Ayatollah Khomeini Regarding Weapons during the Iran-Iraq War, 1988." Council on Foreign Relations, Primary Sources, accessed at http://

www.cfr.org/iran/letter-ayatollah-khomeini-regarding-weapons-during-iran-iraq-war/p11745.

6. Joby Warrick, "IAEA Says Foreign Expertise Has Brought Iran to Threshold of Nuclear Capability," *Washington Post,* November 6, 2011; International Atomic Energy Agency, "Implementation of the NPT Safeguards Agreement and Relevant Provisions of Security Council Resolutions in the Islamic Republic of Iran," Report by the Director General, November 8, 2011; Elaine Sciolino, "Nuclear Aid by Russian to Iranians Suspected," *New York Times,* October 9, 2008.

7. Kroenig, *Exporting the Bomb.*

8. Ibid.

9. Matthew Kroenig, "The Enemy of My Enemy Is My Customer: Why States Provide Sensitive Nuclear Assistance" (PhD diss., University of California, Berkeley, 2007).

CHAPTER 2: WHAT DOES IRAN WANT?

1. Jeffrey Richelson, *Spying on the Bomb: American Nuclear Intelligence from Nazi Germany to Iran and North Korea* (New York: Norton, 2006).

2. "IAEA Reports," *IAEA and Iran.* International Atomic Energy Agency, n.d., accessed at http://www.iaea.org/newscenter/focus/iaeairan/iaea_reports.shtml.

3. "IAEA Safeguards Glossary 2001 Edition," *International Nuclear Verification Series* (IAEA: Austria, June 2002), 23.

4. I will not describe the uranium enrichment process in detail in this book, but readers who are interested can find many good primers online.

5. David Albright, "The Rocky Path to a Long-Term Settlement with Iran," *The Washington Post,* November 25, 2013.

6. Ibid.

7. International Atomic Energy Agency, "Implementation of the NPT Safeguards Agreement and relevant provisions of Security Council resolutions in the Islamic Republic of Iran," Report by the Director General, November 8, 2011.

8. Ibid., 7-11; William Broad, "Inspectors Pierce Iran's Cloak of Nuclear Secrecy," *New York Times,* May 30, 2011; David Albright, Christina Walrond, William Witt, and Houston Wood, "Comments on Wall Street Journal Editorial and Our Breakout Estimates," *ISIS Report,* Institute for Science and International Security, October 30, 2012.

9. William C. Witt, Christina Walrond, David Albright, and Houston Wood, "Iran's Evolving Breakout Potential," *ISIS Report,* Institute for Science and International Security, October 20, 2012, 19-20.

10. US Department of Defense, "Annual Report on Military Power of Iran," US Department of Defense report to Congress, April 2012, accessed at http://www.fas.org/man/eprint/dod-iran.pdf; Anthony H. Cordesman, Alexander Wilner, "Iran and the Gulf Military Balance–I: The Conventional and Asymmetric Dimensions (4th Working Draft)," Center for Strategic and International Studies, June 28, 2012.

11. US Department of Defense, "Annual Report on Military Power of Iran," 3.

12. Ibid.

13. Ibid.
14. William C. Witt, Christina Walrond, David Albright, and Houston Wood, "Iran's Evolving Breakout Potential," *ISIS Report*, Institute for Science and International Affairs, October 20, 2012; "Israel Says Iran Seeking U.S.-Range Missile," Reuters, February 2, 2012; "Pentagon Report: Iran Could Test an Intercontinental Ballistic Missile by 2015," *Defense Update*, April 25, 2013, accessed at http://defense-update.com/20130425_iran_nuclear_icbm.html.
15. Colin Kahl, "Not Time to Attack Iran: Why War Should Be a Last Resort," *Foreign Affairs* 91, no. 2 (March/April 2012).
16. David Albright, Mark Dubowitz, and Orde Kittrie, "Stopping an Undetectable Iranian Bomb," *Wall Street Journal*, March 26, 2013.
17. US Department of Defense, "Annual Report on Military Power of Iran," 2.
18. Scott Sagan, "Why Do States Build Nuclear Weapons? Three Models in Search of a Bomb," *International Security* 21, no. 3 (1996–1997).
19. International Atomic Energy Agency, "Implementation of the NPT Safeguards Agreement," November 8, 2011.
20. National Intelligence Council, "Iran: Nuclear Intentions and Capabilities," *National Intelligence Estimate*, November 2007, accessed via the *New York Times*, http://graphics8.nytimes.com/packages/pdf/international/20071203_release.pdf
21. David Albright and Paul Brannan, "The New National Intelligence Estimate on Iran: A Step in the Right Direction," *ISIS Report*, Institute for Science and International Security, March 22, 2012, 1.
22. George Jahn, "AP Interview: UN Nuke Chief Concerned about IRAN," Associated Press, April 2, 2013.
23. James Risen and Mark Mazetti, "U.S. Agencies See No Move by Iran to Build a Bomb," *New York Times*, February 24, 2012.
24. David Martosko, "Iran Has Not Issued the 'Fatwa' against Nukes That Obama Used to Justify Negotiations, Claim Experts," *Daily Mail*, September 30, 2013, available at: http://www.dailymail.co.uk/news/article-2439490/Middle-East-research-group-Irans-fatwa-nukes-cited-Obama-twice-week-doesnt-exist.html.
25. Emmanuelle Ottolenghi, "Iran and the International Community: Policy Considerations for 2013," Henry Jackson Society and Foundation for Defense of Democracies, January 30, 2013, accessed at http://www.defenddemocracy.org/events/iran-and-the-international-community-policy-considerations-for-2013/.

CHAPTER 3: THE NONSTARTERS

1. "Iranian Nuclear Scientist Shot Dead in Tehran," Al Jazeera English, July 24, 2011, accessed at http://www.aljazeera.com/news/middleeast/2011/07/201172318727723775.html; "Missing or Killed Iran Scientists," Al Jazeera English, November 29, 2010, accessed at http://www.aljazeera.com/news/middleeast/2010/11/2010112911470378903.html.
2. Sadeq Saba, "Israel and US behind Tehran blast—Iranian state media," BBC News, January 12, 2010, accessed at http://news.bbc.co.uk/2/hi/8453401.stm; Karl Vick and Aaron J. Klein,

"Who Assassinated an Iranian Nuclear Scientist? Israel Isn't Telling," *Time,* January 13, 2012, accessed at http://www.time.com/time/world/article/0,8599,2104372,00.html.

3. Roger Howard, *Operation Damocles: Israel's Secret War against Hitler's Scientists, 1951–1967* (New York: Pegasus, 2013); Ian Black and Benny Morris, *Israel's Secret Wars: A History of Israel's Intelligence Services* (New York: Grove Weidenfeld, 1991).

4. William Tobey, "Nuclear Scientists as Assassination Targets," *Bulletin of the Atomic Scientists* 68 (2012): 61–69.

5. Jeremy Bernstein, "'A Solution for the US–Iran Nuclear Standoff': An Exchange," Letter to Editors, *The New York Review of Books,* April 3, 2008, accessed at http://www .nybooks.com/articles/archives/2008/apr/03/a-solution-for-the-usiran-nuclear-standoff -an-exch/?pagination=false; Interview with Gholamreza Aghazadeh, then head of Atomic Energy Organization of Iran, "Iran's Nuclear Chief Explains Nuclear Fuel Cycle, Comments on U.S. Concerns," *Network 2,* April 12, 2006, translated from Persian.

6. David E. Sanger, *Confront and Conceal: Obama's Secret Wars and Surprising Use of American Power* (New York: Crown, 2012), 189.

7. Gary Samore speaking at the Washington Forum of the Foundation for Defense of Democracies in Washington DC, December 10, 2010, reported by CSPAN and contained in PBS program *Need to Know* ("Cracking the Code: Defending against the Superweapons of the 21st Century Cyberwar," (4 minutes into piece)). Accessed at http://www.pbs.org/wnet /need-to-know/security/video-cracking-the-code-defending-against-the-superweapons -of-the-21st-century-cyberwar/9456/

8. David E. Sanger, "Obama Order Sped Up Wave of Cyberattacks against Iran," *New York Times,* June 1, 2012; Sanger, *Confront and Conceal,* 203–208; Peter Beaumont and Nick Hopkins, "US Was 'Key Player in Cyber-attacks on Iran's Nuclear Programme'," *The Guardian,* June 1, 2012.

9. Vincent Manzo, "Stuxnet and the Dangers of Cyberwar," *National Interest,* January 29, 2013, accessed at http://nationalinterest.org/commentary/stuxnet-the-dangers-cyberwar-8030.

10. Sara Sorcher, "Senators Blast Publicity of Cyberattack on Iran," *National Journal,* June 6, 2012.

11. Sanger, *Confront and Conceal,* 197.

12. Richard A. Clarke and Robert K. Knake, *Cyber War: The Next Threat to National Security and What To Do about It* (New York: Ecco, 2010).

13. "Stuxnet 'Hit' Iran Nuclear Plans," BBC News, November 22, 2010, accessed at http://www .bbc.co.uk/news/technology-11809827; Ivanka Barzashka, "Are Cyber-Weapons Effective?" *The RUSI Journal* 158, no. 2 (2013): 48–56; "Stuxnet Worm Aided Iranian Nuclear Program, Researcher Says," *Haaretz,* May 16, 2013, accessed at http://www.haaretz.com /news/diplomacy-defense/stuxnet-worm-aided-iranian-nuclear-program-researcher-says -1.524367.

14. Jacques E. C. Hymans, "Veto Players, Nuclear Energy, and Nonproliferation: Domestic Institutional Barriers to a Japanese Bomb," *International Security* 36, no. 2 (Fall 2011): 154–189.

15. "Diplomacy, Sanctions and a Nearing Red Line with Iran," *Talk of the Nation.* National Public Radio, April 29, 2013, accessed at http://www.npr.org/2013/04/29/179851900/dip lomacy-sanctions-and-a-nearing-red-line-with-iran.

CHAPTER 4: A DEAL WITH THE DEVIL

1. Lydia Saad, "Americans Want a Restrained Iran Strategy," Gallup Polling, November 6, 2007, accessed at http://www.gallup.com/poll/116236/iran.aspx; see also Scott Clement, "Iranian Threat: Public Prefers Sanctions over Bombs," *Washington Post,* March 14, 2012, accessed at http://www.washingtonpost.com/blogs/behind-the-numbers/post/iranian-threat-public -prefers-sanctions-over-bombs/2012/03/07/gIQAmnrXCS_blog.html and "Washington Post-ABC News Poll, March 7–10, 2012, http://www.washingtonpost.com/wp-srv/politics /polls/postabcpoll_031012.html.

2. Julian Borger, "Barack Obama: Administration Willing to Talk to Iran 'without Preconditions'," *The Guardian,* January 21, 2009.

3. Robert H. Mnookin, *Bargaining with the Devil: When to Negotiate, When to Fight* (New York: Simon & Schuster, 2010), 267.

4. Joseph Cirincione, "Lessons of the Iraq War: How the Bush Doctrine Made Proliferation Worse," available at http://www2.gsu.edu/~poljsd/4460/Balance%20Sheet%20Cirincione .pdf.

5. "Full Text of Netanyahu's 2013 Speech to the UN General Assembly: Prime Minister Says the World Must Not Be Fooled by the New Face of the Iranian Regime," *Times of Israel,* October 1, 2013, accessed at http://www.timesofisrael.com/full-text-netanyahus-2013-speech -to-the-un-general-assembly/.

6. "Prohibiting Certain Transactions with Respect to Iran," Executive Order 13059, *Federal Register* 62, no. 162 (August 19, 1997): 44531–4453, accessed at http://www.gpo.gov/fdsys /pkg/FR-1997-08-21/pdf/97-22482.pdf.

7. International Atomic Energy Agency, "Implementation of the NPT Safeguards Agreement and Relevant Provisions of Security Council Resolutions in the Islamic Republic of Iran," Report by the Director General, November 8, 2011.

8. International Atomic Energy Agency, "Implementation of the NPT Safeguards Agreement and Relevant Provisions of Security Council Resolutions in the Islamic Republic of Iran," Report by the Director General, November 16, 2012, 10; "Iran Laying Asphalt at the Suspect Parchin Site," *ISIS Imagery Brief,* Institute for Science and International Security, May 22, 2013; David Albright and Paul Brannan, "Satellite Image of Building Containing High Explosive Test Chamber at Parchin Site in Iran," *ISIS Report,* Institute for Science and International Security, March 13, 2012.

9. Rick Gladstone, "Group Sees Signs of Iran Cleanup at Nuclear Site," *New York Times,* May 9, 2012, accessed at http://www.nytimes.com/2012/05/10/world/middleeast/imagery-said-to -suggest-cleanup-at-iran-nuclear-site.html?_r=0.

10. International Atomic Energy Agency, Resolution, "Implementation of the NPT Safeguards Agreement in the Islamic Republic of Iran," February 4, 2006.

11. Lionel Beehner, "Russia's Nuclear Deal with Iran," *Council on Foreign Relations,* February 28, 2006, accessed at http://www.cfr.org/iran/russias-nuclear-deal-iran/p9985; Karl Vick, "Iran Rejects Russia's Proposal on Uranium," *Washington Post,* March 13, 2006.

12. United Nations Security Council, 5500th Meeting, "Resolution 1696 (2006)," (S/RES/1696), July 31, 2006, accessed at http://www.iaea.org/newscenter/focus/iaeairan/unsc_res1696

-2006.pdf; Amy Reed, "UN Resolution 1696 Moots Iranian Legal Claims," *Proliferation Analysis*, Carnegie Endowment for International Peace, August 21, 2006, accessed at http://carnegieendowment.org/2006/08/21/un-resolution-1696-moots-iranian-legal-claims/2xwe.

13. Peter Crall, "Proposals Offered on Iranian Nuclear Program," *Arms Control Today*, Arms Control Association, June 2008, accessed at http://www.armscontrol.org/node/2931.

14. Peter Crall, "Iran Presented with Revamped Incentives," *Arms Control Today*, Arms Control Association, July/August 2008, accessed at http://www.armscontrol.org/act/2008_07-08/IranIncentives.

15. "Package of Proposals by the Islamic Republic of Iran for Comprehensive and Constructive Negotiations," Islamic Republic of Iran, primary source document accessed at http://www.armscontrol.org/system/files/Iran2009Proposal.pdf; "History of Official Proposals on the Iranian Nuclear Issue," Arms Control Association, January 2013, accessed at http://www.armscontrol.org/factsheets/Iran_Nuclear_Proposals.

16. Trita Parsi, *A Single Roll of the Dice: Obama's Diplomacy with Iran* (New Haven, CT: Yale University Press, 2012), 203–209.

17. United Nations Security Council, 6335th Meeting, "Resolution 1929 (2010)," (S/RES/1929), June 9, 2010, accessed at http://www.iaea.org/newscenter/focus/iaeairan/unsc_res1929-2010.pdf; Colum Lynch and Glenn Kessler, "U.N. Imposes Another Round of Sanctions on Iran," *Washington Post*, June 10, 2010.

18. David Bird, "Sanctions Cut Iran's Oil Exports to 26-Year Low," *Wall Street Journal*, April 29, 2013; "Recent Trends in Oil Supply from Iran," The Institute for Energy Economics, Japan, June 2012, accessed at http://eneken.ieej.or.jp/data/4363.pdf.

19. Carol E. Lee and Keith Johnson, "U.S. Targets Iran's Central Bank," *Wall Street Journal*, January 4, 2012.

20. Rick Gladstone and Stephen Castle, "Global Network Expels as Many as 30 of Iran's Banks in Move to Isolate Its Economy," *New York Times*, March 15, 2012.

21. Jonathan Schanzer, "How Iran Benefits from an Illicit Gold Trade with Turkey," *The Atlantic*, May 17, 2013, accessed at http://www.theatlantic.com/international/archive/2013/05/how-iran-benefits-from-an-illicit-gold-trade-with-turkey/275948/.

22. Mark Dubowitz and Jonathan Schanzer, "Targeting Tehran's Euros," *Wall Street Journal*, February 13, 2013.

23. Matthew Kroenig and Robert McNally, "Iranian Nukes and Global Oil," *The American Interest*, March/April 2013.

24. Ibid.

25. Ladane Nasseri, "Iran's Rial Gains 10% as Government Boosts Dollar Supply," Bloomberg, March 5, 2013.

26. "Iran and Sanctions: When Will It Ever End?" *The Economist*, August 18, 2012.

27. David M. Herszenhorn, "Nuclear Talks with Iran End without Accord or Plans for Another Round," *New York Times*, April 6, 2013.

28. Text of the interim deal available at, "The Iran nuclear deal: full text" CNN.com, November 24, 2013, http://www.cnn.com/2013/11/24/world/meast/iran-deal-text/.

29. Matthew Kroenig, "Now for the Hard Part," Foreign Policy, November 24, 2013, accessed at http://www.foreignpolicy.com/articles/2013/11/24/now_for_the_hard_part.

30. David Albright, "The rocky path to a long-term settlement with Iran," *Washington Post,* November 25, 2013, accessed at http://www.washingtonpost.com/opinions/reaching-a-final-iran-deal-will-be-a-tough-road/2013/11/25/dcc2f752-55ef-11e3-ba82-16ed03681809_story.html.

31. Jeffrey Goldberg, "Obama Weapons Expert: No Chance of Success With Iran," Bloomberg View, February 18, 2014, available at http://www.bloombergview.com/articles/2014-02-18/obama-weapons-expert-no-chance-of-success-with-iran.

32. Paul Kerr, "North Korea Admits Secret Nuclear Weapons Program," *Arms Control Today,* Arms Control Association, November 2002, accessed at http://www.armscontrol.org/act/2002_11/nkoreanov02.

33. David Albright and Christina Walrond, "North Korea's Estimated Stocks of Plutonium and Weapon-Grade Uranium," August 16, 2012, Institute for Science and International Security, accessed at http://isis-online.org/uploads/isis-reports/documents/dprk_fissile_material_production_16Aug2012.pdf.

34. Matthew Kroenig, *Exporting the Bomb: Technology Transfer and the Spread of Nuclear Weapons* (Ithaca, NY: Cornell University Press, 2010).

35. Jeffrey Goldberg, "Obama to Iran and Israel: 'As President of the United States, I Don't Bluff,'" *The Atlantic,* March 2, 2012.

36. For example, see Ted Galen Carpenter and Justin Logan, "U.S Must Offer Iran Diplomatic Deal," *Commentary,* Cato Institute, April 21, 2006, accessed at http://www.cato.org/publications/commentary/us-must-offer-iran-diplomatic-deal.

37. Jeffrey Heller, "Netanyahu Draws 'Red Line' on Iran's Nuclear Program," Reuters, September 27, 2012.

38. Jacques Hymans and Matthew Gratias, "Iran and the Nuclear Threshold," *Nonproliferation Review* 20, no. 1 (2013): 13–38.

39. Goldberg, "Obama to Iran and Israel."

40. For more on this issue see the various reports from JINSA's Gemunder Center Iran Task Force, co-chaired by Ambassador Eric Edelman and Ambassador Dennis Ross: "Strategy to Prevent A Nuclear Iran," (September 2013); "Principles for Diplomacy with Iran," October 2013; and "Assessment of Interim Deal with Iran, January 2014, available at http://www.jinsa.org/gemunder-center-iran-task-force.

CHAPTER 5: IRAN WITH THE BOMB

1. SIPRI Yearbook 2013, Stockholm International Peace Research Institute, available at http://www.sipri.org/yearbook/2013/06.

2. U.S. Department of Defense, "Annual Report on Military Power of Iran," U.S. Department of Defense report to Congress, April 2012, accessed at http://www.fas.org/man/eprint/dod-iran.pdf.

3. "Army Fighter Jet Crashes in Southwestern Iran," FARS News Agency, April 21, 2013, accessed at http://english2.farsnews.com/newstext.php?nn=9107162984.

4. James Burgess, "Iran Says Will Build a Nuclear Submarine—But Can It?" CNBC, July 13, 2012, accessed at http://www.cnbc.com/id/48176321; "Iran Submarine Capabilities," *Nuclear Threat Initiative,* August 8, 2012, accessed at http://www.nti.org/analysis/articles/iran-submarine-capabilities/.

5. Morten Bremer Maerli, "Components of Naval Nuclear Fuel Transparency," NATO-EAPC Fellowship Report, June 2001 (revised January 2002), accessed at http://www.nato.int/acad /fellow/99-01/maerli.pdf.

6. U.S. Department of Defense, 2012; Michael Elleman, "Iran's Ballistic Missile Program," in *The Iran Primer: Power, Politics, and U.S. Policy,* ed. Robin B. Wright (Washington, DC: United States Institute of Peace, 2010); "Iran's Ballistic Missile Capabilities: A Net Assessment," *IISS Strategic Dossier,* International Institute for Strategic Studies, May 10, 2010; Louis Hellman, Lesley McNiesh, Alex Rothman, with Laicie Olson and Kingston Reif, "Fact Sheet: Iran's Nuclear and Ballistic Missile Programs," The Center for Arms-Control and Non-Proliferation, January 2013, accessed at http://armscontrolcenter.org/publications /factsheets/fact_sheet_irans_nuclear_and_ballistic_missile_programs/; Greg Bruno, "Iran's Ballistic Missile Program," Council on Foreign Relations, July 23, 2012, accessed at http:// www.cfr.org/iran/irans-ballistic-missile-program/p20425; "Iran to Unveil Indigenous Ballistic, Cruise Missiles," Press TV, April 27, 2013, accessed at http://www.presstv.com /detail/2013/04/27/300497/iran-to-unveil-ballistic-cruise-missiles/.

7. U.S. Department of Defense, 2012.

8. William C. Witt, Christina Walrond, David Albright, and Houston Wood, "Iran's Evolving Breakout Potential," *ISIS Report,* Institute for Science and International Affairs, October 8, 2012; "Israel Says Iran Seeking U.S.-Range Missile," Reuters, February 2, 2012; "Pentagon Report: Iran Could Test an Intercontinental Ballistic Missile by 2015," Defense Update, April 25, 2013, accessed at http://defense-update.com/20130425_iran_nuclear _icbm.html.

9. David Alexander, Christine Kim, and Narae Kim, "North Korea Can Launch Nuclear Missiles, U.S. Spy Agency Says," Reuters, April 11, 2013.

10. Peter Crail and Jessica Lasky-Fink, "Middle Eastern States Seeking Nuclear Power," *Arms Control Today,* Arms Control Association, May 2008; "Emerging Nuclear Energy Countries," World Nuclear Association, May 21, 2013, accessed at http://www.world-nuclear.org/info /Country-Profiles/Others/Emerging-Nuclear-Energy-Countries/#.Ubd3vfbwJrU.

11. "Report: Saudi Arabia to Buy Nukes if Iran Tests A-bomb," NBC News, February 10, 2012, accessed at http://worldnews.nbcnews.com/_news/2012/02/10/10369793-report-saudi -arabia-to-buy-nukes-if-iran-tests-a-bomb?lite; David Blair, "Israel Says Iran Has Pulled Back from the Brink of Nuclear Weapon—for Now," *The Telegraph,* October 30, 2012; "Saudi Arabia May Need Nuclear Weapons to Fend off Threat from IRAN and Israel, Says Former Intelligence Chief," *Daily Mail,* December 6, 2011, accessed at http://www.dailymail .co.uk/news/article-2070704/Saudi-Arabia-need-nuclear-weapons-fend-threat-Iran-Israel -says-prince.html; Amos Yadlin and Avner Golov, "A Nuclear Iran: The Spur to a Regional Arms Race?" *Strategic Assessment* 15, no. 3 (October 2012): 7–26.

12. Jeffrey Goldberg, "Obama to Iran and Israel: 'As President of the United States, I Don't Bluff'," *The Atlantic,* March 2, 2012.

13. Philipp Bleek, "Does Proliferation Beget Proliferation? Why Nuclear Dominoes Rarely Fall" (PhD diss., Georgetown University, 2010).

14. Matthew Kroenig, *Exporting the Bomb: Technology Transfer and the Spread of Nuclear Weapons* (Ithaca, NY: Cornell University Press, 2010), 31.

15. Eric S. Edelman, Andrew F. Krepinevich, and Evan Braden Montgomery, "The Dangers of a Nuclear Iran," *Foreign Affairs* 90, no. 1 (January/February 2011); Julian Borger, "Pakistan's Bomb and Saudi Arabia," Julian Borger's Global Security Blog, May 11, 2010, accessed at http://www.guardian.co.uk/world/julian-borger-global-security-blog/2010/may/11/paki stan-saudiarabia.

16. Kroenig, *Exporting the Bomb,* 105–108.

17. Ibid.

18. "Venezuela Country Profile," *Nuclear Threat Initiative,* James Martin Center for Nonproliferation Studies, updated August 2012, accessed at http://www.nti.org/country-profiles /venezuela/.

19. Kroenig, *Exporting the Bomb.*

20. See Naser al-Tamimi, "Will Riyadh Get the Bomb? Saudi Arabia's Atomic Ambitions," *Middle East Quarterly* 20, no. 2 (Spring 2013); Eric S. Edelman, Andrew F. Krepinevich, and Evan Braden Montgomery, "The Dangers of a Nuclear Iran: The Limits of Containment," *Foreign Affairs* 90, no. 1 (January/February 2011).

21. Scott D. Sagan and Kenneth N. Waltz, *The Spread of Nuclear Weapons: A Debate Renewed* (New York: Norton, 2002), 88–125 and 155–180.

22. Barbara Starr, "Iranian Boats 'Harass' U.S. Navy, Officials Say," CNN, January 7, 2008; Thom Shanker, "Navy Deploying Laser Weapon Prototype near IRAN," *New York Times,* April 8, 2013.

23. Albert Wohlstetter, "Nuclear Sharing: NATO and the N+1 Country," *Foreign Affairs* 39, no. 3 (April 1961), 355–387.

24. U.S. Department of Defense, "Sustaining U.S. Global Leadership: Priorities for 21st Century Defense," January 2012, accessed at http://www.defense.gov/news/Defense_Strategic _Guidance.pdf; U.S. Department of Defense, "The National Defense Strategy of the United States of America," March 2005, accessed at http://www.defense.gov/news/mar2005 /d20050318nds1.pdf.

25. Chris McGreal, "US Intensifies Pressure on Iran over Strait of Hormuz Threat," *The Guardian,* January 13, 2012; Kenneth Katzman, Neelesh Nerurkar, Ronald O'Rourke, R. Chuck Mason, and Michael Ratner, "Iran's Threat to the Strait of Hormuz," CRS Report for Congress, Congressional Research Service, January 23, 2012, accessed at http://www.fas.org/sgp /crs/mideast/R42335.pdf.

26. Daryl G. Press, *Calculating Credibility: How Leaders Assess Military Threats* (Ithaca, NY: Cornell University Press, 2005).

27. Will Fulton and Ariel Farrar-Wellman, "Qatar-Iran Foreign Relations," *Iran Tracker,* American Enterprise Institute, July 22, 2011, accessed at http://www.irantracker.org/foreign -relations/qatar-iran-foreign-relations.

28. Colin H. Kahl and Kenneth N. Waltz, "Iran and the Bomb," *Foreign Affairs* 91, no. 5 (September/October 2012).

29. This section draws heavily from Matthew Kroenig and Robert McNally, "Iranian Nukes and Global Oil," *The American Interest,* March/April 2013. See also Senator Charles S. Robb and General (ret.) Charles Wald, Co-Chairs, "The Price of Inaction: Analysis of Energy and Economic Effects of a Nuclear Iran," Bipartisan Policy Center, October 2012, accessed at http:// bipartisanpolicy.org/library/report/price-of-inaction.

30. Ibid.

31. Daniel Yergin, "Oil's New World Order," *Washington Post*, October 28, 2011.

32. Nazila Fathi, "Wipe Israel 'Off the Map' Iranian Says," *New York Times*, October 27, 2005; Pete Hegseth, "Stopping Iran's Bomb," *National Review Online*, May 29, 2013, accessed at http://www.nationalreview.com/article/349510/stopping-irans-bomb.

33. Gili Cohen, "Israel Navy Gets Fifth Dolphin-Class Submarine from Germany," *Haaretz*, April 30, 2013.

34. "Rafsanjani Says Muslims Should Use Nuclear Weapon against Israel," Iran Press Service, December 14, 2001, http://www.iran-press-service.com/articles_2001/dec_2001/rafsanjani_nuke_threats_141201.htm.

35. Thomas C. Schelling, "The Reciprocal Fear of Surprise Attack," in *The Strategy of Conflict* (Cambridge, MA: Harvard University, 1981).

36. Thomas C. Schelling, *Arms and Influence* (New Haven, CT: Yale University Press, 2008).

37. For a primer on nuclear brinkmanship, see Matthew Kroenig, "Nuclear Superiority and the Balance of Resolve: Explaining Nuclear Crisis Outcomes," *International Organization* 67, no. 1 (January 2013), 141–171.

38. Ibid.

39. Arthur Bright, "Eyeing Iran, US Details $60 Billion Arms Sale to Saudi Arabia," *Christian Science Monitor*, October 21, 2010, accessed at http://www.csmonitor.com/World/terrorism-security/2010/1021/Eyeing-Iran-US-details-60-billion-arms-sale-to-Saudi-Arabia.

40. Ben Piven, "Map: US Bases Encircle Iran," Al Jazeera English, May 1, 2012, accessed at http://www.aljazeera.com/indepth/interactive/2012/04/2012417131242767298.html.

41. For more on my views on nuclear cuts, see Matthew Kroenig, "Think Again: American Nuclear Disarmament," *Foreign Policy*, September/October 2013.

42. Keir A. Lieber and Daryl G. Press, "The Nukes We Need," *Foreign Affairs* 88, no. 6 (Nov/Dec 2009): 39-51.

43. Joseph Cirincione, Jon B. Wolfsthal, and Miriam Rajkumar, *Deadly Arsenals: Tracking Weapons of Mass Destruction* (Washington, DC: Carnegie Endowment for International Peace, 2002) ; Paul Ingram and Oliver Meier, eds., "Reducing the Role of Tactical Nuclear Weapons in Europe: Perspectives and Proposals on the NATO Policy Debate," An Arms Control Association and British American Security Information Council Report, May 2011; Oliver Meier and Paul Ingram, "The NATO Summit: Recasting the Debate Over U.S. Nuclear Weapons in Europe," *Arms Control Today*, Arms Control Association, May 2012; Mustafa Kibaroglu, "Reassessing the Role of U.S. Nuclear Weapons in Turkey," *Arms Control Today*, Arms Control Association, June 2010; Amy F. Woolf, "Nonstrategic Nuclear Weapons," *CRS Report for Congress*, Congressional Research Service, December 19, 2012, accessed at http://www.fas.org/sgp/crs/nuke/RL32572.pdf.

44. For more on this point, see Victor Gilinsky and Henry Sokolski, "Serious Rules for Nuclear Power without Proliferation," The Nonproliferation Policy Education Center, accessed at http://npolicy.org/article_file/serious_rules_for_nuclear_power_without_proliferation.pdf/.

45. Kroenig, *Exporting the Bomb*.

46. Schelling, *Arms and Influence*; Schelling, *The Strategy of Conflict*.

47. Kroenig, "Nuclear Superiority and the Balance of Resolve."
48. For a thoughtful analysis that comes to a different conclusion, see Kenneth Pollack, *Unthinkable: Iran, the Bomb, and American Strategy* (New York: Simon and Schuster, 2013).

CHAPTER 6: BOMBING IRAN

1. For a video backgrounder on the Massive Ordinance Penetrator, see AviationExplorer, "Boeing Delivers Massive Ordnance Penetrator (MOP) 37,000 LB Bombs to the USAF– GBU-57," November 18, 2011, accessed at http://www.youtube.com/watch?v=WlaIl9J14H4. See also Robert Johnson, "The 30,000-lb Massive Ordnance Penetrator Bomb Works So Well It Earned a Rare Honor," *Business Insider,* September 7, 2012, accessed at http://www .businessinsider.com/this-30000-massive-ordnance-penetrator-bomb-works-so-well- its-design-team-just-won-a-rare-honor-2012-1.
2. Johnson, "The 30,000-lb Massive Ordnance Penetrator Bomb Works So Well It Earned a Rare Honor."
3. For more on the variety of military policy options regarding Iran's nuclear program, see Anthony H. Cordesman and Abdullah Toukan, "Analyzing the Impact of Preventive Strikes against Iran's Nuclear Facilities," Center for Strategic and International Studies, September 10, 2012; Anthony H. Cordesman and Alexander Wilner, "Iran and the Gulf Military Balance I: The Conventional and Asymmetric Dimensions, Fifth Working Draft," Center for Strategic and International Studies, July 11, 2012; Anthony H. Cordesman and Bryan Gold, "US-Iranian Competition: The Gulf Military Balance–II The Missile and Nuclear Dimensions, Twelfth Edition," Center for Strategic and International Studies, April 18, 2013; Whitney Raas and Austin Long, "Osirak Redux? Assessing Israeli Capabilities to Destroy Iranian Nuclear Facilities," *International Security* 31, no. 4 (Spring 2007): 7–33; Austin Long, "Can They?" *Tablet Magazine,* November 18, 2011, accessed at http://www.tabletmag.com /jewish-news-and-politics/83631/can-they; Matthew Kroenig, "Time to Attack Iran," *Foreign Affairs* 91, no. 1 (January/February 2012): 76–86; James Cartwright and Amos Yadlin, "Israeli or U.S. Action against Iran: Who Will Do It If It Must Be Done?" *The Atlantic,* May 28, 2013.; Dov S. Zakheim, "The Military Option," in *The Iran Primer: Power, Politics, and U.S. Policy,* ed. Robin B. Wright (Washington, DC: United States Institute of Peace, 2010); Geoffrey Kemp and John Allen Gay, *War with Iran: Political, Military, and Economic Consequences* (Lanham, MD: Rowman & Littlefield, 2013); "Weighing Benefits and Costs of Military Action against Iran," *The Iran Project,* September 2012; Tony Capaccio, "Iran Attack Would Halt Nuclear Bid for Four Years, Report Says," Bloomberg News, September 12, 2012; Joby Warrick, "Iran's Underground Nuclear Sites Not Immune to U.S. Bunker-Busters, Experts Say," *Washington Post,* February 29, 2012; Isabel Kershner, "Officials in Israel Stress Readiness for a Lone Strike on Iran," *New York Times,* April 18, 2013; Aaron Kalman, "We Have Prepared a Military Option for Iran, US General Says," *Times of Israel,* March 5, 2013.
4. For more on similar air power tactics, see Eric Schmitt, "U.S. Gives Its Air Power Expansive Role in Libya," *New York Times,* March 28, 2011; Jason R. Greenleaf, "The Air War in Libya," *Air & Space Power Journal* 27, no. 2 (March–April 2013): 28–54; Anthony H. Cordesman, "US Airpower in Iraq and Afghanistan: 2004–2007," Center for Strategic and International Studies, December 13, 2007.

5. William C. Witt, Christina Walrond, David Albright, and Houston Wood, "Iran's Evolving Breakout Potential," *ISIS Report,* Institute for Science and International Affairs, October 8, 2012; Tony Capaccio, "Boeing's 30,000-Pound Bunker-Buster Improved, U.S. Says," Bloomberg News, January 14, 2013.

6. Stephen Linch, "30,000-Pound Bomb Reaches Milestone." *Air Force Link,* December 27, 2007, accessed at http://www.ar15.com/archive/topic.html?b=1&f=5&t=655324

7. Long, "Osirak Redux?"; Cordesman and Toukan, "Analyzing the Impact of Preventive Strikes Against Iran's Nuclear Facilities"; Cheryl K. Chumley, "New U.S. Bunker Bombs Take Out Replica Underground Nuclear Site," *Washington Times,* June 7, 2013.

8. Long, "Osirak Redux"; Cordesman, "US Airpower in Iraq and Afghanistan: 2004–2007."

9. "GBU-57/B Massive Ordnance Penetrator (MOP)," GlobalSecurity.org, accessed at http://www.globalsecurity.org/military/systems/munitions/mop.htm; Cordesman and Toukan, "Analyzing the Impact of Preventive Strikes against Iran's Nuclear Facilities."

10. Adam Entous and Julian E. Barnes, "Pentagon Bulks Up 'Bunker Buster' Bomb to Combat Iran," *Wall Street Journal,* May 2, 2013; Cordesman, "US Airpower in Iraq and Afghanistan: 2004–2007."

11. "B-2s Fly Nonstop from US to Korea for Exercise Mission," *Stars and Stripes,* March 28, 2013; "B-2 Bombers Conduct Extended Deterrence Mission to South Korea," *Air Force Link,* March 28, 2013; "B-2 Specifications," GlobalSecurity.org, accessed at http://www.globalsecurity.org/wmd/systems/b-2-specs.htm.

12. For video of a B-2 escorted by F-16s, see "B-2 Fly over Osan," John Jacob, accessed at https://www.youtube.com/watch?v=dUTTH5xWXXA.

13. See endnote 3 in this chapter.

14. Jamie M. Fly and Gary Schmitt, "The Case For Regime Change in Iran," *Foreign Affairs,* January 17, 2012, accessed at http://www.foreignaffairs.com/articles/137038/jamie-m-fly-and-gary-schmitt/the-case-for-regime-change-in-iran.

15. Colin Kahl, "Not Time to Attack Iran," *Foreign Affairs* 91, no. 2 (March/April 2013): 166–173.

16. Wikipedia contributors, "GBU-28," *Wikipedia, The Free Encyclopedia,* http://en.wikipedia.org/wiki/GBU-28

17. Raas and Long, "Osirak Redux?"

18. "Obama Three Times Denied Israel's Request for MOP Bunker-Busters," *World Tribune,* May 7, 2013, accessed at http://www.worldtribune.com/2013/05/07/obama-three-times-denied-israels-request-for-mop-bunker-busters/.

19. Raas and Long, "Osirak Redux?"

20. Ibid.

21. Kroenig, "Time to Attack Iran"; Amos Harel, "Israeli Strike Would Only Delay Iran's Nuclear Program by Two Years," *Haaretz,* August 3, 2012; Kahl, "Not Time to Attack Iran."

22. "'Iran 'Zone of Immunity' Resonating with World'," *Jerusalem Post,* March 19, 2012.

23. Scott Wilson, "Biden Seeks to Reassure AIPAC of U.S. Commitment to Israel," *Washington Post,* March 4, 2013; Gili Cohen, "IDF Chief Benny Gantz lands in U.S. for Talks on Mideast Security Situation," *Haaretz,* February 3, 2013; "Kerry Warns Iran Time for Nuclear Talks Is Limited," BBC News, April 7, 2013; Dave Boyer, "John Kerry: U.S. Won't Stop Israeli Action against Iran," *Washington Times,* April 8, 2013; Thom Shanker and Isabel Kershner, "Hagel, in Israel, Presses U.S. Agenda on Deterring Iran," *New York Times,* April 21, 2013; "Reversing

Policy, US Will Sell Israel Aerial Refueling Planes," *Times of Israel,* April 19, 2013; Gopal Ratnam and Jonathan Ferziger, "U.S. Aircraft Sale Upholds Israel Military Edge: Hagel," Bloomberg News, April 22, 2013; Barak Ravid, "U.S. Presented Netanyahu with Contingency Plan for Iran Strike," *Haaretz,* July 29, 2012.

24. Ali Vaez and Karim Sadjadpour, "Iran's Nuclear Odyssey: Costs and Risks," Carnegie Endowment for International Peace, 2013, accessed at http://carnegieendowment.org/2013/04/02/iran-s-nuclear-odyssey-costs-and-risks/fvui.

25. I thank my colleague Kayhan Barzegar for first bringing this point to my attention.

26. Jacques E. C. Hymans, "Spinning in Place: Iraq's Fruitless Quest for Nuclear Weapons," in *Achieving Nuclear Ambitions: Scientists, Politicians and Proliferation* (Cambridge: Cambridge University Press, 2012), 79–123.

27. "From the Sky," *ISIS Nuclear Iran,* Institute for Science and International Affairs, accessed at http://www.isisnucleariran.org/from-the-sky/.

28. Wade Stone, "Good-bye Dubai? Bombing Iran's Nuclear Facilities Would Leave the Entire Gulf States Region Virtually Uninhabitable," *Global Research,* May 11, 2013, accessed at http://www.globalresearch.ca/good-bye-dubai-bombing-irans-nuclear-facilities-would-leave-the-entire-gulf-states-region-virtually-uninhabitable/5334737.

29. "Iran's Ballistic Missile Capabilities: A Net Assessment," IISS, May 10, 2010, available at http://www.iiss.org/en/publications/strategic%20dossiers/issues/iran—39-s-ballistic-missile-capabilities—a-net-assessment-885a; "Iran, Country Profiles," NTI, available at http://www.nti.org/country-profiles/iran/.

30. "Iran, Country Profiles," NTI.

31. "Iran's Ballistic Missile Capabilities: A Net Assessment," IISS.

32. Stuart Winer, "Millions Don't Have Access to Bomb Shelters, Gas Masks, Army Warns," *Times of Israel,* August 1, 2012, http://www.timesofisrael.com/home-front-command-mulls-inadequate-civilian-readiness-for-war/.

33. Matthew Kroenig and Barry Pavel, "How to Deter Terrorism," *Washington Quarterly* 35, no. 2 (Spring 2012): 21–36.

34. Rafael D. Frankel, "Keeping Hamas and Hezbollah Out of a War with Iran," *Washington Quarterly* 35, no. 4 (Fall 2012): 53–65.

35. Amos Harel, "Defense Ministry Experts Predict 300 Israeli Fatalities in War with Iran, Syria," *Haaretz,* August 2, 2012, accessed at http://www.haaretz.com/news/diplomacy-defense/defense-ministry-experts-predict-300-israeli-fatalities-in-war-with-iran-syria-1.455333.

36. Jerry Markon and Karen DeYoung, "Iran behind Alleged Terrorist Plot, U.S. Says," *Washington Post,* October 11, 2011.

37. Lee Moran, "Iranian Bomber Blows off His Legs in Bangkok as Grenade He Hurled at Police Bounces off Tree and Explodes at His Feet," *Mail Online,* February 14, 2012.

38. Matthew Kroenig and Robert McNally, "Iranian Nukes and Global Oil," *American Interest,* March/April 2013.

39. Kahl, "Not Time to Attack Iran."

40. Caitlin Talmadge, "Closing Time: Assessing the Iranian Threat to the Strait of Hormuz," *International Security* 33, no. 1 (Summer 2008): 82–117.

41. Elisabeth Bumiller, Eric Schmitt, and Thom Shanker, "U.S. Sends Top Iranian Leader a Warning on Strait Threat," *New York Times,* January 12, 2012.

42. Thom Shanker, Helene Cooper, and Ethan Bronner, "U.S. Sees Iran Attacks as Likely if Israel Strikes," *New York Times,* February 29, 2012.

43. Con Coughlin, "Can Iran Close Down the Strait of Hormuz?" *The Telegraph,* January 5, 2012, accessed at http://www.telegraph.co.uk/news/worldnews/middleeast/iran/8995261 /Can-Iran-close-down-the-Strait-of-Hormuz.html.

44. For more on this point, see Michael Eisenstadt and Michael Knights, "Beyond Worst-Case Analysis: Iran's Likely Responses to an Israeli Preventive Strike," *Policy Notes* 11, The Washington Institute for Near East Policy, June 2012.

45. Harel, "Defense Ministry Experts Predict 300 Israeli Fatalities in War with Iran, Syria."

46. Kahl, "Not Time to Attack Iran."

47. Kroenig and McNally, "Iranian Nukes and Global Oil."

48. Joshua Rovner, "After Prevention: Prospects for Deterrence in the Wake of a Military Strike on Iran," *National Interest,* November 28, 2011.

49. John Mueller, "Presidential Popularity from Truman to Johnson," *American Political Science Review* 64, no. 1 (March 1970): 18–34.

50. Matthew Baum, "The Constituent Foundations of the Rally-Round-the-Flag Phenomenon," *International Studies Quarterly* 46 (June 2002): 263–298.

51. Alireza Nader, "Think Again: A Nuclear Iran—Why It Won't Be the End of the World if the Mullahs Get the Bomb," *Foreign Policy,* May 28, 2013, accessed at http://www.foreignpolicy .com/articles/2013/05/28/think_again_a_nuclear_iran.

52. Critics of a strike have argued that these possible post-strike enforcement measures mean that we would have to "deter and contain" Iran whether we strike or acquiesce to a nuclear Iran, but such statements are highly misleading. After all deterring and containing Iran and assuring our regional allies and partners will be much easier if Iran lacks nuclear weapons.

53. Kahl, "Not Time to Attack Iran"; Trita Parsi, "The U.S. and Iran's Mistaken Path to War," *Huffington Post,* June 20, 2012, accessed at http://www.huffingtonpost.com/trita-parsi/the -us-and-irans-mistaken_b_1612874.html.

54. Dennis Jett, "If You Liked Iraq, You'll Love Iran," *Huffington Post,* August 26, 2012, accessed at http://www.huffingtonpost.com/dennis-jett/liked-iraq-love-iran_b_1832020.html.

55. Yuen Foong Khong, *Analogies at War: Korea, Munich, Dien Bien Phu, and the Vietnam Decisions of 1965* (Princeton, NJ: Princeton University Press, 1992).

CHAPTER 7: WHICH IS WORSE?

1. James R. Clapper, "Worldwide Threat Assessment of the US Intelligence Community," *Statement for the Record,* Senate Select Committee on Intelligence, January 29, 2014, accessed at http://www.intelligence.senate.gov/140129/clapper.pdf.

2. Ibid.

3. Colin Kahl, "Not Time to Attack Iran," *Foreign Affairs* 91, no. 2 (March/April 2013), 166–173; Stephen Walt, "The Worst Case for War with Iran," *Foreign Policy,* December 21, 2011, accessed at http://walt.foreignpolicy.com/posts/2011/12/21/the_worst_case_for_war_with _iran; Paul Pillar, "Worst Casing and Best Casing Iran," *The National Interest,* December 22, 2011, accessed at http://nationalinterest.org/blog/paul-pillar/worst-casing-best-casing-iran -6307.

4. Colin H. Kahl and Kenneth N. Waltz, "Iran and the Bomb," *Foreign Affairs* 91, no. 5 (September/October 2012).

CHAPTER 8: CONCLUSION

1. Richard Haass, "The Irony of American Strategy," *Foreign Affairs* 92, no. 3 (May/June 2013).

INDEX

06-12-2014